Energy

and

Power

Fundamental Knowledge

Dr. Les Anderson

INFINITY
PUBLISHING

Copyright © 2010 by Dr. Les Anderson

ISBN 0-7414-6104-8

Printed in the United States of America

Published September 2010

INFINITY PUBLISHING
1094 New DeHaven Street, Suite 100
West Conshohocken, PA 19428-2713
Toll-free (877) BUY BOOK
Local Phone (610) 941-9999
Fax (610) 941-9959
Info@buybooksontheweb.com
www.buybooksontheweb.com

Dedication

This book is dedicated to the people with the helping attitudes that made this project a reality. Pat, my wife, helped with encouragement and the word-to-word proof reading of a compromised text. David and Mark, my sons, helped by providing computer knowledge and literary substance to the author. Linda Sharif, my friend, helped by a thorough total evaluation of a difficult body of text. Dave Schulte helped by reviewing Chapter 21. Their contributions deserve the greatest recognition.

Preface

Goals

The motivation and purpose in writing Power and Energy – Fundamental Knowledge was to selfishly provide needed documentation to the five identified groups associated to my instructional activities. This book is primarily directed at satisfying the information requirement of the five groups:

1. Energy directed students

With the increasing importance of the energy segment in our economy, energy as an educational subject at the university level is being formulated. The evolution of energy education is oriented towards the coalescence of a pervasive energy education independent of established disciplines. The formulation and establishment of information to precisely satisfy the new energy discipline requirements have yet to be determined. The best example is that this text really doesn't, at this time, have a viable educational alternative.

2. Environmentally oriented people

This text provides additional information to the objective nature of the environmental viewpoint. For our text purposes, environmentalists require an education in the vast field of energy. It is important for us to originate energy policy and environmental policy starting from an educated investigation of natural scientific relationships. Those relationships are presented for the common agreement position by everyone. Those relationships are a necessary, but not yet sufficient, path towards of optimum future energy policy. The logical science of Power and Energy – Fundamental Knowledge does not have any optional subjective interpretations.

3. Older citizens

Older people, and I am a member of this group, desire a comprehensive text in energy. Their interest is prompted by the recent public forum regarding energy policies. When they were younger, this group had greater priorities than the comprehensive understanding of energy. Energy, as a defined focus, passed them by. Now, additional education regarding energy is required to bring many elders to a satisfactory level of energy understanding and communication. The largest contribution to elder energy learning is formatting the Power and Energy – Fundamental Knowledge in the larger 14 point print.

4. The scientific community

People actively engaged in the overall energy program have repeatedly requested a copy of the Energy and Power – Fundamental Knowledge proposed text as a beneficial adjunct to their role in the overall energy program. I have no idea as to the extent and value of this text to this energy dedicated group.

5. The general public

The unanswered question, key to goal of this text, is "How much energy knowledge is optimum for the general public?" The current (2010) level of basic energy science in the public is close to zero. But is energy education like algebra? We all learn algebra in high school, but few use it during their lives. Presently, energy education is communicated through the newspaper and TV media. These energy communications are specious and contains gross distortions based upon self-vested conclusions. But maybe this is the true manner in which a democratic society proceeds. Energy and Power – Fundamental Knowledge is understandable by the majority of the public audience.

People working in the energy field are conveniently segregated into four groups: scientists, engineers, businesspersons, and social scientists

The greatest challenge, for education at the university level, is to educate all four groups with a common curriculum.

Social scientists may use this energy introductory text to enhance communications with energy scientists, engineers, and business people. I hope that this text provides value to their work or provides a base for further educational consideration of this important group.

Constraints and Compromise

A reason for adding the constraints and compromises used as guidelines in writing this text is to provide future directed documentation of energy an explicit structure. The following list forms a guideline for future improved energy texts. It is the future author's prerogative to structure text according to his or her inclinations. This text provides a learned evaluation for that text structure. I could not find an existing energy text document to guide content and format.

1. The projected goal of Energy and Power – Fundamental Knowledge is to provide an individual internalized knowledge that is summarized at the end of each chapter as "must knows." An knowledgeable energy individual must be able to fluently converse in the "must know" concepts.

2. Since energy analysis is historically rooted in mathematics, the following compromise was made to encompass a greater number of readers to understand energy concepts. Mathematics is kept to a minimum and all supplied mathematical derivations are conclusive to textural content. The age old process of extensive mathematical analysis until the physical meaning is internalized was not used.

3. A bridge between observable phenomenon and energy concepts is maintained throughout the text. The abstract nature of nuclear energy is an exception. Observable energy phenomenon provides a continuing reinforcement of energy concepts.

4. The text is written in the 1st person. It is similar to a class room lecture. I am poor at this writing technique, but God will understand my lofty intentions. The third person text (from my own experience) separates science from humanity (See Ghandi for the proper quote).

5. There are associated educational topics that are either too advanced for the body of the text or are popular enough to evoke ancillary questions. These

associated topics are substantially abbreviated and included at the end of each chapter. They are called Chapter Insights.

6. The text contains extensive graphics and purposeful "white" space. These presentation techniques provide a better visual retention factor than uninterrupted text. It is unrealistic to consider energy science as entertaining. So we will takc it easy on the reader!

7. The text was repeatedly edited to control the length. This was a very difficult task. The entire energy field is contained in a large library. One has to seriously compromise content and still maintain the overall educational value.

These 7 guidelines were applied to every chapter in Energy and Power – Fundamental Knowledge. Less than half of the final written text remained after editing. One will never know whether the editing increased or decreased the total learned value.

For those reading the entire preface, I hope that this text provides a worthwhile contribution to your goals. I fully expect that every reader will find something lacking in this book. I sincerely hope that the readers will advance their energy and power knowledge in a direction provided by the many excellent available resources.

Dr. Les Anderson

Table of Contents

Chapter 4: Kinetic Energy

Sections

Chapter 5: Gravitational Energy

Sections

Chapter 6: Elastic Energy

Sections

Chapter 7: Heat Energy

Sections

Chapter 8: Chemical Energy

Sections

Chapter 9: Radiant Energy

Sections

Chapter 10: Electrical Energy

Sections

Chapter 11: Gas Pressure-Volume Energy

Sections

Chapter12: Utility Power

Sections

Chapter 13: Petroleum

Sections

Chapter 14: Coal

Sections

Chapter 15: Hydroelectric Power

Sections

Chapter 16: Nuclear Power

Sections

Chapter 17: Solar Power

Sections

Chapter 18 Wind Power

Sections

Chapter 19: Geothermal Power

Sections

Chapter 20: Biofuel Power

Sections

Chapter 21 The Automobile

Sections

Figures

Chapter 1:

Introduction to Energy

ENERGY EDUCATION GOAL

OUR GOAL IS TO SYSTEMATICALLY COMMUNICATE ENERGY KNOWLEDGE THAT IS COHERENTLY ORGANIZED AROUND KEY CONCEPTS AND PRINCIPLES – AND VERIFY THAT THE KNOWLEDGE LEVEL IS ADEQUATE FOR OUR GENERAL SOCIETY.

Sections:

I. Two Reasons to Understand Energy Science

The motivation for understanding energy science primarily originates from the following two conditions and needs in our society:

1. The utilization of energies is the main reason for what the public considers as our modern quality of life. This reality is not understood nor well appreciated by the public. One can speculate that maybe energy science may not be as fascinating when compared with present weather conditions nor as entertaining when compared with investigations of pre-historic dinosaurs.

2. Our modern life is based upon utilization of available coal and petroleum energy, called fossil fuels. The amounts of fossil fuels are limited; so in our near future we will have to develop alternate sources of energy in order to maintain our quality of life. In addition, climate change is alleged to be caused by the carbon dioxide produced by burning fossil fuel. Global warming is a political policy concern that challenges both scientific bodies and political entities. The education of energy science provides a better ability to evaluate the many proposals directed towards energy policy.

These two reasons for energy science education are qualitatively described in sections of this chapter and investigated in detail in the focused chapters of this book.

II. Energy Utilization

Energy utilization is the basis for the modern quality of life. Yes, energy utilization is the basis for our modern quality of life. Then why shouldn't we understand this important body of knowledge!! This fact alone should be reason enough for everyone to be informed and educated about energy.

Interestingly, this fact is not generally appreciated; so we will validate the bold faced statements of the last paragraph. Initially, a description of our recent energy utilization history is presented to confirm and reinforce this concept.

A reasonable comparison can be made between average living conditions of around the year 1810 and around the year 2010. I am listing some living conditions affected by energy utilization. The list of living condition improvements is extensive and your priority may differ from mine, but the overall relationship between energy utilization and improvement in living conditions will be demonstrated by many historical examples. Here are five examples:

1. Heat

Around year 1810 we were still primarily an agrarian society, and our prime source of heat was wood and some coal. The amount of effort sawing, collecting, splitting, and storing wood was substantial. The resulting smoke and soot was substantial. Central heating for home or business was very rare. In general, we were uncomfortable during periods of cold outside temperature.

Around year 2010 we have evolved into an industrial society with distributed energy for heating. The predominant heating energy sources are oil heat, gas heat, and electric heat. We have central heating controlled by a thermostat. We now are so accustomed to our comfort that we even argue about the thermostat setting. **Our improved living conditions resulted from energy utilization.**

2. Light

Around year 1810, our sources of light were primarily bee's wax candles and whale oil lamps. Both sources were supply limited and conservation was a rule. An urban culture response was to frequent a tavern where social interaction occurred in front of fireplace light. The farmer just went to bed.

Around year 2010, electric lighting predominates in our society. A lighting evolution from coal gas to incandescent bulbs to fluorescent bulbs to light emitting diodes has occurred to improve electric lighting efficiency. However, the convenience of adequate lighting is so pervasive that the modern application is not even considered as an historical development by the public. **Our improved living conditions resulted from energy utilization.**

3. Preparing food

Around year 1810, excellent food preparations were already known. However, the cooking task required substantial effort for many reasons. Meat preservation was limited to salt packing and dehydration. This was prior to home and commercial canning. Potatoes, carrots, and corn were preserved in a cool root cellar. Fruits and vegetables were also dehydrated. Food preparation was a major labor component of year 1810 living.

Around year 2010, pervasive food availability occurs without notice due to our energy utilization. Rapid transportation allows fresh food stocks to be available all year. Refrigeration and freezing techniques have eliminated chronic food spoilage problems. Appliances, like mixers and microwaves have substantially reduced labor. **Our improved living conditions resulted from energy utilization.**

4. Transportation

Around year 1810, the ground transportation was horse energy. Ships sailed the waterways to serve commercial (and military) needs. Modes of transportation had been stable for all of recorded history. The concept of travel for pleasure was restricted to few people.

Around year 2010, we observe the automobile for personal transportation, the electromotive train for commercial transportation, and the airplane for fast personal, commercial, and military needs. Each factor in this transportation revolution adds to our pleasure, comfort and convenience (quality of life). **Our improved living conditions resulted from energy utilization.**

5. Electronics

Around the year 1810, electronics did not exist.

Around the year 2010, we have high-definition television, cell phones for communication, global positioning systems (GPS), portable audio/video recorders, digital cameras, etc. I am writing this text on a computer. We also have a full cadre of marketing people advertising the next "electronic wonder." This burst of personal electronic items was and is substantially created from semiconductor technology. One, sort of cynical, observation is that in 1810 people worked long hours to survive and in 2010 people use sports and video games to occupy their free time generated by energy utilization. **Our improved living conditions resulted from energy utilization.**

Repeatedly, the statement, **"Our improved living conditions resulted from energy utilization"** has been objectively demonstrated. I am sure that you can think of other energy process utilizations. Strangely, energy process utilization is rarely mentioned or considered in discussions regarding our quality of life.

III. Universe Dimensions

Energy is difficult to comprehend because it is based upon universe dimensions that we do not understand in terms of underlying causes or identifiable structure.

Typical universe dimensions are distance, time, and mass. We don't spend any effort thinking about these dimensions since we have no knowledge regarding their existence. But, without thinking, we do use the quantified measurements of these dimensions. We do not understand distance, but I am 20.5 miles from home. We do not understand time, but I will be home at 5:00 P.M. We do not understand mass, but I weigh 80 kilograms.

Energy belongs with the category of universal dimensions. Although we sense energy and measure energy, we neither understand any underlying cause nor logical structure of energy in our sensed observations. All energies are related to these basic universe dimensions. The fundamental definition of energy includes "force". Force is related to time, mass and distance. We can measure "force" and energy, but we have no idea what force actually is in terms of underlying causality.

IV. What is Energy?

Energy definition:

There are two historical definitions of energy:

> 1. "Energy is the ability to do work"

> 2. "Energy is force traveling through a distance"

These definitions were appropriate in the historical development of energy science, but presently these definitions are too vague for use as the specific energy definitions required in this text. You deserve an explanation!

The definition of "energy is the ability to do work" ascribes an animate characteristic "ability" to an inanimate process. Energy possesses no animate characteristics. It is only a physical part of the universe.

"Energy is force traveling through a distance" also is the general definition of work. Work is a recognized observation. Historically, the force/work definitions are energy definitions that apply well to mechanical systems and physics in general. However, these energy definitions have difficulty when applied to energy related processes when distance is not observed. Radiant energy from your light bulbs and heat energy from a chemical reaction are examples of energies not clearly defined directly by force/work.

These difficulties are only annoying to trained physical scientists, but create a substantial learning barrier, regarding energy, to the general public.

Let us carefully view and create a definition of energy from a focused perspective of this text. This text explains the following kinds of energies:

Chapter 3 Mechanical

Chapter 4 Kinetic

Chapter 5.Gravitational

Chapter 6 Elastic

Chapter 7 Heat

Chapter 8.Chemical

Chapter 9.Radiant

Chapter 10 Electrical

Chapter 11 Gas Pressure

Chapter 15 Nuclear

While there are more kinds of energies, this text only considers energies related to large scale energy production and usage. The large scale energy systems are called *"utility grade"* energy systems

Each of the energies from the above list can be converted to any other.

This fact allows us to have a better definition of energy:

<u>*"Energy"*, and only *"energy"*, can do work</u>

<u>and</u>

<u>All energies can be converted to do work.</u>

Work is defined, and measured, (as amount of force) x (amount of distance)

We have defined energy. We actually could use any kind of energy measurement to create a definition. However, the work definition, based upon mechanical work, retains the best historical meaning.

V. Practical Use of Energy Knowledge

We often state an overused justification regarding education that an informed public is the foundation of democratic society. This statement is difficult to evaluate. In energy education, the required level of public education is even more difficult to define. Energy proposals and policies are based upon analysis of energy and the analysis requires energy science. <u>Public education to improve the energy logical analysis process is the prime motivation for this text.</u>

Fueled by enthusiasm for future potential energy financial rewards and hyped by media communications and political response, the energy engineering proposals frequently are in stark disagreement with scientific energy facts.

The following paragraph of this section will be explained by real examples. As you progress through this text, you will realize that repeated examples from common observations form the outline skeleton of the entire text.

Examples of proposals:

1. We should air condition our homes using blocks of ice.

2. We should feed termites wood so that they produce methane that can be burned to heat the house.

3. We should place solar panels on top of 18-wheel semi-trucks to replace the diesel engines.

4. We should disconnect from the electrical grid by installing 1000 watt wind turbines in our back yards.

The 4 examples above have been proposed. And there are many more. You should be aware of the "We" and "should" in each proposal.

The sincerity of the proposing individuals is beyond question. Notice that the appropriate responses to these proposals have not been provided. The appropriate responses will become your responsibility. That is a goal of this educational text. However, you need specific tools for evaluating the energy proposals. The educational tools are:

1. Understanding energy science principles
2. Understanding energy science limitations
3. Understanding energy applications (engineering)

The energy educational tools involve a comprehensive coalescence of the diverse energy field. The comprehensive understanding of energy science is aided immensely by using mathematical relationships. Those mathematical relationships must be tempered when recognizing the fact that this text is also directed towards a public audience and not exclusively towards a scientific audience.

A goal of this text is to inform and educate people regarding energy science. The best measure of your internalized information and education in energy science is your ability to evaluate various energy engineering proposals and policies in the future.

VI. The Energy Laws

The greatest tools to integrate a coherent understanding of energy are the Three Laws of Energy, also called the *Three Laws of Thermodynamics*. Don't let the title "Three Laws of Thermodynamics" frighten you. The "Three Laws of Thermodynamics" are only general statements made from ordinary measured observations. We will provide numerous observed examples of these laws in operation within this text. Understanding the principles of the Three Laws of Thermodynamics is essential to understanding the pervasive energy science.

The *1ˢᵗ Law of Thermodynamics* states that energy cannot be created or destroyed

Now what does that mean?

It means that, during any physical process, energy can only be converted from one kind to another kind. Energy cannot be created or destroyed. That is a fundamental property of our universe.

The *2ⁿᵈ Law of Thermodynamics* states the heat energy flows from a higher temperature to a lower temperature.

Now what does that mean?

This observation is sensed by everyone. A hot object always cools down to the temperature of its surroundings. A cool object always warms up to the temperature of its surroundings. The opposite observation is unthinkable.

The *3ʳᵈ Law of Thermodynamics* states that temperature can only get so cold. Absolute zero temperature is a measured -273 degrees Celsius.

Now what does that mean?

Motion of the atoms within matter is temperature. At -273 degrees Celsius, atomic motion stops absolutely. There is no colder temperature.

You do not have to immediately memorize these three laws. They are stated here in case you need them as a reference. By the time you finish this text, they will be memorized due to the repeated examples.

VII. A Typical Energy Analysis

From what we observe by our senses, the 1st Law of Thermodynamics seems intuitively to be incorrect. When we burn a tank of gas, we end up with water and carbon dioxide. When we burn our campfire, we end up with ashes. When we burn up our food, we end up with waste. When we use electricity, we end up with a bill from the energy company.

One often hears; "Don't tell me that we didn't consume energy." Correcting this incorrect public view is one of our educational hurdles.

A sensible observation is that we consume energy during any process. This incorrect observation is based upon our sense evaluation of the process result. The flaw in our everyday evaluation was that we did not account for (and measure) all of the energies. This is particularly true regarding heat energy. However, we will present many evaluations throughout this text using energy measurements that confirm the 1st Law of Thermodynamics. Our evaluations are based upon accurate measurement of energy values during the physical processes. In fact, the 1st Law of Thermodynamics is the primary basis for coherently understanding the many aspects of observed energies.

The qualitative evaluation using the 1st Law of Thermodynamics and 2nd Law of Thermodynamics will be demonstrated by the following example. This non-memorable example is directed only at orientation towards energy science. Quantitative confirmation will be demonstrated throughout the text.

Energy analysis of heating your house:

The energy to heat your home living space typically comes directly from burning oil/natural gas or indirectly from a distributed electrical source. The amount of energy used can be accurately measured (see your fuel bill).

The heat in your house energy process is:

1. Energy is added to your house from a oil/natural gas or electricity source. (Observed as a increase in house temperature)

2. Energy is removed from your house by heat energy passing through the exterior (walls, roof and floor) of the house. (Observed as a decrease in house temperature)

So, when the house temperature with time remains the same (thermostat setting), all we are doing, on a continual basis, is converting oil/natural gas (chemical energy) or electrical energy to heat energy.

A visual diagram of heat flow would look like:

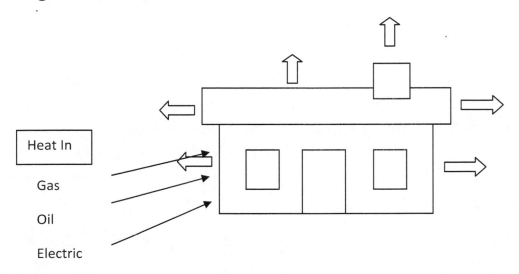

Figure 1.1 Heat Flow

Measurements of energy values are electrical energy (kilowatts), gas energy (therms) or oil energy (Btu's) into your house and heat loss (as hot temperature inside to colder temperature outside) from your house. The heat loss is the same as the heat generated. We apply the 1st Law of Thermodynamics unintentionally when we evaluate our heating bill.

The process energy conservation principle is confirmed by measurement in every physical process.

This underlying concept helps explain many observed energy dynamics in your house. These observations normally do not result in focused thought.

1. You don't keep the house door open long when it is cold outside. The common concept is that it will let the cold air inside. Actually, it is better to

say that you are letting the hot air (energy) inside the house flow to the outside. This would properly express heat flow. Notice that the furnace or electric heater will start soon to replenish the lost energy and maintain the house temperature at the thermostat setting.

2. We observe that heat always flows from matter in a region of higher temperature to a region of lower temperature. Remember the 2nd Law of Thermodynamics. Any other observation is even unthinkable. We heat (raise the temperature) our house because the temperature outside is colder than inside and we would be uncomfortable at the outside temperature. The amount of heat flowing to the outside depends upon the difference between the inside temperature and the outside temperature. Any material that slows the rate of heat flow from hot to cold temperatures is called *insulation*. Slowing heat flow by using better insulation (by definition one that slows heat flow) is a common house feature. Slowing heat energy flow from your house means less need for energy flowing into your house and that means a lower utility (energy) bill.

3. The third observation is that we save on our utility (energy) bill if we turn the temperature thermostat down at night. The amount of heat flow from the house is directly related to the difference between the inside and outside temperature. One can think of this as what will happen if we turn the input energy (heat) OFF. The house inside temperature will eventually reach the outside temperature. When the temperatures are the same, no heat energy flow, from inside to outside or from outside to inside will occur. So, by reducing the difference between inside and outside temperatures, we reduce the house output heat energy and the corresponding input energy.

Note that people usually evaluate energy usage as an economic impact. So if you want to lower your heating bill, lower your thermostat temperature, add insulation, and make sure the windows are closed. This is common economic sense.

The 1st Law of Thermodynamics is universally accepted in this case and we actually measure heat energy loss from the house by conveniently measuring the energy equivalent heat into the house. We only talk about our fuel bill, not our heat loss. Your electric, oil, and/or gas bill reflect this accepted energy conversion. This single qualitative example will not convince everyone about the validity of 1st Law of Thermodynamics, but the many examples in this text will be persuasive.

This example points the way to complete understanding of energy science and engineering applications. Note that we have only qualitatively described the house energy process. A superior method would be to quantitatively describe and analyze the house energy process. I do that every month when I get my energy bill.

VIII The Conversion of Kinds of Energies

The 1st Law of Thermodynamics states that energy is conserved during any physical process. That is an energy science fact. To convert available energy to usable energy is a different story. Converting available energy to usable energy is the essence of energy engineering. Understanding the applications of energy conversions provides a comprehensive view of energy science.

All of the energy utilizations referred to in Section III are the result of successful energy engineering. Energy science and energy engineering are intermingled in all applications. *Energy science* remains the unchanging interpretation of the universe. *Energy engineering* is the dynamic effort directed at the improvement of energy conversions of available energy into usable energy.

Energy engineering activities are sensitive to business and public policies. That sensitivity is very dynamic.

Energy science and energy engineering are intermingled, but a couple of examples will present how to separate the two bodies of knowledge. Don't worry about quickly developing the separation expertise. That will be yours by the end of this text.

1. Solar radiant energy, as it encounters the earth's surface, is estimated to be 1000 watts/square meter. That solar radiant energy will be about 1000 watts/square meter 100 years from now. This is an unchanging fact of energy science.

   Present solar panels (2010), with full sunlight exposure, convert solar radiant energy to usable electricity and produce about 170 watts/square meter. We hope that a breakthrough in engineering solar to electrical conversion can significantly improve this energy conversion (Maybe up to 500 watts/ square meter). This is energy engineering.

However, solar panels can never produce more than 1000 watts/ square meter of electrical energy. That contradicts the 1st Law of Thermodynamics. This unchanging limit is part of energy science.

2. A microwave oven converts electrical energy into radiant energy that converts into heat energy within our food. As understood from the 1st Law of Thermo-dynamics, we cannot heat our cup of tea (convert energy) faster than the energy flow from the electrical source. This is energy science.

   However, we can design a microwave oven has a more efficient electrical energy input to heat energy output. It also could feature a greater operating convenience. That is energy engineering.

Energy engineering is primarily focused upon the conversion of available energy to usable energy. We will develop the ability to separate the energy science from the energy engineering

IX. Conversion Efficiency and Energy Flow Diagrams

There is a compelling reason to dwell upon energy engineering in this energy and power text. Conversion efficiency and energy science are both required in order to properly evaluate proposed energy scenarios.

When using every energy conversion process, the energy conversion *efficiency* is the measured amount of usable energy exiting the process divided by the measured amount of available energy entering the process. Conversion efficiency is important because we pay for the energy input and receive value from the energy output. With higher conversion efficiency, we receive the same value of energy at lower cost. The definition of percent energy efficiency is:

% Conversion Efficiency = (Energy Out / Energy In) x 100

Now we already know that the energy out of a process can never be more than the energy into a process (back to the 1st Law of Thermodynamics). The conversion efficiency can never be greater than 100%. We saw that in the last section with a solar panel operating at about 17%. However, don't be surprised if someone suggests he has invented a solar panel with a conversion percentage of 120%. We are still in the introductory chapter, but we have acquired some ability to evaluate energy systems.

A logical tool to provide focus on our repeated examples of energy flow is the *energy flow diagrams*. They are used in this text to graphically present the kinds of energies. This will reduce the inherent confusion caused by the voluminous topics. Chapters 12 to 20 (power) present the graphical energy flow diagrams each off the utility grade power applications.

An introductory example, Figure 1.2, presents the solar to electrical energy conversion process referred to earlier in this chapter.

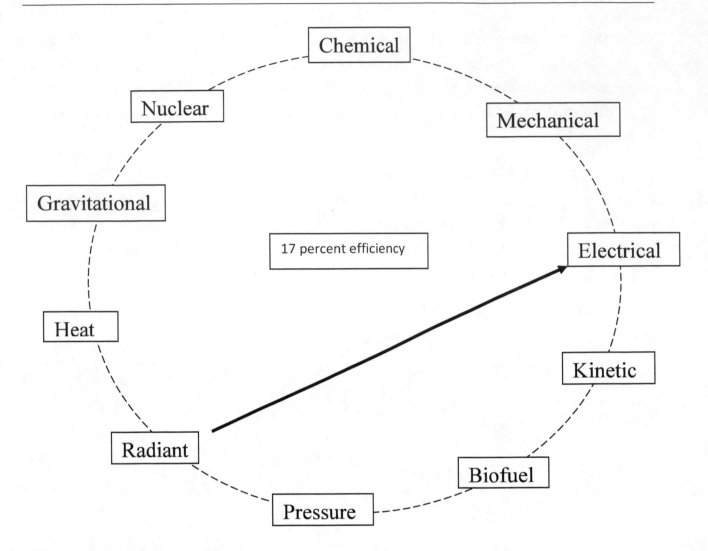

Figure 1.2 Energy Types

Note that the energy diagram is quite complex. This energy flow diagram indicates that we have a long path to our goal of understanding the flow dynamics of the major energy processes.

Energy conversion efficiencies and energy flow diagrams will be used in this text to provide a unified approach to the many aspects of energy (power) science.

X. Chapter 1 Summary

These Section's introductory paragraphs define the scope of the text material and the ending paragraphs define text operational approach. For a Chapter 1 summary, review the chapter subjects and remember the bold-faced type within the text.

As always the case with learning texts, the introductory chapter is much clearer when read after understanding the body of the text.

The must-know elements of the Introductory Chapter are:

    1. Energy is the basis of our quality of life

    2. Public energy education is needed for future public energy policy

    3. The three laws of thermodynamics are embedded in energy science

    4. Energy engineering is efficiently converting available energy to usable energy.

Chapter 2:

Energy Mathematics

Sections:
   I.   **Introduction to Energy Mathematics**
   II.   **Physical Factors and Measurement Standards**
   III.   **Energy Measurement Systems**
   IV.   **Scientific Notation**
   V.   **Scales and Conversions**
   VI.   **Conclusions**

I. Introduction to Energy Mathematics

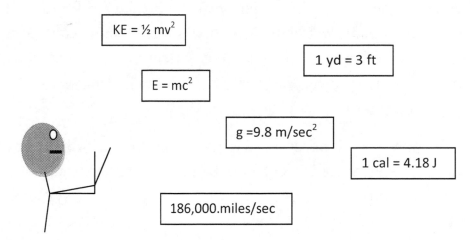

Figure 2.1 Mathematics

There are two fundamental reasons for requiring mathematics in order to clearly understand energy science:

1. Energy science is based upon mathematical descriptions in order to clearly define the kinds of energy. These mathematical descriptions allow us to determine relationships and compare the values between the kinds of energies.

2. The cost of energy is of prime importance to the general consumer (public). Everyone is aware of their electric power bill or the cost per gallon of gasoline. Energy cost considerations can be determined precisely using mathematics when quantifying our energy science and engineering.

The details of how we are going to satisfy these two energy science mathematical requirements are provided in this chapter.

Two deliberate actions have been taken to reduce the mathematical requirement for understanding Energy and Power - Fundamental Knowledge. They are:

1. The mathematical operations used to explain energy have been reduced almost to an intuitive level. Calculus and differential equations have been eliminated from our text. This allows people unfamiliar with scientific analysis to adequately understand the fundamentals of energy. Of course, the mathematical simplification comes with the price of incomplete description. This results in an uncertain compromise (and many rewrites). If you have difficulty in logical mathematical operations, help can come from a knowledgeable friend. It is not the intention of this text to teach mathematics; but specific explanation will be given when we encounter necessary mathematics.

2. Repeated examples of observed energy phenomenon will be presented for each kind of energy and energy applications. These examples furnish the framework for qualitative evaluation of energy related systems and allow you to have a better understanding of the pros and cons of proposed energy application plans.

What you need to do is spend some extra time to understand the energy concepts presented by repeated examples until the underlying concept becomes clear. In other words, think a little about the examples.

The use of mathematics in this text is only slightly beyond the mathematics commonly used presently by consumers. For example:

The "gas mileage' of our automobile is a mathematical term used to communicate the absolute energy efficiency of our automobile and to compare our automobile efficiency with other automobiles. The government measures gasoline miles per gallon (MPG) for automobiles as part of its program to reduce gasoline usage. The MPG number communicates, in distinct terms, our energy efficiency. This is the familiar EPA mileage estimate. The underlying concept is that everyone accepts that a gallon of gasoline provides a standard amount of energy (119,000 Btu's) and that MPG's are an acceptable measure of gas energy to automobile energy conversion. This is done without detailed understanding.

The heating and cooling of our house and workplace is measured (usually monthly) for amounts of usage. Whether we use fuel oil and/or electricity for heating and cooling, we are billed for a measured amount of energy used during the measured period of time. The bill contains a numerical amount of energy consumed. The amount used allows us to consider options in our energy usage and compare our energy usage with other consumers. This is a familiar mathematical process.

The electricity consumer's use, independent of cooling and heating, also is measured according to a strict mathematical process. As stated earlier, turning down the thermostat at night will result in a quantitative reduction in your heating bill.

The mathematical procedures in this text are not significantly more difficult than these familiar mathematical applications.

II. Physical Factors and Measurement Standards

There are basic physical factors (called dimensions on occasion) that cannot be explained in lesser basic terms. Figure 2.2 presents those basic physical factors.

We sense time. But we don't understand what time is itself. We sense mass (or weight). But we don't understand what mass is itself. We sense distance. But we don't understand what distance is itself. These are mysterious dimensions of our existing universe.

Dimension	English	Metric (SI)
Time	Second	Second
Mass		Gram
Weight	Pound	Newton
Distance	Inch, foot, yard, mile	Meter

Figure 2.2 Universal Dimensions

Our scientific advances have been in the universal establishment of the amounts of dimensions and our ability to measure these quantities in comparison to standards. Standards are amounts of specific dimensions whose values are universally accepted by the scientific, business, and public community. We have our favorite TV program at 8:00 P.M. We live 5 miles from our friend. We may weigh 138 pounds. We now measure dimensions in reference to standards. Examples of standards are given below. Where would our society be without standard time, weight, and distance?

III. Energy Measurement Systems

Here is some bad news. The factors that create quantitative energy data (logically and mathematically) are complicated because two major systems have naturally evolved in the measurement and standardization of energy. The two systems were tabulated in Figure 2.2. It is as though two languages are being used to describe energy science. We have all been subject to the confusion resulting from these two separate systems. When I go to Quebec, the speed limit sign is 100 kilometers/hour. I have to think a moment to calculate that speed in miles/hour. When I go to Europe, my baggage limit is 22 kilograms. Now what is 22 kilograms in pounds? And similar to expression in two different languages for communication, no matter which system one uses, the universal values (meanings) are exactly the same.

The English System

Over time, in the 18th and 19th century, a standard measurement of weight, distance, and time was slowly established in England. The units of weight, distance, and time were adopted from business familiarity and necessity. The weight was the pound (and derivatives), the distance was the foot (and derivatives) and the time was the second (and derivatives).

The Metric System

The Metric measurement system was based upon the convenience of using the factor of 10, along with the meter length as a standard. It originated in the French government/scientific community in the year 1799. The Metric System has grown in parallel with the English System for the last century. The Metric system does offer less opportunity for errors when calculating than the English System.

The unit of measurement of mass (not weight) is the gram, the measurement unit of distance is the meter, and the measurement unit of time is the second. The original platinum standard for a meter is kept in Paris.

The English System produced other measurements that exist to this day. The best example is the British Thermal Unit (BTU), a heat energy measurement standard:

> The **BTU** is defined as the amount of heat (energy) required to increase the temperature of one pound of water 1 degree Fahrenheit.

The Metric system produced the **Calorie** heat energy measurement standard, used to this day, as follows:

> A **Calorie** is the amount of heat (energy) required to increase the temperature of 1 gram of water 1 degree centigrade.

The English and Metric measurement standards were established as above. Other physical measurements also furnish substantial scientific and business value and are standardized. They are not universe dimensions nor are they universally familiar. Figure 2.3 presents two sets of physical measurements central to our investigation of energy.

	English	**Metric**
Temperature	Fahrenheit	Centigrade
Heat	BTU	Calorie

Energy	Foot-Pound	Joule
Power	Horsepower	Watt
Volume	Gallon	Liter

Figure 2.3 System Conversions

As visually presented in Figure 2.4, the BTU standard is based upon a significantly larger amount of water.

The definition of energy originates from the heating of water. Water is a universal substance accepted and familiar to everyone. It was an excellent choice for the energy standard.

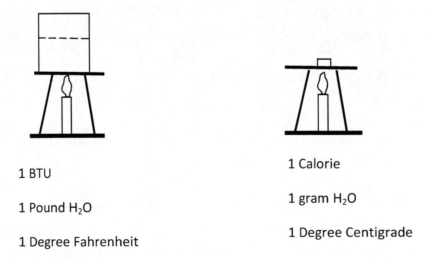

1 BTU

1 Pound H_2O

1 Degree Fahrenheit

1 Calorie

1 gram H_2O

1 Degree Centigrade

Figure 2.4 BTU and Calorie

Using the BTU and calorie standards example, the need for conversions between the two energy measurement systems is obviously required. An appendix is furnished for convenient reference to conversions. For now, 1 BTU of heat energy is the same as 252 calories of heat energy.

The use of Metric and English Systems are included in this text. The strategy in writing under these two systems is:

1. Only one appropriate system is predominantly used within each chapter. For example, the Metric system is used in Chapter 4 and English system is used in Chapter 13. The use of conversions (and possible errors) is kept to a minimum. Quantified energies can always be translated from one system to the other. That activity may be a good method for obtaining scientific energy familiarity, but it does utilize the precious time required to internalize the fundamental energy science concepts.

2. The energy conversion process is described in the later chapters as required. The reason for this late description, after presenting energy fundamentals, is to keep our focus on energy science, rather than spend time on endless system conversions. A factor that supports this strategy is that few energy conversions are actually needed in future practical energy evaluations. For those few people encountering difficulties, you may seek help from an experienced person.

IV. Scientific Notation

Energy and power quantification does have a unique requirement for the use of very large and very small numbers. Our text quantifies energies such as the electrical energy of a single electron attracted to the nucleus of a single atom to the kinetic energy of the earth rotating around the sun. Both of these quantities are expressed in a standard energy amount unit (In this case the joule). These large variations in numbers cause us to use a more convenient numerical system called *scientific notation*.

Here are the calculated energy examples using scientific notation. The benefit of using scientific notation will be obvious.

Figure 2.5 presents a hydrogen atom with and 1 electron where we will remove that electron, separating the attractive charge between the positively charged center and the negatively charged electron.

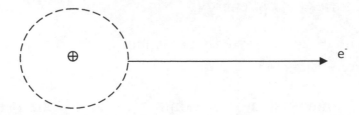

Figure 2.5 Hydrogen Atom Electron Charge Separation

The energy to separate the electron from a single, stable hydrogen atom is:

0. 000, 000, 000, 000, 000, 002.2 joules

This amount of energy for a single electron separation from a hydrogen proton is very small. This is a very small number can be expressed correctly above in a very inconvenient manner.

0. 000, 000, 000, 000, 000, 002.2 joules can be also expressed as the number 2.2 divided by the number 10, 18 times.

2.2 (1/10)(1/10)(1/10)(1/10)(1/10)(1/10)(1/10)(1/10)(1/10)(1/10)(1/10)

(1/10)(1/10)(1/10)(1/10)(1/10)(1/10)(1/10) joules

This numerical division process (called power of tens) is communicated correctly as:

2.2×10^{-18} joules

This is _scientific notation_

Let us look at a very large number.

The energy (kinetic) of the earth in is:

2.700, 000, 000, 000, 000, 000, 000, 000, 000, 000, 000 joules

Figure 2.6 presents a graphic of our earth traveling around the sun.

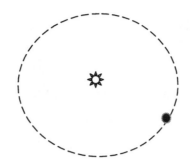

Figure 2.6 Earth Circling Sun

This is a very large number expressed correctly above in a very inconvenient manner.

2.700, 000, 000, 000, 000, 000, 000, 000, 000, 000, 000 joules can also be expressed as the number 2.7 multiplied by 10, 33 times.

2.7(10)(10)(10)(10)(10)(10)(10)(10)(10)(10)(10)(10)(10)(10)(10)(10)
(10)(10)(10)(10)(10)(10)(10)(10)(10)(10)(10)(10)(10)(10)(10)(10)(10)

This numerical multiplication process (called power of tens) is communicated correctly as:

2.7×10^{33} joules - This is a lot of energy! !

This is *scientific notation*.

This is a very convenient method of expressing large numbers.

If you are unfamiliar with the power of ten (also sometimes called scientific notation) of numbers, it will initially require some time with a knowledgeable person to become fluent. Here are some examples:

1) 9.2×10^{7} miles – distance earth to sun
2) 3×10^{8} meters/sec – velocity of light
3) 400×10^{-9} meter – wavelength of purple light
4) 6.5×10^{9} people – number of people in the world

For those unfamiliar with scientific notation, take a moment and expand the scientific notation to our familiar decimal notation. Remember, the numerically expressed values are exactly the same as decimal notation, no matter how they are expressed.

V. Scales and Conversions

Two prime reasons for confusion and errors in the quantitative evaluation of energy systems are 1) the use of two energy measurement systems (SI and British) and 2) the prolific use of measurement standards and scales.

An appendix is provided to facilitate Metric/English conversions. It is intended that within the text, when Metric/English conversions are required, that a comprehensive explanation of the conversion process will be provided at that point. Energy system conversions should not disrupt our focus on energy science.

VI. Conclusions

In Chapters 3 – 11, the energy science is explained in terms of physical dimensions and simple mathematical relationships. At the conclusion of each chapter, the kind of energy described in the chapter will be given in terms of 1) measurement technique of the dimensions and 2) the resulting energy of the specific example in terms of a mathematical equation. You should (must) clearly understand the measurement process and mathematical relationship to calculate energy for each kind of energy. That is our goal.

The must-know elements of energy mathematics are:

> **1, Mathematics is required to clearly define kinds of energies and provide information regarding energy (power) financial comparisons.**
>
> **2. Two systems (English and Metric) are used to quantify energy (power).**
>
> **3. Standards evolved from universal experiences (heating water) that are familiar and acceptable to everyone.**
>
> **4. Scientific notation is extensively used in energy quantification.**

Chapter 3:

Mechanical Energy

Sections

I. Introduction to Mechanical Energy:

Mechanical energy in this chapter is defined as a measurable force times a measurable distance within a solid object. Be careful - that definition may not match the definition of mechanical energy within other texts. Mechanical energy is historically the simplest form and is defined as the amount of energy present is the amount of force times the amount of distance. Mechanical energy is sensed by people in unending examples. Mechanical energy has the oldest and most universally observed energy applications. Chapter 3 reviews the history of this commonly observed kind of energy.

Three observable examples are provided to establish the orientation of this chapter:

1. The available rotational force x distance of our garage door electrical motor is converted to a usable force x distance of opening the garage door.
2. The available muscle force x distance of our bodies is converted to a usable force x distance to open a bottle cap.

3. The available muscle force x distance of our bodies is converted to a usable force x distance when we raise the car with a jack.

II. Levers

Levers are the simplest tools known to mankind. So, if someone calls you a "lever", you may safely assume that not to be a compliment. Early humans discovered that they could lift or pry objects (here a rock as an example) that were too heavy to lift directly, by using a simple rod (lever). This would increase the force. Figure 3.1 presents this pre-historic discovery.

Figure 3.1 Caveman

Not much thought was given to analyzing the lever process. Cavemen just wanted to move the rock away from the center of the cave. By trial and error, the early humans intuitively concluded, the force times the distance from the lever pivot point on one side of the lever was sort of equal to the force times the distance from the pivot point on the other side of the lever. Even monkeys have discovered that one can pry things around with a stick. However, without mathematics and measurement standards, the lever operation became only a limited part of primitive culture.

With the development of mathematics and measurement standards, a more complete understanding of the lever process evolved. This more complete understanding has led to greater applications for our society. Figure 3.2 presents the modern analysis of the lever operation.

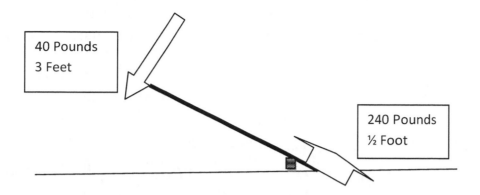

Figure 3.2 Rock Lifting (Modern Interpretation)

1. Numbers are used to quantify the forces and distances. Figure 3.2 presents the rock weighing 240 pounds being raised upward ½ ft by applying a downward force of 40 pounds for 3 ft to the other end of the lever.

2. Observe that in Figure 3.2 the energy on the left side of the pivot point (3 ft x 40 lbs) is equal to the energy on the right side of the pivot point (1/2 ft x 240 lbs). Energy is conserved. This (force x distance) transformation, without energy loss, is the basis of mechanical energy.

3. The definition of mechanical energy is force times distance. The caveman inputted 120 foot-pounds of energy (3 feet x 40 pounds) and outputted 120 foot-pounds of energy (1/2 ft x 240 pounds) during the process of lifting the rock. A lever only exchanges force and distance. Energy is always conserved according to the 1st Law of Thermodynamics.

4. Note that the applied force and resultant force of the lever rotates around a central point. In Figure 3.1 the rotational point was called the "pivot point" with the lever resting on top. The rotational aspect during lever operation was temporarily ignored. In Figure 3.2 the "pivot point" was replaced with a rotating "shaft" and the forces are indicated as rotating around the shaft. The "shaft" is the basis of modern mechanical energy applications.

The engineering aspect is that the actual total length of the entire lever for force amplification is only a practical application. The caveman couldn't fit a 20 foot lever into the cave. The caveman also couldn't use a 4 foot lever and still get the

36" of distance required to move the rock 6" upward. So a practical length of a lever for the caveman would be about 7 feet, with 6 feet on the input side and 1 foot on the output side. The caveman engineered the proper energy application.

Let us shift from the prehistoric example of lifting a rock to the modern example of removing a nail. Figure 3.3 presents a bent lever (claw hammer) that increases the force (pull) upon the nail for a small distance by moving the hammer handle with a smaller force over a larger distance. This is the origin of the words "applying leverage." The bend lever (dotted line) is superimposed upon the hammer.

The mechanical energy conversion is defined by the available biological force of our arms (actually bodies) and the usable application of removing a nail from the material. With a claw hammer, we can amplify our biological force into a physical force capable of removing the nail. Only the force numbers are included in Figure 3.3. What are the distances to the pivot (shaft)?

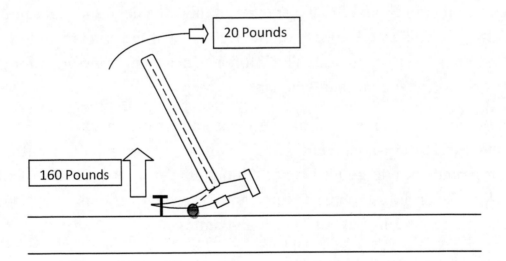

Figure 3.3 Claw Hammer

Two features of the nail removal by the hammer are fundamental:

1. The applied force and the resultant force rotate around a single point called the "pivot point." The "pivot point" and the "shaft" are the same physical location where available energy (force times distance) is converted to a more usable energy (force times distance.).

2. The rotating forces around the "pivot point" or "shaft' means that mechanical force and distance conversion can only occur in a circular manner. The circular motion is obvious when using a claw hammer to remove nails. The removed nails are usually bent in circles.

The engineering considerations of the force needed to remove a typical nail, the size of the claw hammer convenient for operation, the distance required to remove the nail, and the input (pull) force required for operation are part of designing the most suitable claw hammer. A general observation is that various engineered designs of claw hammers have produced almost identical products. There are many examples of applied lever processes. The lever operation clearly describes the concepts of force amplification and the process conservation of energy.

III. Mechanical Rotational Energy

Mechanical rotational energy is an integrated part of our large utility grade energy production systems. Two aspects of mechanical energy must be clearly understood:

1. Mechanical energy can be transferred from one (feet x distance) to another (feet x distance) more suitable to a specific application. Energy is not created nor destroyed in this process. The common noun for mechanical to mechanical energy transfer systems is *machines*.

2. Mechanical energy occurs only during the transfer of energy.   Mechanical energy cannot be stored.

Keeping these two aspects in mind, mechanical rotational energy is visually presented in Figure 3.4.

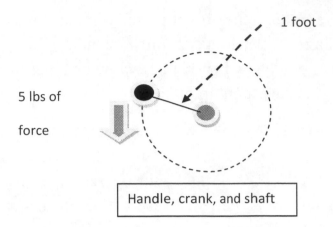

5 lbs of

force

1 foot

Handle, crank, and shaft

Figure 3.4 Shaft Energy Input

Figure 3.4 presents a mechanical device that uses a *"crank* and *handle"* to transmit energy into a *"shaft"*. The "crank and handle" are a rotating lever. The "shaft" in Figure 3.4 is directed into the page. The shaft is the round circle in the middle of Figure 3.4.

The amount of energy transmitted during each turn into the shaft is the force applied to the handle multiplied by the distance traveled by the handle in each turn.

Some elementary mathematics is required in order to clearly describe the machine. The input energy to the shaft is now calculated for a simple example. The amounts of force and distance traveled each turn are chosen only as an example.

First, the input force, in a counter-clockwise direction around the shaft, is arbitrarily given as 5 pounds. This would be a reasonable amount for an average person's cranking force.

Next, we must calculate the distance traveled by the handle each turn of the shaft. In Figure 3.4, the crank distance (from shaft center to the handle) is given as 1 foot. The circular distance (dotted line) around the shaft created by the handle in one turn is 6.28 feet. The 6.28 feet are derived from the universal relationship between the shaft center to the handle distance (radius) and the length of the path created by rotating the radius. The distance around a circle is always the diameter of the circle multiplied by 3.14. In this case 2 feet x 3.14 equals 6.28 feet.

In the Figure 3.4 example, the energy transmitted into the shaft for each turn is (5 pounds) multiplied by (6.28 feet) or 31 foot-pounds.

Be sure you are comfortable with this calculation.

Each turn has 31 foot-pounds of energy transmitted into the shaft. Now where did that energy go? The 1st Law of Thermodynamics states that energy cannot just disappear (as into the page in Figure 3.4). Figure 3.5 presents options where the 31 foot-pounds might have gone. We can choose only one rope-drum as an option (A, B, or C).

Figure 3.5 presents a side view of the handle, crank, and shaft along with where the 31 foot-pounds of energy per turn may have gone (A, B, or C). The shaft is kept in place by bearings which support at each end.

Three drums (A, B, and C) rotate around the shaft 1 turn for 1 turn of the input rotation presented in Figure 3.4. Each drum has a rope attached to it so that the ropes wrap around the drums when it is turned. The distance around a drum is always 2π (6.28) times the radius of the drum. Π is 3.14. In this example, the input distance of force travel is 2π x 1 foot or 6.28 feet per turn.

Figure 3.5 presents options A, B, or C to utilize the 31 foot-pounds of mechanical energy transmitted from the shaft in each turn.

For each turn:

    Drum "A" has a diameter of 1 foot. The rope travels 3.14 feet per turn.
    Drum "B" has a diameter of 2 feet. The rope travels 6.28 feet per turn.
    Drum "C" has a diameter of 3 feet. The rope travels 9.42 feet per turn.

A force upward on each rope (only one at a time) is supplied by the input shaft with an energy of 31 foot-pounds per rotation. An equivalent force of 31 foot-pounds per rotation must be downward to conserve the energy of the system.

    Drum "A" 31 ft-lbs / 3.14 ft is 9.9 pounds
    Drum "B" 31 ft-lbs / 6.28 ft is 4.9 pounds
    Drum "C" 31 ft-lbs / 9.42 ft is 3.3 pounds.

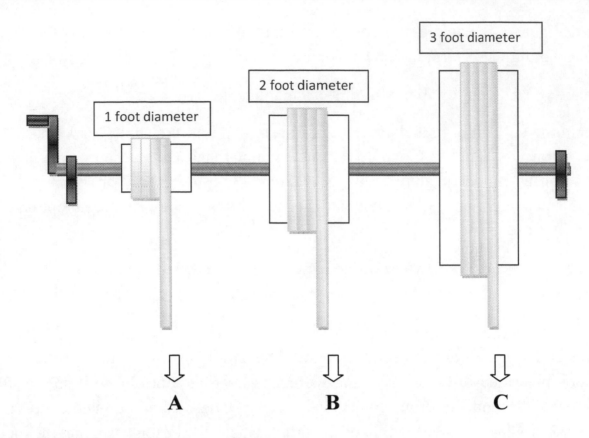

Figure 3.5 Crank shaft and ropes

The Figure 3.5 analysis is charted in Figure 3.6. Note that in every option for using a specific rope, the energy is always conserved. The unifying concept regarding rotational shaft energy is that available energy can be converted into usable energy.

	Force on rope	Length per turn	Energy per turn
"A"	9.9 pounds	3.14 feet	31 foot-pounds
"B"	4.9 pounds	6.28 feet	31 foot-pounds
"C"	3.3 pounds	9.42 feet	31 foot-pounds

Figure 3.6 Energy Output

Two examples of familiar rotational mechanical energy conversion are presented to reinforce the rotational mechanical energy concept.

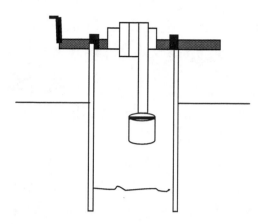

Figure 3.7 The Water Well

Water, in rural areas of the world, may be obtained by lowering a bucket into an open well, and pulling the water-bucket to the surface. The crank and shaft are very similar to the example analyzed in Figure 3.7 above. The open well bucket system in modern society has been relegated to be a romantic ornament in the back yard.

Using what we have learned from energy science:

A small bucket full of water weights about 15 lbs. From the energy science described above, and using the same 5 lb crank force, with 31 ft-lbs of energy per rotation, we would need about 2/3 foot diameter rope puller around the output shaft. The distance traveled by the rope is 2.2 feet per rotation. That means that the force pulling up on the rope will be 14 lbs. (**14 lbs x 2.2 ft is 31 ft-lbs.**) That is close enough to do the job of water retrieval.

Here is the engineering specification:

Handle Diameter	Handle Force	Energy per turn (in)	Water Weight	Length per turn	Energy per turn (out)
2 feet	5 pounds	31 ft-lbs	14 pounds	2.2 feet	31 ft-lbs

The lesson here is not that we can engineer a water bucket system. The proper water bucket system was first founded by common sense without mathematical rigor. The lesson here is that mechanical rotational energy fundamentals are energy science and those scientific principles will apply to engineering for societal benefit.

Figure 3.8 is a stickwoman riding a bicycle. In order to propel the bicycle, she must apply a force to the pedal through a distance (energy). The energy is transmitted to the back wheel (force x distance) where the force part of the energy pushes against the road and propels the bicycle forward. The bold lines trace the energy flow (force x distance). There is a dynamic opposing force between the pedal sprocket and the rear wheel sprocket that obeys the force x distance energy conservation. The amount of force at the rear wheel to road interface varies considerably due to many factors. Examples are road slope, wind, road surface roughness, speed etc. Because of the large variation in rear wheel to road force required, the shaft force to distance conversion is engineered into the bicycle. An example is the 12-speed bicycle. The engineering aspects are too complex for comment in this text. However, you should think about this application with energy science insight.

Figure 3.8 Bicycle

IV. The Horsepower - A Mechanical Power Standard

The mechanical shaft is a basic element of energy science. However, the main physical characteristic of a shaft is rotation, and the universal characterization of a shaft is rotation with time. Note, that in the last section, the element of **time** it took to raise the water bucket did not have to be included in the energy analysis. The natural evolution of energy science in mechanical science was to measure energy over time.

By definition, energy for a period of time is power.

Energy over a period of Time is Power

The mechanical rotational shaft provided the basis for understanding power in quantized terms and provided a standard basis of energy accepted by society. Here is how these events evolved.

James Watt (1736 – 1819) invented a way to provide continuous power to a mechanical shaft. He built a "working" steam engine around 1790. Steam engine energy is described in Chapter 11. The steam engine invented by James Watt used heat energy from burning coal to produce steam pressure that created energy (force at a distance) on a shaft (Figure 3.10). James Watt had a difficult time marketing the steam engine's power and effectiveness since a measurement of power did not exist. But James Watt knew his invention was in direct economic competition with horses in lifting coal from underground mines. James Watt then established a quantitative mechanical energy standard.

James measured the average lifting ability of horses lifting coal from the mines and estimated that they lifted, on the average, 550 pounds 1 foot per second. He established 550 ft-lbs/sec to be a standard 1 horsepower. This is often stated as the equivalent 33,000 ft-lbs/min. Note that power includes distance, force, and time. James Watt's genius is that he standardized energy in terms of the universe dimensions of feet, pounds, and seconds. And now everyone could precisely understand power in those familiar terms. The actual name horsepower was only given as a marketing tool.

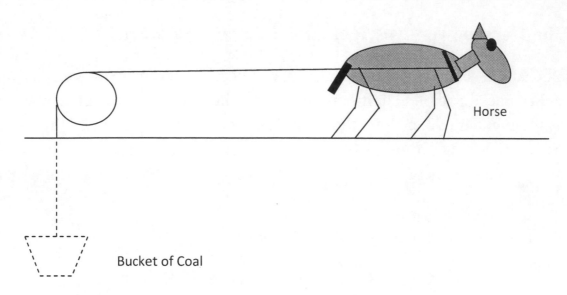

Horse

Bucket of Coal

Figure 3.9 Horsepower

James Watt invented a revolutionary (excuse the pun) application. Not only could the steam engines work (energy) 24 hours per day (power), one could depend upon the steam engine power to perform as specified by the steam manufacturer. One also could compare steam engine costs of purchase, maintenance, and operation. This removed business variables from the coal mining operations.

James Watt's successful coal driven steam engines soon found other applications where continuous power available on a mechanical shaft was needed. The most notable application was the steam engines used in train locomotives. Today, the major utility grade power generation is through heat energy conversion into steam energy conversion into mechanical energy conversion into usable electrical energy. The energy standard horsepower was kept in future applications. James Watt's name was immortalized by his efforts. And we also measure our home electricity energy (actually power) usage in (kilo) *Watts*. We see his name each month on our energy bill.

We also now measure automobile engine power by *horsepower*. The standardization of power means that everyone agrees to the meaning of the horsepower measurement. Automobiles are still sold and compared by horsepower.

V. Horsepower Measurement

Power is the proper noun of utility grade energy with time production. Power in the English system is measured in horsepower. A horsepower is defined as 550 ft-lbs/sec (that's energy over time). Power is defined in the Metric system as a watt. A Metric unit of energy is a joule (1 Newton x 1 meter of distance) and power is a watt. A watt is 1 joule of energy during one second (energy over time). The familiar unit of power is a kilowatt.

Conversion between the power measurement systems is detailed. The mathematical procedure of this conversion is given in Chapter 3 Insight.

1 Horsepower is equal to 746 watts

The reason we will retain both horsepower and watts as power measurements is that both systems exist due to the historical establishment. All people agree with these two standards.

The measurement of shaft horsepower has been greatly simplified as visually presented by the steam engine presented in Figure 3.10. The simplifying factors are:

1. The revolutions per minute (RPM) of a shaft has become an accurate and common measurement. Most automobiles have an RPM gauge. RPM measurement gauges are called *tachometers*. Knowing RPM's, the **distance** that a force travels with time can be precisely calculated.

2. The amount of **force** generated by an internal combustion engine can be measured precisely at any distance from the engine shaft.

The results are an easily obtained engine power determination. All we have to do is take the force at a distance from the shaft and multiply the distance the force is traveling.

In honor of James Watt, Figure 3.10 presents the internal mechanical fundamentals of the steam engine.

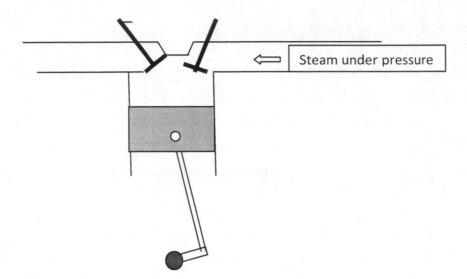

Steam under pressure

Figure 3.10 Steam Engine

James Watt's steam engine is not much different from our water well example. The hand force on the input handle has been replaced by the force of steam pressure. The rotating shaft in the steam engine is now called the *crankshaft*. However the versatility of the steam engine crankshaft in providing reliable horsepower has produced many notable applications.

VI. Practical Applications

The mechanical shaft is utilized often in the generation of utility grade power. The mechanical shaft has a convenient attribute of allowing a flexible way of obtaining the best force and distance. In this section, common force-distance designs for shafts are mentioned.

Remember, mechanical energy cannot be stored; it can only be used to convert other kinds of available energy into usable kinds of energies.

Conversion of shaft speeds (RPM's) to meet application requirements is so common that we hardly notice that application.

Figure 3.11 presents two shaft sprockets connected by a chain. Each sprocket connects to the chain with "teeth" on the perimeter of each sprocket to keep the chain from slipping.

The sprocket chain allows us to maximize the force-distance from the input power to the force-distance of the output power. We saw an excellent example in Figure 3.8 where we could shift gears to establish our best bicycle force being applied to the road.

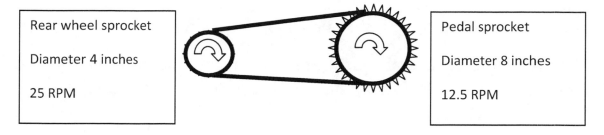

Rear wheel sprocket	Pedal sprocket
Diameter 4 inches	Diameter 8 inches
25 RPM	12.5 RPM

Figure 3.11 Sprocket Chain

This is one speed on your bicycle chain and sprockets. All 12 speeds are not included, it would be too complicated.

A belt is fundamentally a sprocket-chain without teeth. Again, optimum force-distances can be chosen for any specific application.

Figure 3.12 presents a typical belt within an automobile that is driven by the main crankshaft. The belt turns the water pump, the power steering, the electrical generator, and the air conditioning pump. The size of the belt pulleys for each application is determined by the best RPM value and direction for the specific application during the automobile operation.

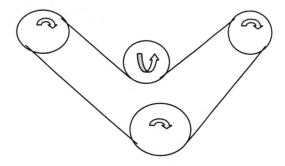

Figure 3.12 Automobile Belt

Gears are commonly used to achieve the best force and distance for power. The great advantages of gears are that they cannot slip and they are relatively durable.

Figure 3.13 presents a typical gear system that transmits power from one shaft to another. Observations about gears are:

1. Note that the distance between gear teeth in both the input gear and output gear must be equal. (Or else the gears will not mesh, and quickly wear out)

2. The input shaft and output shaft turn in opposite directions.

3. In every gear contact, the input gear teeth must slide upon the output gear teeth while operating. Lubrication is always needed with gears to minimize wear caused by this sliding.

4. You may have heard about many specialized gears, such as worm, hypoid, differential, and synchronized. They all have been developed using our simple principles.

5. The ratio of the rpm's during operation of the input shaft relative to the rpm's of the output shaft is called the *gear ratio*. In this example, one gear has 16 teeth and the other 32 teeth, the same as the sprocket in Figure 3-10. Of trivial significance is that a gear set will change the direction of rotation.

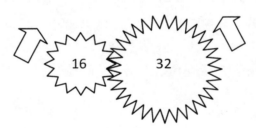

Figure 3.13 Gears

The common application of gears to optimize force and distance is the automobile transmission. When we start moving an automobile, we need a high force applied to the wheels on the pavement. We start in low gear where we have a high engine crankshaft to driving wheel gear ratio. This increases the drive wheel force and helps to accelerate the automobile to its desired speed. But the engine can only rotate so fast; the driveshaft must shift into a lower gear ratio (engine to wheel) as the high engine rotational speed limit approaches. Now we have a lower force at the drive wheels with a greater distance at the same engine rotation. Eventually, we will change to the driveshaft the lowest gear ratio (high gear), where we only have to sustain the selected automobile speed. We have transformed available mechanical energy into usable mechanical energy. The automobile is quite a machine.

This process is done for us by the automobile automatic transmission.

Other common applications use a winch. A winch is the same fundamentally as the water well in Figure 3.7. Other observed uses of the winch are those mounted on the front of jeeps and the winch used to pull boats out of the lake unto trailers. Both utilizations use gear ratios to amplify the force to a usable level.

VII. Conclusions

Mechanical energy, as defined in the introduction, is a measurable force times a measurable distance traveling through a solid object. The observed examples are called "machines."

The must-know elements of mechanical energy are:

1. Mechanical energy is force x distance.

2. Mechanical energy in English system is measured in foot-pounds.

3. Mechanical energy in Metric is measured in joules. (or capital J)

4. Power is energy over time.

5. English system power is measured in horsepower.

6. Metric power is measured in watts. (Usually stated as kilowatts)

Mechanical energy has a long history of applications. From the simple lever to the present gear technology, energy transfer by mechanical means has been the basis of the modern industrial revolution and energy utilization. The concept of mechanical energy being available as a flexible force x distance conversion is also fundamental to engineerng.

Chapter 3 Insight

The Conversion of Horsepower to Kilowatts

An internal source of confusion exists because the public uses the English System of weight (pounds) and the public also uses the Metric System of mass (grams) to express the same physical measurement.

Example: An automobile with a measurement weight of 3000 lbs will also have a measurement mass of 1364 kg (kilograms). But weight and mass do not possess the same universal dimensions. Pounds are a measure of earth's gravitational force on matter and grams are a measure of mass, a basic property of matter!

And this perpetuated institutionalized confusion remains without resolution; not even on the internet. The conversion of horsepower to kilowatts is not logically derived (mathematically), but the conversion factor alone is supplied without explanation.

The derivation is slightly beyond the requirement of understanding mechanical energy.

First, force (F), by definition, is mass (m) x acceleration (a).

F = ma

This equation applies to all matter (m) in our universe.

English System $F \text{ (pounds)} = ma = (XXXXX)(32.2 \text{ feet/sec}^2)$

Metric System $F(\text{Newtons}) = ma = (\text{kilograms})(9.81 \text{ meters/sec}^2)$

Newtons and (XXXXX) are very unfamiliar. But values in Newtons are required in the mathematical equation to retain universal dimensions. A *Newton* is the weight of mass (grams) in our earth's gravitational force field. Metric newtons are equivalent to English pounds.

Second, gather the equations that we need:

    1. 1 joule = 1 newton x 1 meter

    2. 1 Watt = 1 joule / 1 second

    3. 1 lb = 454 grams = 0.454 kg

Third, substitute Metric equivalent values into Watt's horsepower equation.

1 horsepower = 550 ft x 1 lb / sec (Watt's standard)

Newtons of force in 1 pound

    Force (newtons) = kilograms x gravitational acceleration

    = 0.454 kg x (9.81 meters / sec^2)

    = 4.45 newtons (in 1 pound)

Meters distance in 550 feet

    550 feet x 0.3048 meters / ft = **167.6 meters (in 550 feet)**

So, 1 Horsepower = 167.6 meters x 4.45 Newtons / sec

= 746 joules / sec = 746 watts of power

Fortunately, this specific measurement conversion has minimal impact upon our energy description. See Chapter 5 Insight for more details.

Chapter 4:

Kinetic Energy

Sections:

I. Introduction to Kinetic Energy

Kinetic energy is the energy of material (mass) in motion (distance in time). Kinetic energy is a fundamental part of our universe.

Kinetic energy is observed in an unending number of events. Kinetic energy is observed (felt) when you bump your knee. Kinetic energy is observed when you see a golf shot. Kinetic energy is observed when you see a fender-bender accident. Kinetic energy is the primary attribute of our favorite football running back. Kinetic energy pushes our sailboat through the water. What we generally observe is conversion of other forms of energy to and from kinetic energy. However, kinetic energy in itself is rarely discussed. Why, I do not know. That is one good reason for having kinetic energy basics within this text.

Kinetic energy is primarily observed when converting other forms of energy into kinetic energy and when converting kinetic energy into other forms of energy. All examples of kinetic energy phenomenon in this chapter follow these observations. Kinetic energy is easiest to understand by its measurement. And fortunately, kinetic energy is easy to measure.

In every example of kinetic energy, we can calculate the amount of energy if we just know the mass (weight) and the velocity (speed). This is a big deal. It allows us to compare kinetic energies to other kinetic energies and to other forms of energy. For example, in a later chapter, we will calculate the amount of electrical energy produced by wind. Wind is a simple form of kinetic energy. Wind has mass and velocity. This calculation process is simple enough so everyone can understand. We just have to learn a few things.

The unit for measurement of kinetic energy is a joule. Let me repeat, the unit for measurement of kinetic energy is a joule. Joule is pronounced jewel like in jewelry. What a horrible way to start a text! I am presenting a vague idea using an obscure (for now) proper noun. A quick way to establish a feel for the magnitude of a joule is to lift this book (about 1000 grams) upward against gravity 40 inches (about 1 meter). That took about 10 joules of energy.

The joule is the standard unit of measurement for kinetic energy. And yes, following the 1st Law of Thermodynamics, all kinds of energies can be measured with the same scale. All kinds of energies can and most often are presented in joules.

The prime goal of this text is to explain the elements of energy, and we will not get too involved with energy measurement systems. The physical dimensions for our kinetic energy calculations are:

1. Kinetic energy (Joules)

2. Mass (Kilograms) (That is 1 gram x 1000) or (about 2.2 pounds).

3, Velocity (Meters/sec)

The formula for the measurement of kinetic energy is:

K.E. (joules) = ½mv^2

= ½ mass (kilograms) x velocity (meters/sec) x velocity (meters/sec)

There are two areas of learning involved in understanding kinetic energy:

1) The dimensions used to calculate kinetic energy exclusively use the Metric Energy measurement system. The Metric Energy measurement system is unfamiliar to most individuals in the United States because we use English physical dimensions.

2) Kinetic energy is always calculated from the measured values of mass and velocity. Some examples will familiarize us to the kinetic energy concept.

II Kinetic Energy Universal Observations

A universal observation of kinetic energy is the balls during the sports games of baseball, basketball, football, bowling, etc. All of these sports games feature a ball (mass) that travels at a speed (velocity). We have abundant examples of kinetic energy! As repetitive learning examples, we will calculate some kinetic energies:

A. Baseball

Figure 4.1 Baseball Pitcher

Watching TV, the announcer says that the last pitch was a 95 Miles per Hour (MPH) fastball. It was measured to be 95 MPH by radar behind home plate. "What was the kinetic energy of the baseball at 95 MPH?" The answer to the question will be given by executing the following steps:

Step #1: **Determine the mass of the moving object in kilograms.**

The specified mass of baseball is can be obtained from the internet.

The internet states that the weight of a baseball is <u>5 ounces.</u>

Convert ounces to grams for use in the K.E. formula. (See the Conversion Appendix)

5 ounces x 28.4 grams/ounce= 142 grams

142 grams x 1 kilogram/ 1000 grams = **<u>0.142 kilogram</u>**

We know the mass of the baseball in kilograms.

Step #2: **Determine the velocity of the moving object.**

The announcer said the velocity of the baseball was 95 MPH.

Convert MPH to meters/sec for use in the K.E. formula.(See the Conversion Appendix)

95 miles/hr x 0.44 meters/sec / miles/hour = **<u>42 meters/sec</u>**

We know the velocity of the baseball in meters/sec.

Step #3: **Determine the kinetic energy of the moving object**

Using the proper dimensions, we calculate the kinetic energy of the baseball.

K.E. = ½ (mass)(velocity)(velocity)

K.E. (Joules) = ½ (0.142 kg)(42 meter/sec)(42 meter/sec)

Kinetic energy = <u>125 Joules</u>

Now we know the kinetic energy of the baseball in joules.

Baseball insight:

Knowing the kinetic energy of the baseball leads to many interesting insights. For instance, a major league pitcher can throw about 110 pitches before he becomes tired. It is easy to calculate the total amount of energy an average pitcher can convert from his body (chemical energy) to kinetic energy before tiring. This is the measure of athletic stamina.

110 pitches x 125 Joules/pitch = 13,800 Joules/game

(1.3×10^4 joules/game in scientific notation)

Now this amount of energy is expended if only fastballs were thrown. And in reality, we know that fastball "closers" (those only pitching the last couple of innings) can only throw about 20 maximum velocity pitches while keeping adequate control and velocity of the baseball. Is this reasonable?? Actually, kinetic energy evaluations will provide reasonable expectations. But few people mention kinetic energy. My friend says kinetic energy evaluations take the fun out of baseball.

B. Automobile

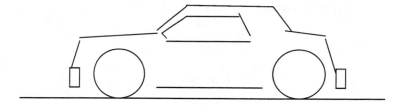

Figure 4.2 Automobile

An automobile is a very familiar example of observed kinetic energy. We will measure the kinetic energy of a typical automobile and present some insights into this familiar energy system.

Step #1: **Determine the mass of the moving object in   kilograms.**

> Automobiles have a large range of weights (masses). So we will designate a reasonable weight for our automobile as 3200 lbs. Convert lbs to kilograms for use in the K.E. formula. (See appendix conversion chart)
>
> 3200 lbs x 1kg/2.2 lbs = **1400 kg**
>
> We have the mass of the automobile in kilograms

Step #2: **Determine the velocity of the moving object.**

Automobiles have a large range of speeds (velocities).We will designate the highway velocity of the automobile at 60 miles per hour (MPH). The speedometer indicates 60 MPH.

Convert MPH to meters/sec for use in the K.E. formula. See Conversion Appendix)

60 MPH x 0.44 meters/sec/MPH = **26 meters/sec**

We have the velocity of the automobile in meters/sec.

Step #3: **Determine the kinetic energy of the moving object**

Using the proper dimensions, we calculate the kinetic energy

K.E. = ½ (m)(v²)

K.E. = ½ (1400 kg)(26m/s)(26m/s) = 480,000 joules

(4.8 x 10⁵ joules in scientific notation)

We know the kinetic energy of the automobile in joules.

Automobile insight:

We have just determined that a 3200 pound automobile traveling at a velocity of 60 MPH has a kinetic energy of 480,000 joules. When we started from the garage, the automobile had zero kinetic energy. We converted 480,000 joules of energy from the gasoline chemical energy into kinetic energy. Now, in order to stop the automobile (back to zero kinetic energy), we have to convert the 480,000 joules of kinetic energy to heat energy in the brakes. This is a crude approximation that will be described in detail later. The important idea is that energy only flowed from one kind to another kind during this automobile process. Energy was neither created nor destroyed. This idea is central to the understanding of the universal energy conservation.

This automobile insight was added as an afterthought. The energy flow model presented does not include a common automobile observation. If we were traveling at 60 MPH on a level road and placed our automobile in neutral, we would notice that the automobile's speed would decrease and eventually we would stop moving. The kinetic energy of the automobile would be decreasing. The kinetic energy is being transferred to heat energy through tire resistance and kinetic energy through wind resistance. If your automobile was in outer space, without the tire and wind energy loss, it would maintain its speed and kinetic energy forever.

C. The Glass Door

Ouch!

Figure 4.3 Glass Door

A memorable and painful shared experience of kinetic energy involves running into a glass door. This personal example was chosen because of its lasting impression.

I was running towards my outdoor patio. Steaks were burning on the grill. I thought the door was open; but I surprisingly encountered a glass door and converted my kinetic energy painfully into my body.

What was the amount of this kinetic energy?

Step #1: **Determine the mass of the moving object in kilograms.**

My weight is about 200 pounds.

Convert lbs to mass for use in the K.E. formula. (See the Conversion Appendix)

200 lbs x 1 kg/2.2 lbs = **91 kg**

We have the mass of my body in kilograms.

Step #2: **Determine the velocity of the moving object.**

My velocity was about 5 MPH.

Convert MPH to meters/sec for use in the K.E. formula. (See the Conversion Appendix)

5 MPH x 0.44 meters/sec/MPH = **2.2 meters/sec**

We have the velocity of my body

Step #3: **Determine the kinetic energy of the moving object**

$$\text{K.E.} = \tfrac{1}{2} \, mv^2$$

$$\text{K.E.} = \tfrac{1}{2} \, (91 \text{ kg})(2.2 \text{ m/sec})(2.2 \text{ m/sec}) = \underline{220 \text{ joules}}$$

We know the kinetic energy of my body in joules.

Glass door insights

Bumps and bruises are universal experiences shared by everyone. All are caused by kinetic energy. Of course, common sense dictates that walking into a glass door or even being hit by a fast baseball is not as serious as being hit by an automobile traveling at 60 MPH. Check out the joules.

Kinetic energy observations summary - What have we learned.

1. Kinetic energy can be always calculated by three steps. All the examples are repetition of this procedure. Measurement of kinetic energy is the key to understanding energy conversion and kinetic energy applications.

2. The cohesive energy concepts of energy conservation and energy conversion are explicit in our observed examples.

III. An Important Kinetic Energy Evaluation

What will cause more damage and corresponding pain in your leg, being hit by a 95 MPH baseball, being hit by a driver golf shot, or being hit by a 22 caliber long rifle bullet? This is important trivia information.

We have already calculated the 95 MPH baseball to have 125 joules of kinetic energy. Note that you don't have to calculate (or even check) existing energy data. As you become more familiar with energy values, incorrect values will become instantaneously apparent.

The kinetic energy for a golf ball needs to be determined.

The source of the golf ball mass and the golf ball tee shot velocity is the internet. The internet is a plentiful source of data.

The calculation of kinetic energy will follow the three steps presented in the last section.

Figure 4.4 Stickwoman Golfer

Step #1: **Determine the mass of the moving object.**

The mass is given as **46 grams.** No measurement system conversion is required.

Convert grams to kilograms for use in the K.E. formula.

46 grams x 1 kilogram/1000 grams = **0.046 kg**

We have the mass of the golf ball in kilograms.

Step #2: **Determine the velocity of the moving object**

The velocity is given as 76 meters/second (**76m/s).** No measurement system conversion is required.

We have the velocity of the golf ball.

Step #3: **Determine the kinetic energy of the moving object**

K.E. = ½ mv²

Kinetic energy (joules) = ½ (0.046 kg)(76 m/s)(76 m/s)

Kinetic energy (joules) = 133 joules

We know the kinetic energy of the golf ball in joules.

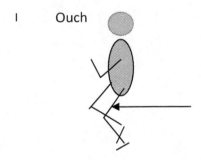

I   Ouch

Figure 4.5 Stickman - What was that?

Third, the kinetic energy of a 22 long rifle bullet needs to be determined.

The mass, velocity and kinetic energy data of a 22 caliber long rifle bullet was found on the internet. I was shocked to find that all pertinent data was available in the Metric Energy measurement system format. The mass was 2.3 grams and the velocity was 330 m/s. And the energy was given as 141 joules!! Just for practice, we will double check the internet kinetic energy value.

K.E. = ½ mv²

Kinetic energy (joules) = ½ (0.0023 kg)(330 m/s)(330 m/s)

Kinetic energy (joules) = <u>142 joules</u> (close enough)

We have confirmed that the 22 caliber long rifle bullet kinetic energy, as internet given, to be 141 joules.

Kinetic energy evaluation conclusions:

Our investigation is best presented as a data consolidation chart:

	Mass(kg)	Velocity(m/s)	K.E. (joules)
Baseball	0.142	42	125
Golf ball	0.046	76	133
22 LR bullet	0.0023	330	141

A comparison of the measured values of the observed kinetic energies allow us to conclude the following:

1. The kinetic energy of all three objects is roughly the same. Without additional information, one could not distinguish what projectile contacted your leg.

2. The 22 LR bullet has a small size and therefore a greater penetrating ability. To make a fair comparison, a bullet proof material must be worn on the leg. This would spread the kinetic energy over an area similar to the baseball and golf ball. Let us for now imagine that all three objects hit an area in the leg that had a wallet made of material that stopped the 22 LR bullet. Including the required conditions, the kinetic energy being converted is approximately the same over the same area of the leg.

3. The answer to our original question about the most bodily damage, all three are about the same. The bullet has the ability to penetrate because of its smaller size.

4. Avoid kinetic objects.

IV. Rotational Kinetic Energy

An application of kinetic energy, one which we do not visually observe for safety considerations, is the internal combustion engine flywheel. An operational aspect of our internal combustion engines is that energy is transmitted to the mechanical engine shafts only during the power stroke. This periodic pulse of power is smoothed for the engine power output in the following manner. The shaft is connected to a rotating mass (the flywheel) that absorbs kinetic energy during the power stroke of the engine and releases it as mechanical energy to the engine crankshaft, decreasing kinetic energy, during the time between power strokes. Flywheels do not transfer any power away from the engine, they only create a smooth power flow from the engine.

The yo-yo toy is an example of rotational kinetic energy in action. By periodically adding kinetic energy to the yo-yo by applying mechanical energy (force x distance) to the string, we can observe many entertaining actions.

V. Conclusions

Kinetic energy is the energy of material (mass) in motion. The concept of kinetic energy has not become part of our modern languages. However, kinetic energy is a crucial part of understanding the cohesive energy concepts of 1) the conservation of energy, 2) the conversion of energy forms, and 3) the flow of stored and dynamic energies.

The must-know elements of kinetic energy are:

> **1. Kinetic Energy = ½ mv^2**
>
> > **a. In universal dimension terms = ½ (m)(d/t)(d/t)**
>
> **2. Kinetic Energy is calculated from measured quantities**
>
> **3. Mass and velocity are the measured quantities.**
>
> **4. The KE disciplined calculation procedure**
>
> > **a. Determine the mass**

b. Determine the velocity

c. Determine the energy

5. Kinetic energy is a basis for utility power.

The use of kinetic energy in later chapters of this comprehensive energy investigation will demonstrate its importance in integrating the entire energy discipline.

Chapter 4 Insight

The Derivation of Kinetic Energy

The underlying physical nature of kinetic energy is difficult to determine from observation alone. However, based upon elementary physics and a little calculus, the universe constants of kinetic energy can be derived:

Elementary physics: acceleration (a) = dv (velocity) /dt (time)

If $a = dv/dt$, then $v = \int a\, dt = at + c_1$

Now, if at time 0 we let $c_1 = 0$, then $v = at + v_0$ (Equation 1)

Velocity is equal to distance divided by time.

$v = dx$ (distance) $/ dt$ (time)

$x = \int v\, dt = \int (at + v_0) dt = \frac{1}{2} at^2 + v_0 t + c_2$ (distance)

At time 0, $x = c_2$, so $x = x_0 + v_0 t + \frac{1}{2} at^2$

And if we start at a zero distance $x = v_0 t + \frac{1}{2} at^2$ (Equation2)

Rearrange Equation 1, so $t = v - v_0 / a$, and substitute that in Equation2:

$x = v_0 (v - v_0) / a + \frac{1}{2} a (v - v_0)^2 / a^2$

or $2ax = 2v_0 v - 2v_0^2 + v^2 - 2v_0 v + v_0^2$

$= v^2 - v_0^2$

or $v^2 = v_0^2 + 2ax$ (Whew!) (Equation 3)

Now remember Force = (Mass)(Acceleration) or **F=ma**

a = F/m, and Equation 3 is now $v^2 = v_0^2 + 2Fx / m$

But Fx is force through a distance, by definition the energy we are looking for!!!

Just rearrange the last equation:

$Fx = \frac{1}{2} mv^2 - \frac{1}{2} mv_0^2 =$ Kinetic Energy (In its complete form)

$KE = \frac{1}{2} mv^2$

This is a very important physical derivation. It is recognized that without calculus tools, this derivation would be impossible to achieve. That is the reason the derivation is placed in the Chapter 4 Insight. One really doesn't need to understand physical derivations to understand utility grade energy and power. But whether it is part of a wind turbine or a hydroelectric power plant, kinetic energy is based upon established, unchanging science.

Chapter 5:

Gravitational Energy

Sections:

I. Introduction to Gravitational Energy

Gravitational energy is based upon a fundamental force in nature. Gravity is the mutual attraction between all masses in the universe. That attraction is a force. Gravitational force by itself is not energy; <u>When the gravitational force moves masses a distance towards each other, that is energy</u>. And energy can be stored in gravity (a gravitational field) by first "forcing" masses, using energy, against the gravity field a "distance", then later regaining the energy as the masses return to their original position. A definition of energy is work (a force through a distance).

The precise behavior of gravitational force was deduced by Isaac Newton. That deduction was a flash of genius romantically recorded as Isaac Newton's observation of an apple falling from a tree (Figure 5.1). Isaac defined gravitational force and the universal law of gravity in this simple mathematical equation:

This gravitational relationship was expressed in mathematical terms. The equations for the gravitational relationship are given below. You are not required to know the Universal Law of Gravity to become fluent in utility grade energy. The Universal

Law of Gravity is presented only to demonstrate that basic science provides a solid background of gravitational energy and power.

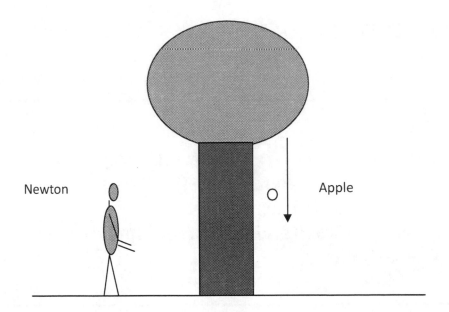

Newton

Apple

Figure 5.1 Newton's Apple

Universal Law of Gravity

    $F = G\,(m_1 m_2 \,/\, r^2)$

    F = Force of attraction

    m_1 = Mass of one object

    m_2 = Mass of another object

    r = Distance between the objects

    G = Mathematical constant so force (F) can be properly expressed in usable standard terms.

Newton's apple is a good reference, whether it is a true story or not. It takes energy to lift the apple to the height of the tree limb (force against gravity). And the same amount of energy (gravitational) is converted to kinetic energy when the apple drops toward the ground.

You do not have to remember the *Universal Law of Gravity* to understand the concept of gravitational energy. But some explanation needs to be devoted to hopefully clarify the confusing evolution of the gravitational concept:

1. Isaac Newton deduced the relationship between gravitational force and masses. However, any underlying reason for gravitational forces to exist in nature is not known.

2. Gravity is a force of attraction. The universal force of gravity between two objects with masses naturally will force the two objects with mass towards each other. This attractive force exists between all masses in the universe.

   This attraction is confirmed precisely by the measurements of our planetary motions. A force moving a mass is one of the basic definitions of energy (underlined above). The static surroundings that we observe are where gravitational forces have attracted masses to their closest position. The atoms on the earth cannot be squeezed together further by gravitational force. The atoms also will not separate from the earth unless an energy greater than gravitational energy can force them apart. We realize this every time we encounter something too "heavy" to lift.

   We can also force (with another kind of energy) objects against the gravitational force field away from each other. The energy will now be available or "stored" for the future as gravitational energy. We can pedal our bicycle up the hill in the morning and coast down the hill in the afternoon.

3. Since gravitation energy was originally considered as occurring within a force field that could **store energy** for future use, it was called historically **potential energy**.

The historical classifications of energies were only kinetic (moving) and potential (stored). However, the more precise contemporary classifications of energy within this text cannot be accommodated by the two simplistic historic classifications. Potential energy, as in the historical classification, would cause extensive confusion within the comprehensive scope of this text.

"*Potential Energy*" will not be used as a proper noun within this text. Instead "*Stored Energy*" will always be used as the proper noun when appropriate.

II. Gravitational Energy Observations

Stored gravitation energy provides many observations when co-existing with kinetic energy:

1. Everything falls down! (After some kind of energy forced it up)

2. Water flows downhill. (After evaporation, then condensation, forced the water up)

3. Arrows return to earth. (After we forced them up by elastic energy into the air)

4. Skiers slide down the slope. (After being raised up by the mechanical energy ski lift)

I am sure that you can supply many other observable examples of gravitational energy. The four examples present gravitational energy dynamically converting to kinetic energy. The gravitational energy is actually stored at the point of maximum distance "up" against the gravitation attraction of the mass to the earth. One of the most ominous examples of gravitational energy is observed when we travel in the mountains. Below steep, long downhill grades there are run-away truck ramps. The concept is to halt a speeding truck without braking capacity into a bed of loose rock in order to dissipate the truck's kinetic energy into heat energy. The kinetic energy was converted from gravitational energy on the way down the mountain. That must be a frightful experience.

Let's analyze the conversion between gravitational energy and kinetic energy:

Figure 5-2 presents a simple conversion between gravitation energy at a measured height and conversion of that gravitational energy to kinetic energy.

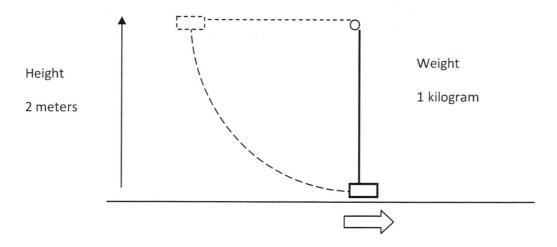

Figure 5.2 Gravitational Energy Converted to Potential Energy

A brick is attached to a wire 2 meters in length. The brick is allowed to swing at the end of the wire downward in an arc to its lowest point (2 meters lower). The gravitational energy of the brick dropping 2 meters is converted to kinetic energy in the brick.

The amount of gravitational energy of any object on the surface of the earth is:

Gravitational Energy = Height x mass x force = hmg

= hmg (or simply weight x height)

The mass, (m), is measurement compared to a standard. The standard gram exists in Paris, France.

The measured mass attraction, (g), at the earth's surface, between any mass on the surface of the earth and the total mass of the earth, has been determined to be 9.8 meters/ (second)(second).

(Further information regarding gravity is given in the Chapter 5 Insight)

Remember this gravitational energy equation!

Gravitational energy = hmg using Metric System measurements

The reason we are using Metric System measurements to investigate gravitational energy is that gravitational energy (joules) can then be compared with kinetic energy (joules) without energy system conversion.

"The Falling Brick"

Figure 5.2 has some measured values so that we can calculate the gravitational energy:

1. Height = 2 meters

2. Weight = 1000 grams (a 2.2 pound brick) = 1 kilogram

Gravitational Energy = hmg = (2 meters)(1 KG)(9.8 meters/(sec)(sec))

= 19.6 joules

When the brick reaches the lowest point, Gravitational energy (19.6 joules) is totally converted to kinetic energy (19.6 joules). The experimental process converted 19.6 joules of gravitational energy into 19.6 joules of kinetic energy.

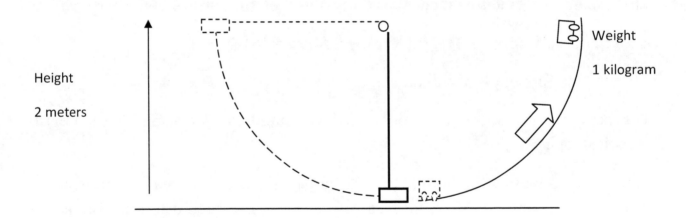

Height

2 meters

Weight

1 kilogram

Figure 5.3 The Toy Car

In Figure 5.3 we allow the brick to contact a resting toy car with 1kg of mass. The brick stops dead as it transfers the 19.2 joules of kinetic energy to the car.

Kinetic energy itself does not distinguish between a brick and a toy car. The toy car proceeds up the solid arc ramp to a height of 2 meters where the brick started its fall. Energy is always conserved (figure 5.3).

III Conversion Efficiency

Ideally, if there were no energy losses during the Figure 5.3 experimental process (100% efficient conversion), this conversion sequence would continue forever. And if a skier had no energy loss during the skiing process, he or she could ski up and down the mountains across a valley all day without the ski lift (energy input).

I should really stay away from using skiing as an example. Skiing personally has a considerable negative content. I tried skiing by attempting to transverse the "beginners" slope. I was never able to ski across that slope. It is very humiliating to be repeatedly raised to one's vertical position by a couple of six-year old strangers. And what is worse, I can view this ski slope from my present house window.

Let us get back to reality. Energy conversion is never 100% and a skier never goes all day without energy input from a ski lift or by walking up the mountain. Figure 5.3 presented an experiment that allowed us to demonstrate a fictional 100% conversion of kinds of energies.

Figure 5.4 presents the real situation where the gravitational energy to toy car energy back to gravitational energy did not return the 1000 gram toy car back to the 2 meter starting height. Some energy was converted to other kinds of energies during the conversion process. Loses include sonic energy (we can hear the brick hit the car) and heat energy (the car has axel friction heat loss). Let's give a good estimate that the car only traveled up the ramp 1.7 meters. The 1000 gram car was 1.7 meters above the bottom when it stopped. It had:

1. Height = 1.7 meters

2. Weight = 1 kilogram

Gravitational energy (joules) = (1.7 meters) x (1kg) x (9.3 meters / (sec)(sec))

   = 15.8 joules

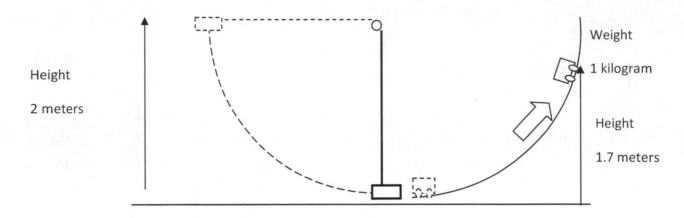

Figure 5.4 Real Conversion

Remember our conversion efficiency equation?

Conversion efficiency= (energy out / energy in) x 100

= (15.8 joules / 19.6 joules) x 100 = **81% efficiency**

3.8 joules of energy was converted to other kinds of unmeasured energies during this process. The likely energy "losses" were to kinetic (air resistance), heat (material impact), and sound (noise). The "energy loss" may incorrectly convey an idea that during the process energy was not conserved. Energy is always conserved. The 3.8 missing joules went somewhere.

The use of the Figure 5.4 experiment will be used in other chapters to demonstrate other energy conversions and energy conversion efficiencies.

IV. Familiar Gravitational Energy Applications

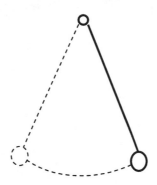

Figure 5.5 The Pendulum Clock

A most familiar observation is the "grandfather" clock used as decorative piece of furniture in many houses. This universal application of the gravitational/kinetic energy process predates the understanding of the basic energy systems.

The basic energy flow of the pendulum clock is as simple as the brick/toy car experiment presented above. However, the generalization of the pendulum clock description leads to a qualitative explanation.

The frequency in which the pendulum swings back and forth is precisely determined by physical law.

A small amount of energy needs to be introduced into the pendulum clock system during each swing of its operation. This small amount of energy is required in order to compensate for the energy loss during the gravitational energy – kinetic energy cyclic conversions. This additional energy keeps the gears of the clock and pendulum moving. Usually grandfather clocks are supplied additional energy by a weight which is lifted to a higher position once a week (gravitational energy) or a windup spring (elastic energy). This is the same energy input needed to compensate for gravitational energy conversion to kinetic energy conversion efficiency loss considered in our experiment in Figure 5.4.

Remember, a small amount of energy is added to the system upon each cycle to compensate for the energy conversion loss during the pendulum cycle. Again, the word "loss" unfortunately conveys the meaning that energy is destroyed during the pendulum process. That is not true. The 1st Law of Thermodynamics always applies. The clock process is accompanied by the comforting "tick" and "tock" as time passes. And those sounds require very little energy.

Although complete descriptions of existing gravitational energy sources are presented in Chapter 15 (Hydroelectric Power), a short description of the existing gravitational energy applications will temporarily demonstrate the value to utility grade energy production.

1. Energy production

The hydroelectric (gravitational) energy source is the river of water falling from a higher to a lower height under the force provided by gravity. The river was created by water vapor/liquid lifted to a higher level by atmospheric convection. Energy is always preserved.

The application of water as a source of energy (power) is very old. We are all familiar with water wheels. However, all older applications required that the water power applications had to be next to the river. Also, the use of water dams to create efficient power utilization was essentially unknown. The discovery of electricity and electrical power transmission were the tools for large scale energy exploitation. The history of the development of the hydroelectric facility at Niagra Falls provides a fascinating story about this pioneering effort.

2. Energy storage

Energy storage in the dam is an integral part of hydroelectric power production. This feature has not gone unnoticed. The alternate utility grade energy sources of solar and wind power have intermittent energy production. Schemes (called Pumped Storage) to integrate hydroelectric power with solar and wind power are not hard to imagine. The goal is to produce the optimum comprehensive energy system. The efficiency of sustainable energy sources must consider the water/gravitational storage option.

V. Conclusions

Gravitational energy originates with the mutual universal attraction (gravitational force) between all masses within our universe. The conclusion of Chapter 5 is slightly more complex than the other chapters; although the gravitational subject matter is not complex. The underlying complexity is that the gravitational energies, historically derived from measurements, stems from the differences between the English and Metric energy measurement systems. The Chapter 5 Insight offers additional explanation of the differences, if you are interested. A quantitative example of each measurement and calculations are given as a reference.

The must-know elements of gravitational energy are:

1. Gravitational energy (Metric) = (In joules)

    a. (height)(mass)(gravitational constant) = hmg

    b. (meters)(kilograms)(9.8 meters/sec)

2. Gravitational Energy (English) = (In foot-pounds)

    a. (height)(weight)

    b. (feet)(pounds)

3. Gravitational energy – Kinetic energy conversion examples

4. Hydroelectric utility grade energy production.

Chapter 5 Insight

A Demonstration of Weight versus Mass

An excellent observation of weight vs. mass has been supplied during our lunar visits. It is entertaining to see our lunar astronauts jump upward 6 feet with apparent ease. I was going to write "6 feet into the air" when I realized there is no air on the moon.

The explanation for lower weight on the moon is simple:

1. Universal Force = mass x acceleration

2. The surface of the earth has a gravitational acceleration of 9.81 meters / sec^2.

3. The surface of the moon has a gravitational acceleration of 1.63 meters / sec^2.

So the force of attraction towards the moon's center when standing on the moon's surface, for the same amount of mass, will be (1.63 m / sec^2) / (9.81 m / sec^2) = 0.166 or 1/6 as great standing on the earth's surface.

Newton's Law of gravitation always applies. The reason we weigh less on the moon is because the moon has less mass than the earth to attract our human mass.

But as explained in Chapter 3 Insight, we have institutionalized a significant difference in the utilization of gravitational force measurements between the English and SI measurement systems. The public usage has taken the most convenient, and divisive, path.

Chapter 6:

Elastic Energy

Sections:

---

1. Introduction to Elastic Energy

Elastic energy is the restoring force of an object returning a distance to its lowest energy equilibrium position. This is clearly defined in the classical definition of energy being a force through a distance.

Elastic energy is not being considered as a significant contributor to our utility grade energy production. However, the understanding of elastic energy helps our total energy view in the following manner.

1. Since elastic energy is familiar from the many observations in our lives, it well deserves explanation.

2. The understanding of elastic energy reinforces the concept of the historical view of energy as a force through a distance.

3. Elastic energy also serves as an excellent working model for general energy phenomenon.

4. Elastic energy is used several times, as a minor contributor, in the explanation of the major kinds of utility grade power sources.

There are many observed elastic energies. The common recognition of elastic energy is a spring. We have springs on our car. We have springs in our mattress. We have spring in our rubber bands. We have spring in our hunting bows. We have springs in our computer keyboard letters.

A few words must be dedicated to the origination of elastic energy. Figure 6.1 presents the general case. Figure 6.1 presents a small strip of spring steel being deformed by force (F) away from its equilibrium position a distance (D).

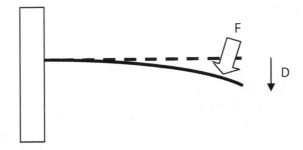

Figure 6.1 Elastic Energy

Elastic energy originates from atomic bonds in material being deformed by force away from their lowest energy position in the material. The electrical bonds (attraction) that hold the material in place are being stretched from their lowest energy position. The atomic bonds remain and retain over time a counter force equal to the deformation force. A requirement of elastic energy applications is that the material will return to its equilibrium state at a later time. In nature, elastic materials are predominately polymeric organic compounds such as natural rubber and sponges. The wooden hunting bow is a familiar example. In nature, few inorganic compounds possess useful elastic properties. While inorganic crystals deform with force, the usefulness in energy storage is limited. The deformation of natural inorganic compounds to produce elastic energy applications essentially does not exist.

The modern development of "spring steel" has revolutionized elastic energy. We can now obtain, within limits, spring steel that meets our specific elastic materials requirement. Most observed examples in this chapter stem from the spring steel development.

II. Elastic Force

It is easier to explain elastic energy by investigating the force component.

Figure 6.2 presents a graphic of spring behavior based upon our sensed observation:

Figure 6.2(A) Spring in equilibrium position

Figure 6.2(A) presents a spring in its equilibrium position. No elastic energy exists within the spring at this point.

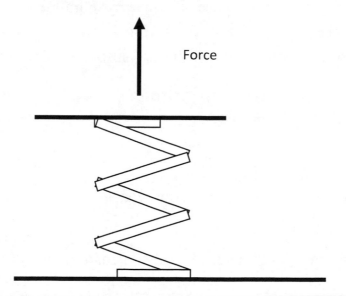

Figure 6.2(B) Spring stretched

Figure 6.2(B) presents a spring where a force is applied to deform (stretch) the spring away from its equilibrium position.

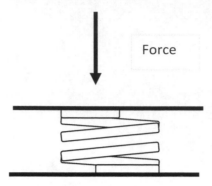

Force

Figure 6.2(C) Spring Compressed

Figure 6.2(C) presents the same spring compressed a distance by a force. That is energy by definition.

The restoring force of a spring is the stiffness of the spring multiplied by the distance the spring is from equilibrium. Spring stiffness is defined below. We have to mention once that springs do have an "elastic limit", where the spring will not return to its original position because it is overly compressed (crushed) or over-stretched. We are here assuming that the spring is compressed or stretched within its working limits to return to its equilibrium position.

The simple mathematical relationship for spring force is: Force = Spring stiffness (k) x distance from equilibrium (d)

or **F= - kd**

F = -kd means that the restoration force increases as we move further away from equilibrium.

The stiffness of a spring (k) is determined by measurement of force and distance. Figure 6.3 presents a typical (k) measurement process.

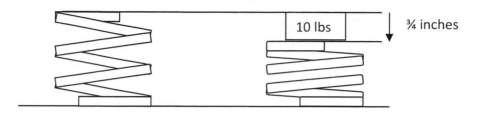

Figure 6.3 Spring Stiffness Measurement

A spring is placed in its equilibrium position. A 10 pound weight (force) is placed upon the spring. The spring is measured to have compressed ¾ inches.

Since above, F = -kd, then k = -F/d

k = - 10 pounds / ¾ inches or 13.3 pounds /inch

Simply put, the spring compresses 1 inch every 13.3 lbs.

This quantification of a spring indicates that a spring will compress in relationship to the applied force (weight). After the single measurement and determination of stiffness constant (k), we can simply measure the spring compression at any distance or spring stretch at any distance and determine the restoring force. This is true of our automobile springs and for our bed mattress springs. The only difference is the value of stiffness (k). The minus sign only means stretching rather than compressing the force from equilibrium. With an ideal spring, when we apply twice the force, we get twice the spring compression (or stretch). This generality is for all springs.

Note that the restoring force increases with spring distance from equilibrium.

III. Elastic Energy

We have demonstrated in the last section that elastic force F = -kd where:

1. (+ or -) = direction of force back to equilibrium

2. k = spring stiffness constant

3. d = distance from equilibrium

In keeping with the commitment not to use calculus in this text, only the actual must-know formula for elastic energy is now given.

Energy = ½ kd²

    1. (k) is the <u>measured</u> stiffness constant of (pounds force)/foot deflection).

    2. d = distance in feet of compression or stretch

Chapter 6 uses the English energy system of feet and pounds; but the Metric energy system (in joules) would work just as well.

IV. Elastic Energy Observations

The conversion of elastic energy to kinetic energy can be demonstrated in the process of shooting a bow and arrow.

Figure 6.4 presents a bow and arrow ready to send an arrow towards a target. A "sport" bow in the United States may require about 10 pounds of force to deflect the bowstring 14 inches. The dotted image is the equilibrium position of the bow. The solid image is the stretched bow.

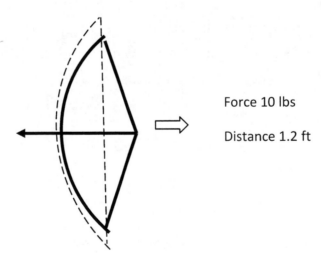

Force 10 lbs

Distance 1.2 ft

Figure 6.4 Bow and Arrow

We first measure and calculate (k) for this specific bow and arrow:

    (k) = force/deflection = 10 lbs/1.2 ft = <u>8.3 lbs/ft</u>

We now can calculate the energy:

$$\text{Energy} = \tfrac{1}{2}\,kx^2 = (1/2)(8.3\text{lbs/ft})(1.2\text{ ft})(1.2\text{ ft}) = \underline{6.0\text{ ft-lbs}}$$

When the bow is released, ideally the 6.0 ft-lbs of elastic energy will be converted to the kinetic energy of the arrow. This assumes that the energy transfer was 100% efficient.

You can now determine the energy of one kind of energy (elastic) and then calculate a component (velocity) of another kind (kinetic) of energy. Now, if we only knew the weight of the arrow?

If we did know he weight of the arrow. We could estimate the maximum velocity obtainable from this bow. Since conversion efficiency (elastic energy to kinetic energy) is less than 100%, it will always be less than the maximum limit.

In elastic energy, the deformation force increased with distance, yet the force was constant in our basic definition of mechanical energy. When yet to be discovered, this elastic energy relationship (called Hooke's Law or $E = \tfrac{1}{2}\,kd^2$) was very difficult to understand. We must learn that different forces (fields) exist for different kinds of energies.

V. Types of Springs

This section is written to provide awareness and recognition of the various elastic energies commonly observed.

1. Flat material

Automobiles: Flat "leaf" springs were used exclusively in early automobiles. They have been replaced with coil springs as described below. The compact coil springs are easier to use in the modern designs. Trucks still use flat leaf springs where heavier weight capacities are required.

Diving boards: A diving board is a universal application of elastic energy. By cyclically transferring muscle energy (force through a distance) into the diving board, one can store increasing amounts of elastic energy within the board. Elastic energy is then transferred to kinetic energy upward into the diver. The kinetic energy from the stored elastic energy is much greater than the diver's single jump of muscle energy. That's why we have diving boards!

Bridges: Highway bridges are built specifically with elasticity in their design. The bridges are designed to absorb energy from the vehicular traffic and natural mechanical forces (stresses). The energy absorption is necessary for the long term reliability of the bridges.

Buildings: Taller buildings have a designed elasticity to withstand forces and absorb energies such as earthquakes and wind. Many stories are told about how a building swayed in an earthquake. The external mechanical energy is converted to elastic energy within the building. The elastic energy is then slowly converted to heat energy within the building.

2. Torsion elasticity

Figure 6.5 presents torsion elasticity. By twisting a rod, in this case made of spring steel, on one end while the other end is stationary, one can convert mechanical energy from the twisting action to elastic energy stored in the deformation of the rod.

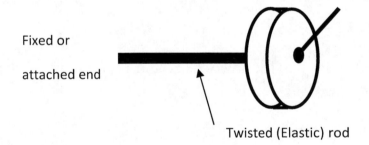

Fixed or

attached end

Twisted (Elastic) rod

Figure 6.5 Torsion Spring

Torsion bar springs have been used directly in automobiles with success.

We have many familiar elastic energy observations. Some are:

1. Coil springs (as presented in Figure 6.2) are very familiar to everyone. They are just wrapped torsion bar springs:

2. Automobiles: Automobile springs are used to absorb the energy transmitted from the rough road surface into the car. No additional information is required.

3. Mattresses: The excellence standard for a mattress involves the use of coil springs. The coils remain elastic for years.

4. Door returns: Most doors have a spring return. Sometimes the spring returns are not obvious, but they are there.

VI. Force Measurements

The universal use of elastic behavior is in the measurement of force itself. The force of gravity (weight) is conveniently measured using a spring. Unfortunately, the word "*scale*" has been the proper noun used to label these devices.

Spring based scales are used for weighing measurements. When baking a cake or buying bananas at the store, it may necessary to weigh the amounts of material.

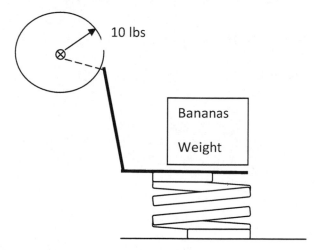

Figure 6.6 Weighing Scale

Figure 6.6 presents a simple spring scale whose weight is standardized and calibrated to a standard by law. As we investigated in the last chapter, weight is the English equivalent of force x acceleration of gravity at the earth's surface. English "force" uses the gravitational weight of a pound as the standard unit of measure. That is a lot of bananas.

The forces described in Chapter 3 can be conveniently measured by the English measurement system using a spring scale. One can either push on the lever or pull on the lever with pounds of force measured by a spring scale.

VII. Conclusions

Elastic energy is the restoring force of an object returning a distance to its lowest energy equilibrium position. Although elastic energy played a small role in our production of utility grade power, it does add significantly to our comprehensive knowledge of energy science. The numerous observations of elastic energy make energy science come alive and focus our thoughts on cohesive principles.

The must-know elements of elastic energy are:

   1. Elastic energy = ½ kd^2

   a. In universal dimensions = ½ (F/d)(d)(d)

   2. The stiffness constant k is a measured value

   3. Elastic energy has many applications.

The primary goal of presenting elastic energy is to unify important elements of energy science.

Chapter 6 Insight

Damped Oscillations and Vibrations

We have an opportunity to investigate a global feature of alternating energy conversion within dynamic systems. That feature is ***damped oscillation and vibration.***

Figure 5.4 demonstrated that the gravitational energy of 19.6 joules was converted to a gravitational energy of only 15.8 joules when we converted the gravitational energy to kinetic energy and back to gravitational energy. This is the energy flow during this ½ of a complete cycle. The energy efficiency of the complete cycle is 66%. That is 81% of 19.6 J = 3.8 J on the first ½ cycle and 81% of 15.8 J = 3.0 J on the 2nd ½ cycle. The energy leaving the system was 6.8 J / 19.6 J x 100 = 34%. The amount of energy converted to other kinds of energy was 6.8J. This was one complete cycle.

This repetitive cycle applies to all gravitational-kinetic cycles such as the pendulum in Figure 5.5. The observed result is that the pendulum or brick/toy car cycles with less and less total (gravitational plus kinetic) energy until cycles stop with zero gravitational and kinetic energy.

The total energy diagram below graphically presents Figure 5.4 with the gravitational-kinetic energy system. It also represents the elastic systems in Chapter 6 where elastic energy oscillates with converting kinetic energy around the restoration point. An example is the bow released without transferring energy to the arrow. The result is that the bow string vibrates around the elastic restoration point until energy losses return it to rest.

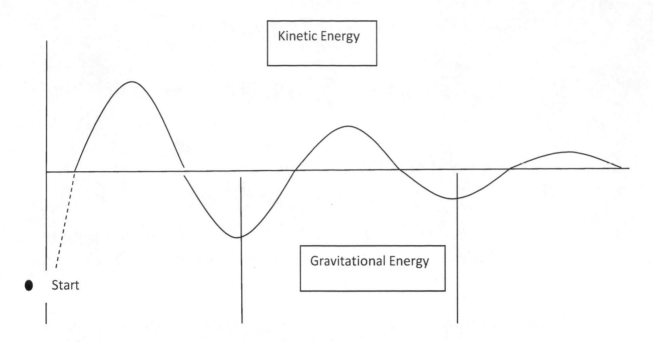

Figure 6.7 Damped Oscillation

The oscillating systems that lose a substantial amount of total energy during each cycle (Figure 5.4 is 34% per cycle) will come to rest after few cycles. A typical "grandfathers" pendulum clock is designed to minimize energy loss during the oscillating motion. Jeweled bearings and slim pendulum weights are typical engineering designs. One can imagine that pendulum operation within a vacuum, with the absence of air resistance would minimize energy loss. A first approximation of energy loss is that my clock's ten pound weight has to be lifted 4 feet for my clock to run for a week. The important concept is that energy is conserved. The 40 foot-pounds of energy converted to clock motion is exactly the energy loss of the clock in one week. This is a confirmation of the 1st Law of Thermodynamics.

The key ideas of the Chapter 6 Insight are:

1. The total observed energy is kinetic energy plus gravitational energy.

2. The energy escaping the system (loss, a bad descriptor) is determined by the lessening of energy with time. This is called a damped oscillation (electrical) or damped vibration (mechanical).

Chapter 7:

Heat Energy

Sections:

I. Introduction to Heat Energy

In the last four chapters, we quantified energy through the measurement of universe dimensions: $E = (force)(d)$, $E = \frac{1}{2} m(d/t)(d/t)$, $E = (m)(g)(d)$, $E = \frac{1}{2} (force/d)d^2$. Heat energy is more difficult to understand since the underlying factors are neither realized directly by universe dimensions nor by sensible observations. The underlying factors that compose heat energy only include validated phenomenon from scientific investigations. Several logical steps (sections) must be taken to arrive at an adequate heat energy description.

II. The Thermometer (Step #1)

Temperature, particularly outside (ambient) temperature, is a significant subject in our conversations. Our bodies sense "cold" and "hot" as a key factor in their preservation. The quantitative measure of temperature has occurred only in recent history. An arbitrary standard was established to quantitatively compare or measure temperature. Figure 7.1 presents the two major measurement scales (Fahrenheit and Celsius) that are generated from the following conditions:

When subjected to a common (standard) pressure, water will freeze at a specific temperature and water will boil at a specific temperature. Freezing and boiling water are universal observations by everyone.

Figure 7.1 presents a linear (evenly spaced) scale between the freezing point and boiling point of water.

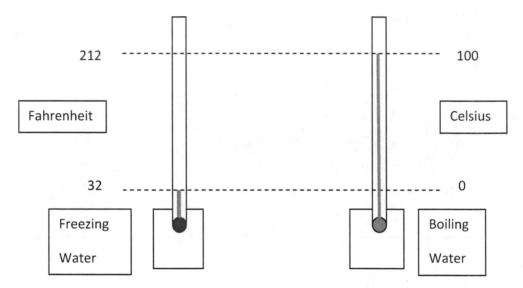

Figure 7.1 Thermometers

The English system, Fahrenheit, sets the scale when freezing at 32 degrees and when boiling at 212 degrees. There are 180 divisions in the scale between freezing and boiling.

The Metric system, Celsius, sets the scale when freezing at 0 degrees and when boiling at 100 degrees. There are 100 divisions in the scale between freezing and boiling.

 The liquid thermometer operates as follows:

The sensing bulb is filled with a liquid (historically mercury) that expands with increasing temperature. The expanding liquid pushes up the capillary where the amount of expansion is measured as the bulb temperature. Note that the scale is arbitrary. In fact, some liquid thermometers are marked Fahrenheit on one side and Celsius on the other side of the same thermometer.

Mechanical spring thermometers (baking thermometers) and electrical resistance (automobile engine temperature) are common. All thermometers are calibrated (we hope) and compared with an accurate standard system.

The advent of the thermometer to measure temperature bought scientific reasoning to the general public. A thermometer is now used to quantitatively determine body temperature rather than feeling a forehead to determine a fever. We also learned how all healthy humans have a very precise healthy body temperature, 98.6 degrees Fahrenheit.

Note that we have not adequately defined temperature at this point. We have only related temperature to a natural water standard.

III. Heat Standards (Step #2)

If you do not immediately grasp the relationship between the sensory awareness and thermometric measurement of temperature and heat energy, don't worry. It took capable scientists years to comprehend this subtle relationship.

The standards for heat energy measurements originated from early chemistry developments. Chemical reaction heat and energy is the key to understanding chemistry. The chemical heat energy measurement standards were made before anyone realized that all kinds of energy could be related to a common standard by the 1st Law of Thermodynamics. Not only that, but two independent measurement systems were independently established that remain to this date. They are the English and the Metric systems.

Here are the standards of energy measurements:

1. In the "English" system, the standard unit of heat energy is the *British Thermal Unit (BTU)*. One BTU is the amount of heat energy that will raise the temperature of 1 pound of water 1 degree Fahrenheit. Since all kinds of energies are convertible, it follows that BTU's can be used to measure all

energies. My monthly gas bill is in "Therms". A Therm is a convenient heat energy unit of 100,000 Btu's.

2. In the Metric system, a standard unit of heat energy is the Calorie. One *Calorie* is the amount of heat energy that will raise the temperature of 1 gram of water 1 degree Celsius. Since all of the kinds of energies are convertible, it follows that the calorie could be a measure for all the kinds of energies.

1 Btu has been measured to be equal to 252 calories. It is not hard to imagine that these two standards conveniently originated in the chemistry laboratories. One must remember that before available electricity, with its precise measurements, the measurement of heat energy values was difficult and confined to chemistry. At this point we can measure temperature, but we still have not determined the essence of temperature.

IV. The Mechanical Equivalent of Heat Energy (Step #3)

James Joule was an Englishman born in 1818. During his lifetime in the middle 19th century, many scientific discoveries were made. Although James Joule was actually a brewer in Manchester, England and not a dedicated scientist; his contributions to physical science were outstanding. James Joule discovered, through experiments, that all kinds of energy are related. This is the origination of the 1st Law of Thermodynamics. He had an interest in developing the newly discovered electrical energy into useful applications. He discovered that heat produced from electricity was precisely equivalent to the (current) x (current) x (resistance). This is Heat $= I^2R$, now known as Joule's Law.

One of his experiments, known as the Joule paddle wheel experiment, is presented in Figure 7.2. By releasing the weights, the gravitational energy was converted into mechanical shaft energy that converted into heat energy by paddles in the water within the insulated bucket. By carefully measuring the temperature before and after the drop in weights, knowing the gravitational energy, and the BTU standard definition; James Joule calculated the number of BTU's in terms of foot-pounds. At that time, he determined that 1 BTU = 772 ft-lbs of mechanical energy. This was an outstanding individual achievement. It is ironic that James Joule, the centerpiece of English system thermodynamic development, should be immortalized by having the

Metric System unit, not English System, of energy named in his honor. James Joule's history, available on the internet, is an interesting story.

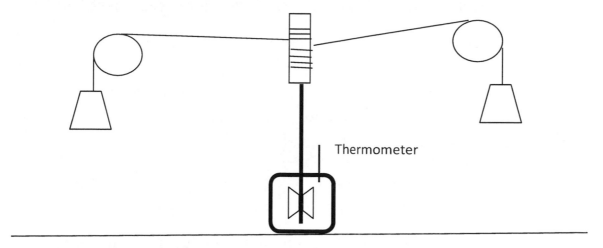

Thermometer

Figure 7.2 Joule's Paddlewheel Experiment

In reading the history of James Joule, there is an unsubstantiated account that on his honeymoon in France he went out to measure the temperature above a waterfall and below that waterfall in order to determine the temperature raise in the water. I personally believe that James Joule just drank some of his fine beer and enjoyed the company of his new wife when they were in France. James Joule was a genius, but there is no sign that he was mentally unbalanced.

The measurement of heat energy equivalence soon became much easier with the precise values of electrical energy. We will demonstrate that below.

After James Joule's pioneering work, the advent of precise electrical energy measurements has confirmed:

1 BTU = 252 Calories (by standard measurement)

(Verified by measurement of system conversions)

1 Calorie (Heat Energy) = 4.18 J (Mechanical energy)

(Verified by measurement during Joule's paddlewheel experiment}

At this point, we have still not defined heat energy in terms of universe dimensions.

V. What is Heat Energy? (Step #4)

With our background of Step 1, 2, and 3, we can develop a reasonable explanation of heat energy.

Heat energy within a mass is the total energy contributed by the kinetic energy of every individual atom and molecule within a mass. Movements of atoms and molecules are not our sensed observations at our larger scale. Scientists worked hard and long to understand the fundamentals of heat energy.

So what are the energies of individual atoms and molecules? There are three ways that atoms and molecules can possess intrinsic, ongoing energy:

1. Translation – on a very small scale, atoms and molecules will possess kinetic energy with the amount exactly as we calculated in Chapter 4: $KE = \frac{1}{2} mv^2$, and we do know the mass and the distribution of velocities for these small particles.

2. Rotation – on a very small scale, molecules will possess Kinetic Energy as rotational energy exactly as we calculated for the flywheel in Chapter4. Molecules rotate as little flywheels.

3. Vibration – the bonds that connect atoms within molecules can store vibrating elastic energy that is specifically determined by bond strength (stiffness – Chapter 6) and the frequency of vibration.

Although they are basically true, using these three simple concepts to calculate heat energy is impossible for the following reasons:

1. On an atomic scale, only certain fixed energies are allowed as governed by the laws of quantum mechanics. For instance, atoms can only translate at one fixed energy or another fixed energy, and nothing in between. For instance, molecules can only rotate at one speed or another, and nothing in between. For instance, bonds can only vibrate at one frequency or another, and nothing in between. Quantum mechanics is a bizarre subject. Fortunately, we don't have to include this subject in our text.

The direct impact upon heat energy calculations is that different atoms and molecules have varying energy storage capacities available and this eliminates a convenient calculation process.

2. The existence of gaseous, liquid, and solid states of material places even more variation upon three basic energy storages (listed above) contributing to heat. In order to clarify this statement the following states of materials are presented below with graphics.

Neon is a monoatomic gas. A gas like neon exists as single atoms that can be considered, at room temperature, as tiny spheres traveling with a distribution of speeds. Neon can be considered to be like very small ping-pong balls that travel around in a Bingo cage. And the translational distribution of velocities substantiates that neon behaves like a huge collection of small kinetic energies as we observe at in large kinetic systems like we presented in Chapter 4. So far, so good!

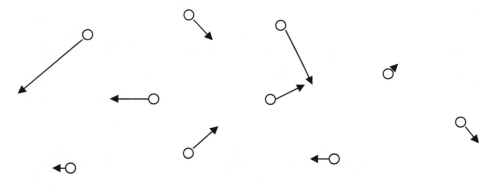

Figure 7.3 Neon Gas Energy

Figure 7.3, presents visually the random velocity distribution of neon gas at room temperature (The velocities and directions are random). Neon gas is called a monoatomic gas because it exists entirely of singular atoms. There are no energetic connections among neon atoms.

The heat energy of neon gas is exactly equivalent to our large scale conception of Kinetic Energy (miniature baseballs). Of course, there is nothing to rotate or to vibrate. If we need, the heat energy of neon gas can be both calculated and measured with great precision.

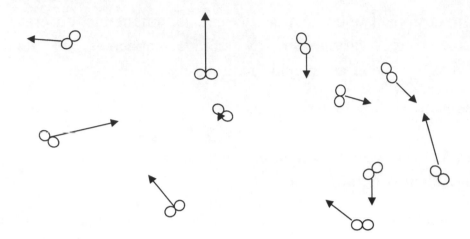

Figure 7.4 Nitrogen Gas Energy

Figure 7.4 presents a graphic of a nitrogen molecule. Nitrogen gas is called a diatomic gas because it exists as a pair of atoms in each molecule. The velocity distribution of nitrogen molecules is similar to the velocity distribution of neon presented in Figure 7.3.

The heat energy of nitrogen gas contains contributions from translation, rotation, and vibration. The energy contribution from vibration is small at room temperature. Note that the energy of rotation is independent of the energy of translation.

Using this heat contribution model for energy, one should find that the heat content of nitrogen should be higher than neon because there is an extra energy mechanism (rotational) in nitrogen. And, not surprisingly, that is exactly what we find.

The behavior of gases is very predictable based upon large scale observable energies. This predictable behavior has led to the label *"ideal gases"*. Gaseous energy can be calculated for any temperature.

Water, at standard atmospheric pressure, exists as a gas, above 212 $^{\circ}$F or 100 $^{\circ}$C. The energy content of steam has essentially the same translational and rotational components, along with a some vibrating energy.

When gaseous atoms and molecules cool sufficiently, they condense into a liquid. The energy of molecular attraction is then greater than the energy of translation (and rotation).

Liquids have limited translation and rotation and the allowed vibrations between atoms and molecules become more predominant. The ability to precisely predict energies in the liquid state becomes impossible. There are too many variable factors. Figure 7.5 presents 10 nitrogen molecules in a condensed state. The translational movements are too small to graphically depict.

Figure 7.5 Liquid Nitrogen

Figure 7.5 presents a liquid material where, the heat content is extremely more complicated. Liquids exist because the shorter range attractions (and energies) between atoms or molecules are greater than the long range translational and rotational energies of the gas.

But the atoms and molecules within a liquid do translate and rotate to some extent. The extent of translation and rotation within a liquid is primarily dependent upon the composition of the liquid. It is not "ideal" in any sense.

Liquids "freeze" into a solid upon cooling. The kinetic energy within a solid can be considered as a mixture of limited translational energy and predominantly vibrating energy. The absolute energy is impossible to calculate based upon underlying terms.

Even by a careful investigation, we still do not have a crisp understanding of heat energy. So what can we do!!!

The universal answer is: "By using the same technique, only modernized, that James Joule (Section IV) used to determine the mechanical equivalent of heat, we can determine the heat energy content of all compounds."

Figure 7.6 presents the modern *calorimeter*.

The modern calorimeter has a very accurate measure of input energy through an electric heater. Also, the temperature can be determined to a fine degree (excuse the pun).

By placing a sample of material in the calorimeter, we can accurately measure the amount of energy, supplied by the electric heater, converted to heat energy, used to raise 1 gram of the material 1 degree Celsius on the Celsius temperature scale. The calorimeter is based upon the 1st Law of Thermodynamics. Since that amount of energy is specific to the measured material, it is called *Specific Heat.*

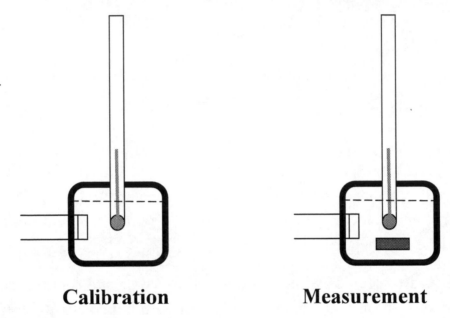

Calibration   **Measurement**

Figure 7.6 The Calorimeter

Specific Heat = **Energy (joules)/ (grams of material)(°C change in temperature)**

Some examples of *Specific Heat* are:

Water (liquid)	4.18 Joules / gram x °C(change)
Iron (Solid)	0.45 Joules / gram x °C(change)
Aluminum (Solid)	0.90 Joules / gram x °C(change)

Note that the specific heat of liquid water originated from the standard definition of heat and the mechanical equivalent of energy.

A short example of a heat-energy observed example is given for memory association. This text is focused on energy and not physics; so this will be short.

Figure 7.7 presents a kitchen energy application where we warm a quart (944 grams) of water in a 2 pound (908 grams) aluminum pan from 25 °C (room temperature) to 100 °C (boiling) before we add the oatmeal. What is the heating energy?

Water heat = (4.18 J / gram x °C[change]) x (944 grams)(75 °C[change])

= 295,000 J

Pan Heat = (0.90 J / gram x °C [change]) x (908 grams)(75 °C[change])

= 61,300 J

The total heat required to warm the water and warm the pan to 100 °C is 356,000 J.

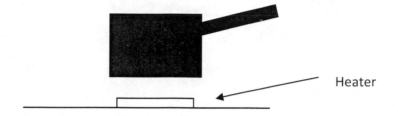

Heater

Figure 7.7 Pan and Water

The lessons from this abbreviated exercise are:

1. Water contains, relatively, a large amount of specific heat energy.

2. Heat energy can be precisely determined.

3. Energy flow always obeys the 1st Law of Thermodynamics

Heat content of materials, even though it cannot be fundamentally calculated, can be accurately measured. We only have to find it the correct source of data.

At this point we can define heat energy. _Heat energy is the total amount of energy of mass movements at the atomic level (specific to individual materials)._ This is not much different than we originally stated at the beginning of this section.

Temperature has a unique attribute in that heat always flows in a material from the higher temperature to a lower temperature. That is the 2nd Law of

Thermodynamics. Physically, that means that, materials with the same temperature have the same level of energy intensity.

The key distinction between heat and temperature is that two materials of equal mass with the same temperature (atomistic energy level intensity) do not necessarily have the same total amount of energy (atomistic heat energy amount). Some materials just have more ways to accommodate the energetic atomic movement.

Think of temperature in terms of energy intensity and heat in terms of energy amount.

VI. Interesting Heat Information

Section V was rather confusing and potentially boring as we struggled through the distinction between temperature and heat. However there are a few interesting investigations in the heat energy area.

When we remove energy by various means from a material, it reduces the heat energy and temperature. Getting colder and colder, gases turn to liquid and then liquids turn into solids. The coldest temperature is absolute zero, or - 278.15 °C. At that temperature all atomic motion stops and there is neither temperature nor heat energy. That agrees completely with our model presented in the last section. Lots of strange things happen as we approach absolute zero.

As we undergo phase changes (i.e. – go from gas to liquid and liquid to solid) the heat energy content of a material changes, but not the temperature. We observe that ice water remains at 0 degrees Celsius until all of the ice in the glass is melted. We observe that boiling water remains at 100 degrees Celsius until all of the water is boiled away. The common energy exchange during material phase change is called *Heat of Fusion* (melting) and *Heat of Evaporation* (boiling). It requires heat to melt solids and heat to boil liquids (without a change in temperature). The only significance to this topic is that energy can be stored within a phase due to this natural phenomenon of melting and boiling. This energy storage is called *"latent heat."* The reasons for latent heats we implicitly presented in the phase discussions in Section V. Latent heat can simple be understood as the change in a materials kinetic energy when it changes from gas to liquid to solid.

Phase changes obey the 1st Law of Thermodynamics. The same amount of energy to melt a gram of water (ice) is released when we freeze the gram of water. The reason we spray fruit trees is to prevent them from freezing. The temperature of the fruit tree can not drop to below 32 ^{o}F until all of the water spray freezes. So we keep on spraying.

Although it is far from the purpose of this text, we have been exposed to the three central laws of thermodynamics. We will restate them:

1. The 1st Law of Thermodynamics states that energy is always conserved, it cannot be created nor destroyed.

2. The 2nd Law of Thermodynamics states the thermal energy always flows from a region of higher temperature to a region of lower temperature.

3. The 3rd Law of Thermodynamics states that the coldest temperature possible is minus 278.15 ^{o}C.

All three laws make logical sense as part of our temperature and heat investigation. The three laws were established by our consistent conclusions from scientific observations. They state a comprehensive description of our natural universe.

We can't pass up this opportunity to recognize the unique nature of water. Our life itself depends upon water. As noted in the specific heats listed above, water has, by far, the highest specific heat.

The reason for water's high specific heat is visually presented in Figure 7.8. Water molecules are shaped like little boomerangs with the partial negative oxygen in the middle and the two partially positive hydrogen at each end. When in a liquid, the positive hydrogen ends of one water molecule will be attracted to the negative oxygen centers of another water molecule. This phenomenon is called *hydrogen bonding*. Hydrogen bonding contributes to the relative (to other liquids) lower energy content of the liquid water. When heated, this hydrogen bonding energy must be overcome in order to separate hydrogen to oxygen attractions, both in the water liquid expansion and when we change the water liquid into water gas (steam).

The high specific heat content of water is crucial to our biological processes. It allows us to perspire in order to maintain our precise body temperature. It stabilizes the change in outside ambient temperature in order to maintain our body temperature.

Hydrogen bonding is also responsible for the relatively high boiling point of water. The ocean's water stabilized to the right amount for our planet's average temperature. The heat capacity of water is just perfect.

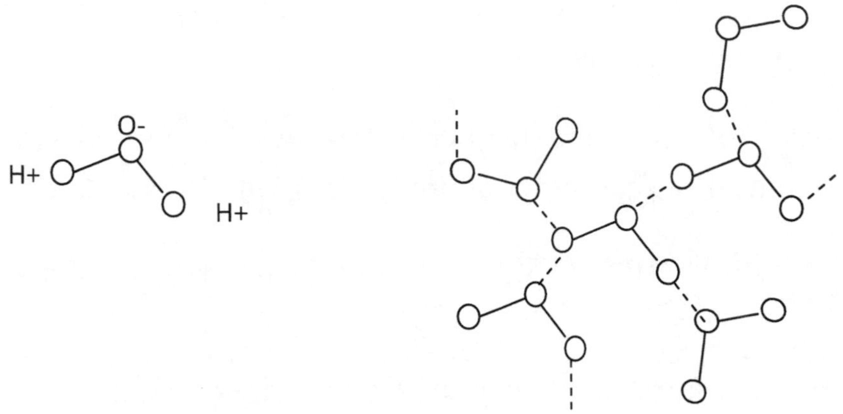

Figure 7.8 Hydrogen Bonding

Heat energy is not understood by the majority of public individuals. Yet this aspect is a crucial element in our national utility grade energy planning. That means that you should clearly understand this section. That means that you should clearly understand this section.

VII. Bad Heat Energy News

The "Bad News" is that only a fraction of available heat energy can be converted and used as other kinds of energy. And our predominant utilization of heat energy is conversion to pressure energy to mechanical energy.

This natural aspect is implicit in the 2nd Law of Thermodynamics. Heat energy only flows from a higher temperature to a lower temperature. We can only convert heat energy to other kinds of energy during the heat flow process from higher temperature to lower temperature. Since the lower temperature is always above absolute zero, we can only convert a fraction of our available heat energy.

The question is, "Where can we find cold enough matter to allow our heat energy in hot matter to efficiently flow into low temperature matter?" I am sorry for the bad English. This is the most important question in all of energy science. And the clear answer is, "We can't".

Rather than lecture upon the proof of this simple statement in the subject of Thermodynamics, we will continue on with observed and mostly ignored observations.

1. Wouldn't it be nice to heat our house in the winter with the absolute heat energy that exists in our swimming pool. But the adequate house temperature is greater than the swimming pool temperature, so we can't do that. Heat energy will only flow from the house to the pool.

2. Wouldn't it be nice to provide electricity for the city of Chicago by extracting the absolute heat energy from Lake Michigan. However, we can't find a workable spot (thermal sink) at a colder temperature than Lake Michigan's temperature, If we don't have a colder thermal sink, we don't have heat flow and the possibility of extracting energy.

3. If our automobile's exhaust temperature were cooler, we could develop a more efficient internal combustion engine, all other things being equal. But exhaust temperatures are hot. That should be the first clue that the heat energy efficiency is an annoying problem.

When in Chapter 1 we used the example of a typical house being heated by energy sources, we conveniently ignored where the heat went. "Outside" is not a good answer. It "heated the universe" is the correct answer.

When heat flows to a lower temperature, there isn't an option for the heat energy flow path except to remain as low temperature energy.

The universe is slowly becoming a lower temperature energy heat sink.

To make matters worse, the only viable process of heat energy conversion to mechanical energy is through conversion to air pressure energy. We really haven't progressed since James Watt's steam engine. This is unfortunate, since our major utility grade energies are produced from the vast available heat energy sources.

Rather than be repetitive during the explanation of power from Chapter 13 to Chapter 19, the limit imposed by this natural aspect of heat energy is presented now.

By investigating the flow of heat energy, it has been determined that the greatest amount of energy that can be converted to mechanical energy (this is called a heat engine) is:

Maximum heat energy to mechanical energy conversion efficiency:

$$\textbf{Eff}_{\textbf{max}} = \textbf{(Hot Temp – Low Temp / Hot Temp) x 100}$$

This is the Carnot cycle equation and is explained in the Chapter 7 Insight.

A steam engine runs at about an efficiency of 25%. This is not good. We are fortunate to have substantial amounts of coal.

This confirmed heat efficiency equation has enormous practical significance. The equation clearly states that a significant fraction of heat energy, which is our predominant utility grade energy source, will be lost to the universe during the process of converting available energy into usable kinds of energy. And we will never engineer around this reality.

There are many sincere and inquisitive questions and answers associated with this heat energy aspect. It is not possible to anticipate the initial and spontaneous response within Energy and Power – Fundamental Knowledge.

VIII. Conclusions

Heat energy within a mass is the total energy contributed by the movements of every individual atom and molecule. Heat energy involves two measureable attributes: One is the very familiar measurement of temperature and the other is the unfamiliar, yet accurate, measure of specific heat. Temperature is considered the <u>intensity</u> of energy that is related to the natural rule that heat energy always flows from a higher temperature to lower temperature. Heat energy is the measured <u>amount</u> of heat capacity within a material. Heat capacity is normally presented as the amount of heat energy required to increase 1 gram of the material 1 degree Celsius.

The must-know elements of Heat energy are:

1. **Heat energy is not determined using universe constants. Heat energy is measured directly and quantified by the *Specific Heat* of any material.**

2. **The thermometer standardization process**

3. **The Fahrenheit and Celsius temperature scales**

4. **The calorimeter Specific Heat measurement process**

5. **The concept of Latent Heat**

6. **The limit of heat energy to mechanical energy conversion**

7. **Again, the limit of heat energy to mechanical energy conversion (Carnot Cycle – Chapter 7 Insight)**

Heat energy is difficult to internalize based upon observable processes. It has been thoroughly investigated and validated by more abstract mathematical proofs. Heat energy is the keystone of our utility grade energy production.

Chapter 7 Insight

The Carnot Cycle

In 1824, a French engineer named Sadi Carnot, asked himself the question, "What is the maximum mechanical energy that one can convert from heat?" And he answered that question, forever, without the analytical tools currently available in thermodynamic science.

Knowledge of our ideal gas law, $PV = nRT$ (Chapter 11), and elementary calculus is required to precisely quantify the Carnot heat to mechanical energy cycle. However, it is important to qualitatively understand this key aspect of this energy science.

Carnot proposed a four stroke heat engine as presented in the graphics below:

Stroke 1:

Gas within the cylinder is heated until the gas reaches the high source temperature. The volume of the gas increases from an initial volume (v_1) to a larger volume (v_2). This expansion produces mechanical energy (PV) external to the engine.

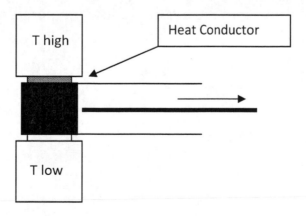

Figure 7.9 Isothermal Expansion (at v_1)

Stroke 2:

Additional mechanical energy can be obtained by allowing the gas at v_2 to further expand (to v_3) without the heat conductor energy from the high temperature source. This external PV energy is converted from the internal heat energy of the gas. This stroke expansion energy will cool the gas, ideally to the low temperature of the heat engine.

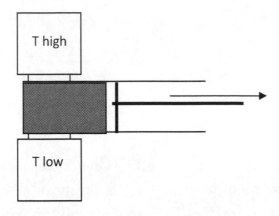

Figure 7.10 Adiabatic Expansion (at v_2)

Stroke 3:

Stroke 3 allows us to transfer heat energy in the gas to the available low temperature. By compressing the gas, which requires external mechanical energy, an increased gas temperature results and heat flows to the available low temperature. Note that a heat conductor now exists between the gas and available low temperature. Heat flows into the available low temperature.

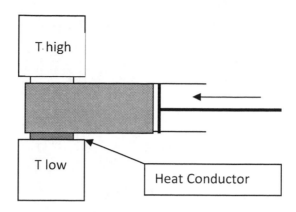

Figure 7.11 Isothermal Compression (v₃)

Stroke 4:

The heat engine stroke 4 is compressing the gas without heat flow from the high temperature source or to the available low temperature. The compression, from external mechanical energy, returns the gas to its starting pressure, temperature, and volume (v_1). The engine is now ready for another 4 stroke cycle.

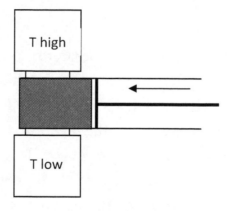

Figure 7.12 Adiabatic Compression (v₄)

The Carnot engine can be conveniently displayed on a PV (pressure – volume) diagram.

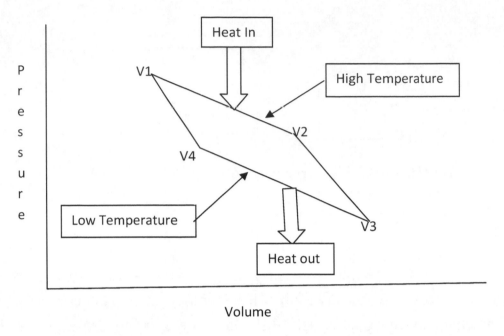

Figure 7.13 The Carnot Cycle

The heat energy flow from the high temperature source to the available low temperature is interrupted by the Carnot cycle, where mechanical energy is extracted during each cycle. The area enclosed by the Carnot cycle strokes is the mechanical energy (PV) extracted from the heat flow during each cycle. The Carnot cycle is based upon ideal gas behavior. It determines the maximum conversion of heat energy to mechanical energy. All heat engines (See chapter 11) are modeled after the Carnot cycle. Heat energy conversion to mechanical energy conversion efficiency can never be better than the Carnot cycle.

Chapter 8:

Chemical Energy

I. Introduction to Chemical Energy

Chemical energy is based upon the attraction between positive charges (protons) and negative charges (electrons) that exist within atoms. It is a part of the inherent atomistic behavior. The explanation of chemical energy requires some chemical background information in order to achieve a clear concept of this kind of energy. The chemical background information will be limited to the large scale energy systems that use hydrocarbons and coal. The detailed in depth portion of energy chemistry is called *thermochemistry* and is beyond the scope of this text. The following sections will provide only the required background information. You do not have to be a knowledgeable chemist to understand the energy aspects of chemistry.

II. Chemistry Basics

The universe provides us with 92 naturally occurring types of atoms. These 92 naturally occurring atoms provide the basics of the science of understanding atomic behavior, called *Chemistry*. Chemistry science is a great example of the collective intellectual achievements of mankind.

1. Sub -atomic Components

We will start from the simplest particles, and work from the "bottom up." All atoms are composed of three (3) distinct particles in distinct proportions. With only three distinct particles, our analysis of atoms is not that difficult. A particle is something that has mass. The constituent sub-atomic particles are electrons, protons, and neutrons. Figure 8.1 charts the physical properties of the three basic sub-atomic components for the atoms of interest for us in chemical energy. The masses are measured relative to a mass unit standard and are therefore relative to each other.

Particle	Mass (amu)	Charge
Electron	4.5×10^{-4}	Negative (-1)
Proton	1.007	Positive (+1)
Neutron	1.009	Neutral (0)

Figure 8.1 Atom components

The charge existing with each component is an existing property of our universe. *Charge* is a proper name given to the observed force interaction between particles. Note that there are only three different natural charges; negative, positive, and neutral. The underlying reasons for charge are not known.

AMU is the standard atomic mass unit. For simplicity, the proton and neutron are considered to have a mass (standard mass unit of AMU) of 1.0 AMU and the mass of an electron is considered to be 0.0 AMU. Our chemical energy explanation does not depend upon a precise value of sub-atomic particle masses.

2. Describing selected atoms

Our method of determining atomic structure does apply to all of the 92 types of atoms. We will limit our description of atoms to only those important to utility grade energy because our focus is upon energy and not chemistry. We will only explain those atoms essential to chemical energies derived from fossil fuels, petroleum and coal. Those atoms are hydrogen, carbon, and oxygen.

Hydrogen:

Figure 8.2 presents a single proton and a single electron in forming an atom. That atom is the hydrogen atom. Hydrogen is the smallest and simplest atom. Hydrogen has one proton and one electron.

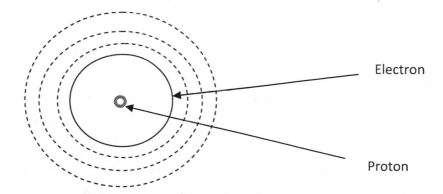

Figure 8.2 Hydrogen Atom

Opposite charges attract and we would expect that the electron would just crash into the proton. However, at very small distances, strange particle behavior happens. Instead of crashing into the proton, the electron appears to go into orbit around the proton. That is reasonable since the mass of the proton is much greater than the electron. Energy is conserved.

The orbiting of an electron(s) around a central proton(s), similar to the earth around the sun, is called the *Bohr model* of an atom. Although the Bohr atom is not precisely correct, it will provide us an adequate model in understanding chemical energy.

Carbon:

The next atom that we will describe is Carbon. Carbon is composed of 6 electrons, 6 protons, and 6 neutrons. Figure 8.3 presents a Bohr model of a carbon atom with 2-dimensional orbits.

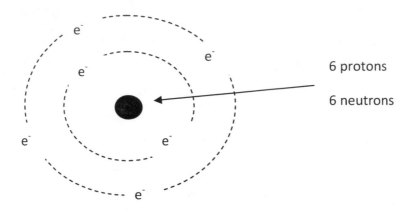

Figure 8.3 Carbon Atom

Atoms containing more than one proton have even stranger behavior. This unique non-intuitive behavior of an atom was determined over many years by excellent scientists. We have discovered that all protons within each atom exist in the center of the atom and that the electrons within each atom exist in specific energy shells around the exterior of the atom.

1. All positive charges (protons) of an atom exist in the center in an extremely small volume. That small central volume is called the *nucleus*. The energy to contain these protons (binding energy) is tremendous compared to our everyday sensed energy.

   The reason that the protons can exist next to each other in a very small volume is that the neutrons "glue" these protons into a stable unit within each atom. The number of neutrons required to glue protons together has been determined for kinds of all atoms.

2. As the electrons travel towards the stabilized nucleus, even stranger things occur. Note that the orbits in carbon now have energy layers (shells) at a distance away from the nucleus. The "allowed" energy shells, as determined by quantum theory, are presented without explanation in Figure

8.3. We can only have at most 2 electrons in the first energy shell (N=1) and at most 8 electrons in the second energy shell (N=2). Carbon has 2 electrons in the inner shell (N=1) and 4 electrons in the outer shell (N=2). That is all that is allowed. The reason for this strange arrangement has been determined by the equally strange science of quantum mechanics. We will just pass on quantum mechanics for now.

Oxygen:

The last atom for presentation is Oxygen. Figure 8.4 is a Bohr atom model of oxygen.

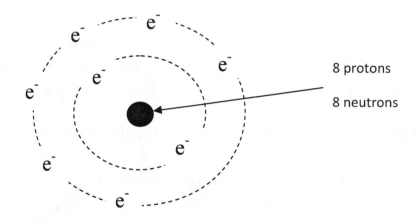

Figure 8.4 Oxygen

The oxygen atom has 8 protons, 8 neutrons, and 8 electrons. 2 electrons are in the first energy shell (N=1) and 6 electrons are in the second energy shell (N=2). Figure 8.4 presents the second layer as missing two electrons (there are only 6 now) in order to complete N=2 with 8 electrons.

Now that we are finished fabricating our atoms of interest, we will just mention once that all atoms isolated are neutral in charge. That means that all atoms contain the same number of protons as electrons. There are no "loose" electrons in our examples of chemical elements.

III. Chemical Bonding and Energy

Enough chemistry, let's move on to chemical energy. The reason for chemical energy production is that the negative charges (electrons) of one atom are "allowed" to exist closer to the positive charges (protons in the nucleus) of the next atom. This allows the total energy of combined atoms to be lower than the total energy of separated atoms. <u>Atoms can form molecules and release energy in the process</u>!!! When this energy lowering condition occurs mutually between two atoms it is called a *chemical bond*. When bonds are formed, energy is released. Figures 8.3, 8.4, and 8.5 present the Bohr models of hydrogen, carbon, and oxygen. Hydrogen, carbon, and oxygen atoms present an opportunity for energy production when they combine with other atoms to form molecules. This is the connection with the classic definition of energy as a force x a distance. This energy produced is called *bonding energy*. The bonded atoms (a molecule now) still must comply with quantum mechanical principles. Please read this paragraph at least twice.

A basic rule of chemical bonding is that atoms combine to form the lowest energy when the "allowed" shells of electrons (Bohr model) are filled. Only the outermost shell can form a bond. We only have to know that the first shell (N=1) has two electrons to be complete and the next shell (N=2) has 8 electrons to be complete. Hydrogen has one electron in N=1, and carbon and oxygen have a complete N=1 with two electrons. But as we will see below, the N=1 electrons in carbon and oxygen do not form chemical bonds and can be ignored. This is a point of confusion for non-chemists.

Let's construct some familiar chemical molecules fundamental to the production of utility grade energy:

Methane is a molecule with 4 hydrogen and 1 carbon. Carbon has 4 electrons in its outer shell (N=2) and hydrogen has 1 (N=1). Methane completes the carbon's 2nd orbit (N=2).to eight electrons. It also completes the 4 hydrogen orbits (N=1) to two electrons. This arrangement produces the lowest energy possible for one carbon and four hydrogen. This lowest energy atomic configuration within a molecule is called the *ground state*. The ground states are our stable molecules of chemicals at room temperature. As the one carbon atom and the four hydrogen atoms form methane, they release heat energy.

Two electrons shared between atoms is called a chemical bond. Methane has 4 (carbon to hydrogen) bonds. The energy released when each of these 4 bonds are formed is precisely known. Figure 8.5 presents the common chemical visual description of methane.

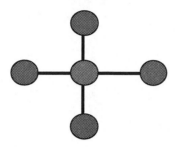

Figure 8.5 Methane Molecule

Oxygen gas exists in nature as two oxygen atoms bonded together. We already noted in Figure 8.4 that an oxygen atom needed only 2 more electrons to complete the octet outer shell. So an oxygen atom only exists until it finds another oxygen atom to share two electrons. Then the lowest energy oxygen molecule, O_2, forms with a stable configuration. Oxygen exists as O_2 in our atmosphere.

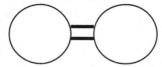

Figure 8.6 Oxygen Molecule

Figure 8.7 presents the molecule of H_2O, or water. The oxygen atom is now bonded to two hydrogen atoms. The N=1 energy of the hydrogen is complete and the N=2 energy of the oxygen is complete. This is the lowest energy state of hydrogen and oxygen. Note that the water molecule is bent like a boomerang. That is due to the bizarre chemical behavior explained by quantum mechanics. The same boomerang shape caused a specific heat energy factor explained in Chapter 7.

Figure 8.7 Water Molecule

Figure 8.8 presents a carbon dioxide molecule CO_2. Carbon dioxide has a straight shape. The carbon has a double bond connecting it to each oxygen molecule. The N=2 shells are complete for the two oxygen and the one carbon.

Figure 8.8 Carbon Dioxide

Now that we have presented molecules in Figure 8.5 to Figure 8.8, we can visually present a chemical reaction of the available chemical energy used as a source of utility grade electrical energy. This is the same reaction of natural gas with oxygen in our kitchen stoves. Natural gas is methane.

Figure 8.9 presents graphically the following chemical reaction:

$$CH_4 + 2O_2 \rightarrow 2H_2O + CO_2$$

Figure 8.9 Burning Methane

All we have done is exchange chemical bonds (count them!).In this section we explained chemical bonding using methane as an example. This example applies to all chemical reactions.

IV. Chemical Energy Conversion to Heat Energy

Burning methane (Figure 8.9) is an appropriate example of available energy for our utility grade applications. Methane is a significant available fuel. The heat energy from burning methane is used in residential heating, industrial heating, and electricity production.

Figure 8.9 depicts a mysterious interchange of molecular (atomic) bonds and does not mention energy. This section explains in a logical model how heat energy is produced from this chemical equation.

Figure 8.10 presents a logical accounting for bond energies and the determination of heat energy generated. It is a heat diagram. The chemical expression for this generated heat is the *heat of reaction*.

View Figure 8.10 in the following steps:

Step #1. A methane molecule and two oxygen molecules are available and ready for action (actually, reaction) (at the kitchen stove).

Step #2. We apply a spark to start the reaction. The bonds in the methane and two oxygen molecules "break" to create independent atoms. This requires us to overcome methane and oxygen bond energies.

Step #3. We "make" all of the bonds on the carbon dioxide and water. This will release all of the bond energies as heat. Some of the heat energy is used to break more methane and oxygen molecules into atoms. Excess heat is transferred to the surroundings. The excess heat energy is the heat of reaction. If we didn't have excess energy, methane and oxygen would not react. But we do need to have some energy (spark) to get the first bonds broken. Don't light a match when you smell methane gas!

Since energy is conserved, the heat energy of methane reaction (Figure 8.10) is:

Heat energy = (sum of bonds energies "made") – (sum of energy bonds "broken")

We could calculate heat of reaction if we only knew the bond energies. And we are in luck! We know bond energies precisely. They exist in every university level chemistry book. They are precise values that only have to be determined one time. Included below are the energies for all the bonds used when we burn methane. The values of energies are presented in KJ / mole, an unfamiliar measurement value for everyone outside of chemistry. Rather than learn yet another energy measurement, the energy amount for the specific methane reaction (Figure 8.9) will be explained for you below.

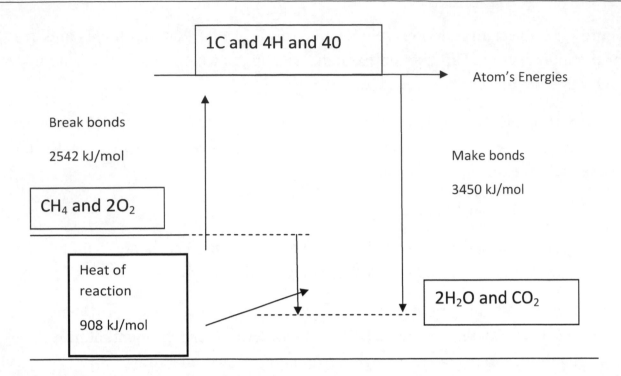

Figure 8.10 Heat Diagram

Bond Energies (kJ/mol)

C-H	413
O=O	495
O-H	463
C=O	799

Here is the stepwise calculation:

Step #1: State the chemical reaction

$$CH_4 + 2O_2 = 2H_2O + CO_2$$

Step #2: (energy needed to break methane and oxygen bonds) kJ / mole

Methane (C-H)	4 x 413	1652
Oxygen (O-O)	2 x 495	990
		2542

Step #3: (bonds released when bonding water and carbon dioxide) kJ / mole

Water (O-H)	4 x 463	1852
Carbon Dioxide (C=O)	2 x 799	1598
		3450

Heat of reaction = 3450 - 2542 = 908 kJ / mol of methane

The metric mole is strange to all except chemists. A *mole* is the specific molecular weight in grams. Or simply, 1 mole of methane is 16 grams of mass. So, stated in a different way, 16 grams of methane produces 908 kJ of heat when burned.

The burning of other available fuels such as propane, gasoline, and coal can be simply analyzed as the methane example. Those examples were included and then later removed. It quickly becomes a boring, repetitive process. If the fundamental chemical heat of reaction is unclear, read this section again. It is important that you understand the chemical energy to heat energy conversion. The actual values of heats of combustions of various fuels have already been evaluated and are readily available. It is important that you understand where the chemical energy exists, and the fundamental structure of a chemical energy diagram.

V. Related Chemical Energy Topics

Several interesting aspects of the chemical energy to heat conversion are needed for awareness by the general public:

1. Natural Gas (Methane) is a pure compound that can be analyzed in a precise manner. Liquid petroleum and coal are mixtures of fossil fuels that are processed to produce useful energy sources. Because of the variation in refined petroleum and coal, assessment of these energy sources produces a range of values. For example, we can find several values for the heat energy per ton of coal in the existing literature. But unless we have a complete understanding how a value was obtained, conclusions based upon a single sample are approximate generalities. Be very careful of energy data from mixtures or variable sources.

2. Note that carbon dioxide (at -1598 kJ/mol) and water (at -926 kJ/mol) have, in common language, all of the available chemical energy squeezed out of them. That is the vernacular way of stating that carbon dioxide and water have very high bonding energy. Carbon dioxide and water cannot react with any other molecules to produce heat energy. That agrees with our observation that we use carbon dioxide and water as fire extinguishers. I have encountered plans that use water or carbon dioxide as an available energy source. What can one say!!

3. Plants do chemically convert the high energy bonds of carbon dioxide to chemicals of lower energy bonds by converting radiant energy (sunlight-next chapter). This is how fossil fuels originated. Proposals for energy sources produced by plants are discussed in Chapter 20 as Biofuels. Fossil fuel chemistry can be crisply evaluated, as in this chapter. Biofuel chemistry requires a significant investment in time for education about a very broad and variable energy subject.

VI. Conclusions:

Chemical energy is the energy inherent and available within atomic behavior. The energy source is based upon the universe dimension of charge attraction between electrons (-) and protons (+).

A chemical reaction is an exchange of chemical bonds. All electrons in our chemical energy examples are bound to equivalent charges by protons. The electrons are fixed within each atom. There are no flowing electrons. The chemical heat of reaction can be understood visually (Figure 8.10) as the "breaking" of existing bonds and the "making" of new bonds. The burning of fossil fuels is universally observed with the generation of heat energy.

The values of bond energies are given only for our molecules of interest. Our chemistry was limited to hydrogen, oxygen, and carbon.

The must-know elements of chemical energy are:

1. Chemical energy exists within molecular bonds.

2. A chemical reaction that produces heat energy is an exchange of chemical bonds.

3. Energy is produced when bonds allow a closer distance between negative particles (electrons) and positive particles (protons).

4. Energy (thermal) values for our chemical reactions are precisely known.

5. Chemical energy is a prime example of the 1st Law of Thermodynamics.

Chapter 8 Insight

The Electrical Energy Storage Battery

The electrical energy storage battery stores electrical energy through a chemical reaction. A universal example is the lead-acid battery used in our automobiles. There are many kinds of batteries using different chemicals; but the principles of operation are the same as the common lead-acid battery.

Figure 8.11 presents a fresh lead acid battery cell where we insert one plate (electrode) of lead and another plate (electrode) of lead oxide into a liquid (electrolyte) of sulfuric acid. Both of the electrodes remain as a solid and do not dissolve into the sulfuric acid.

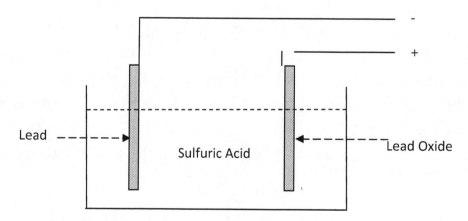

Figure 8.11 New Battery

The following chemical reactions occur at the electrodes; but only if we let electrons flow through an external electrical energy load.

$$PbO_2 + HSO_4^- + 3\,H^+ + 2e^- > PbSO_4 + 2\,H_2O$$

$$Pb + HSO_4^- > PbSO_4 + H^+ + 2e^-$$

The PbO_2 electrode requires 2 electrons for the chemical reaction to proceed and the Pb electrode will give up 2 electrons when the chemical reaction proceeds.

Nothing happens when the external electrodes are not connected. This is like how your car battery exists overnight. In the morning, when you turn on your starter, Figure 8.12 happens:

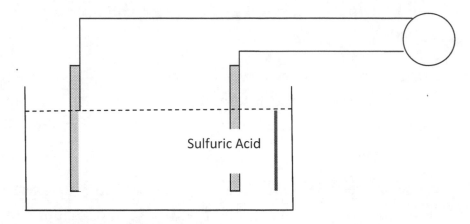

Sulfuric Acid

Figure 8.12 Discharged Battery

The electric connection to the starter allows electrons to flow from the Pb electrode to the PbO_2 electrode. The chemical energy of the two electrodes reaction is transferred to the starter motor. As the electrons (and energy) flow to the starter, the Pb electrode is being converted to $PbSO_4$ and the PbO_2 is being converted to $PbSO_4$. If your car doesn't start soon, the battery will use all the sulfuric acid and the electrodes will become completely coated with $PbSO_4$. You will have a "dead" battery.

The valuable aspect of a lead-acid battery is that it can be recharged back to its original state (Figure 8.11) by reversing the electron flow. This is accomplished automatically by the alternator after your automobile starts.

Chapter 9:

Radiant Energy

Sections:

I. Introduction to Radiant Energy

Radiant energy exists without the need for mass (matter). Radiant energy is a familiar to us as sunshine, our eyesight, light bulbs, x-rays, cell telephones, microwave ovens, lasers, quartz heaters, etc. Radiant energy cannot be defined by the classical definition of (force x distance). Radiant energy consists of magnetic force fields, electric force fields, and velocity. The underlying structure of radiant energy in terms of universe dimensions is unknown. However, the quantified behavior of radiant energy is well understood. Chapter 9 focuses upon radiant energy in relationship to our large (utility) grade energy sources. An effort has been made to minimize the mathematical treatments utilized to explain radiant energy.

II. An Individual Ray of Energy

Figure 9.1 presents a unit (quantum) of radiant energy. The scientific term is *electromagnetic radiant energy*.

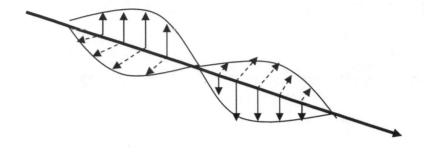

Dotted lines are magnetic field components

Solid lines are electrical field components

Figure 9.1 Electromagnetic Wave

Figure 9.1 is an extremely simplified model of an electromagnetic wave. The wave is moving in the direction of the arrow. The wave has two components. The electrical field is moving up and down. The magnetic field is moving horizontally back and forth. Without mass, the electromagnet wave lacks our sense of shape. Figure 9.1 is drawn only to communicate the electromagnetic wave concept.

Several attributes of an electromagnetic wave must be learned in order to achieve an overall understanding of this kind of energy:

1. Electromagnetic waves and their energy move independent of matter (but they also can move through and interact with matter). This is different than our other kinds of energy.

2. All electromagnetic waves in space travel at a fixed velocity. That velocity is 186,000 miles per second and is called the *"speed of light."* Remember that all light is radiant energy. All radiant energy in space travels at this speed. This is a property of our universe.

3. Radiant waves, in order to provide a visual reference, are modeled after our observed material waves (such as in a lake). Waves in a lake are observed to

move up and down with a forward velocity. Similarly, radiant energy waves swing up and down and back and forth (vibrates) in sync at a certain frequency while moving forward at a light-speed velocity. Radiant energy exists with two complementary components; a vibrating electric field and a vibrating magnetic field. That is why it is called an *electromagnetic wave.* The electric field and magnetic field travel foreword together in sync without any loss of energy, until they react with something (usually matter). It is a neat way of transporting energy from the sun to our earth.

4. The radiant energy we sense is composed of individual independent packets of energy. Each packet has a very little energy and the number of packets of energy in our measured radiant energy applications is very large. The packets of energy are called *quanta.*

5. The amount of energy within each quantum packet depends only upon the wave frequency of the quantum packet. This greatly simplifies assists our understanding and quantification of radiant energy behavior. Unfortunately, the wonderful science developed around radiant energy would require many texts and time to properly communicate. For now, we have to present only appropriate essentials.

6. Radiant energy has a broad range of quantum energies (wavelengths or frequencies). We have observed the effects of everything from high energy (x-rays) to medium energy (visual light) to low energy (electric stove element). They are all radiant energies.

It is essential that you clearly understand and memorize the six attributes of radiant energy. If the attributes are not clear, please reread this section.

III. Radiant Energy Interacting with Matter

The complete understanding of the interaction of electromagnetic (radiant) energy with matter is extremely complex. Our simplified model is presented only because it is adequate for our utility grade energy topic.

Using our sunshine as an observed example, there are three predominant ways that radiant energy interacts with matter:

1. Transmission (essentially no interaction)

   Our atmosphere and windows are transparent to sunshine radiation in our visible eye detection range.

2. Reflection

   Matter with "loose" electrons (like metals) reflect radiation by efficient absorption and emission of quanta. Think about your mirrors.

3. Absorption

   Radiant quanta interact with the allowed energy levels in matter and the absorbed quanta energy is converted to chemical and kinetic energy.

This section is written as orientation to the radiant energy processes.

IV. Observations

The best way to integrate radiant energy into our comprehensive energy science is to provide familiar radiant energy observations that occur without focused thought. This will be an easy investigation.

1. Sunshine

   The sun has been worshiped as a god and cursed for causing sunburn. The sun provides a most familiar example of radiant energy.

   Figure 9.2 presents the radiant energy we receive from the sun:

   Figure 9.2 is the solar spectrum. The quanta emitted from the sun have quantum wavelengths (energies) that are plotted across the bottom of the graphic. The frequency of the quanta and energy units may be unfamiliar. The quantitative calculation of radiant energy is explained in Chapter 9 Insight.

   The sun is about 92,000,000 miles from earth and the quanta always travel at 186,000 miles per second. It takes about 495 seconds for a single quantum to reach the earth from the sun.

   The total amount of radiant energy (power) reaching earth (Figure 9.2), before the sun's radiant energy enters the atmosphere, is 1344 watts per square meter. The average amount of solar energy (from the entire solar spectrum) reaching the surface of the earth is about 1000 watts per square meter. The 344 watt difference in energy is the average amount of radiant energy reflected from or absorbed by our atmosphere. We are very fortunate to have the sun as an available energy source.

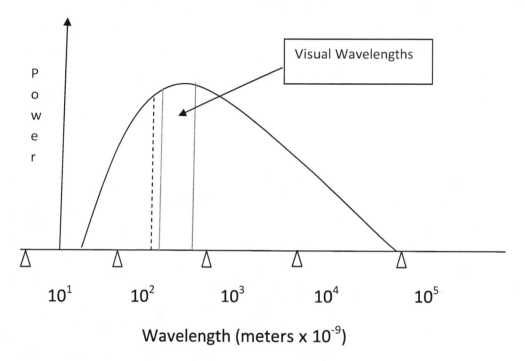

Figure 9.2 Solar Energy Spectrum (Before Entering Earth's Atmosphere)

2. Vision

It is not surprising that humans have evolved to sense the variation in radiant energy emitted by the sun. Figure 9.2 presents our limits of sight within the entire solar spectrum. Our visual range of radiant color discrimination is given by the blue and red wavelength markers. Figure 9.3 is the solar spectrum presented in relationship to the quanta energy discrimination that we have biologically evolved.

Figure 9.3 is presented with our optical limits of detection. These are the colors of the rainbow. Note that the measurement scale is given in wavelength (meters). Photon wavelength and energy is explained in Chapter 9 Insight.

Human color (optic) discrimination is our brain's sensatory input. The energy mechanism for vision is the charge separation (electron from a molecule) caused by energy quanta entering our eye. The mechanism of charge separation is fascinating, but also requires significant education not appropriate in this text. Our eyes can discriminate among quanta frequencies, giving us the sense of color. Those of us possessing normal color must have true sympathy for those whom are color-blind or have visual impairment.

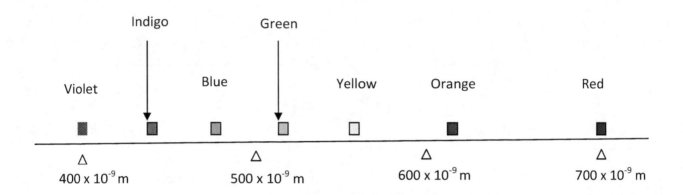

Photon Wavelength

Figure 9.3 Visual Spectrum

3. Ozone UV protection

Figure 9.2 also presents (the dotted line) the solar radiation below 320×10^{-9} meters of wavelength that does not reach earth because the earth's atmosphere has ozone that absorbs essentially all of that radiant energy. The ozone layer shields all biological species from greater quantum energies of radiation. The earth's biological systems have evolved without these energies of radiation, and we would now be in peril if we destroyed the ozone layer.

4. Microwave

The microwave oven is a modern convenience based upon radiant energy (here produced to a specific energy) that efficiently and effectively heat water and hydrocarbon materials. This is electromagnetic radiation engineered to make our lives more convenient. The wave length of the microwave radiation is typically around 2 centimeters.

5. Modern electronics

My first obvious observation is that this computer is "wirelessly" connected to the central computer system. The "wireless" applications are as commonplace as our radio, television, cell phones, garage door openers, and highway radar. All of these applications rely upon electromagnetic radiation.

V. Generating Photons

According to the 1st Law of Thermodynamics, all photons originate (or are converted) from another kind of energy.

Heat energy:

Heat energy converts to radiant energy. You have observed this often, but have not analyzed this conversion. Objects feel hot even when you are not in thermal energy contact (conduction) with them. A good example is an electric stove top "burner". When you turn the "burner" on, as it increases temperature it visually changes from black to a red glow.

Here is what is happening. The electric energy converts to heat energy that increases the temperature of the stove heating element. With the increase in temperature, a larger fraction of the stove heating element's atoms are boosted into the exited energy state from the ground state. When these atom's exited states return to their ground states, they emit photons. With increased temperatures, the stove "burner" not only emits a larger quantity of photons, but also emits photons with larger individual energies. The element turns red. We can feel the radiant energy.

If the element becomes very hot, we will see only "white" heat or photon energy across the entire visible spectrum. That is exactly what happens in an incandescent light bulb. Electricity energy heats a wire within the light bulb to a very high temperature. The light bulb's transmitted electromagnetic spectrum is similar to the solar spectrum. The incandescent (that means hot) light bulb has very comforting light, but it is very energy conversion (electricity to photons) inefficient. It should be called an electric heat bulb.

This paragraph is reluctantly added to this section because this concept adds little to our understanding of utility grade energy, but is the answer to a frequently asked question. At what temperature does matter stop transmitting radiant energy? The answer is at absolute zero (the 3rd Law of Thermodynamics). As long as matter has a temperature (and heat), a small fraction of electrons are "boosted" to energy states above their "ground state" by the kinetic energy within the matter. When they return to the ground state, the electrons radiate electromagnetic energy. Yes, ice does radiate energy!!

The sun generates, on a continuing basis, large amounts of nuclear energy. The way that the sun maintains an energy balance, and maintains a relatively stable temperature, is by radiating that energy into space. The interior of the sun is too hot to generate the solar spectrum presented in Figure 9.2. The simple reason is that the temperature is so high that all electrons are independent of associated protons. This condition is called a *plasma*. In fact, the interior of the sun has all electrons separated from nuclei. In this condition, the sun's interior cannot emit the atomistic quanta. Only the surface of the sun is cool enough to generate the solar spectrum. The sun's surface is called the *photosphere*. The cooler surface permits "allowed" transitions in the solar atoms. If we heat material to 5200 $^\circ$ C, we can closely match the solar surface photon emission spectrum. This is the same mechanism of heat generating quanta as our stove top, only hotter.

Electrical energy:

The electrical energy conversion to photons cannot be observed by our biological senses. The electrical energy conversion to photons is understood through scientific discoveries when investigating our universe.

Figure 9.4 presents an electrical energy device that is commonly called an garage door opener. If we force electrons into the device antenna at a specific frequency, we create and transmit an electric field and wave the same as presented in Figure 9.1. The 1st Law of Thermodynamics applies. We convert electrical energy into electromagnetic energy. At the specific frequency (your favorite radio station) of this electromagnetic energy, it is received (captured) by another antenna. This "wireless" transmission of energy is very common, but rarely understood by the public. TV remote controls are considered mysterious devices, with radiant energy never considered.

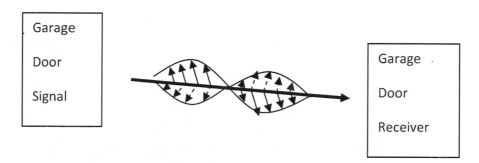

Figure 9.4 Radiation Antenna

VI. The Amount of Photon Energy

From here on we will call the quanta ***photons.*** Photons are used as the common proper name for electromagnetic radiation. It was mentioned in Section I that the energy of a photon was only dependent upon its frequency of vibration. That physical fact is explained, for those interested, in the Chapter 9 Insight. For now, what is relevant is that scientists have precisely determined the energy for photons of different frequencies. The following observables can be explained in terms of this precise individual photon energy calculation:

1. The visible color spectrum

   Yellow color (see Figure 9.3) = 570 x 10^{-19} m wavelength
   570 x 10^{-19} m wavelength = 5.26 x 10^{14} waves per second
   Energy = (6.63 x 10^{-34} J-sec)(5.26 x 10^{14} / sec) = **3.48 x 10^{-19} J**

2. Designed wavelength of radiation
   = 12.2 x 10^{-2} m wavelength
   12.2 x 10^{-2} wavelength = 2.46 x 10^{9} waves per second
   Energy = (6.63 x 10^{-34} J-sec)(2.46 x 10^{9} / sec) = **1.63 x 10^{-24} J**

3. Ozone creation
   Solar photon that has enough energy to break an oxygen bond
   From lab experiments, this energy value has been determined to be
   8.22 x 10^{-19} J / oxygen bond

   Waves per second = (8.22 x 10^{-19}J / 6.63 x 10^{-34} J-sec)
   = 1.24 x 10^{15} / sec
   Photon wavelength = (3.00 x 10^{8} m/s) / (1.24 x 10^{15} / s)
   = 242 x 10^{-9} m

The ability to calculate photon energy is not important to our understanding of utility grade energy. However, consider the following:

1. The accuracy of determining photon is outstanding.

2. Our eyes cannot "see" the radiant microwave energy. The microwave energy wavelength is too long. Our eyes cannot "see" the oxygen breaking wavelength. The oxygen breaking wavelength is too short. The key idea is that we only biologically sense (see) a small portion of the radiant energy around us.

VII. Photon Energy Absorption

Photon energy absorption by matter occurs when the electron energy level change is equal to the energy of the photon. Energy photon spectrum absorption is a common method of chemical element identification. Also, the unique photon emissions are used as chemical element identification. We can identify elements within suns millions of miles from our earth by energy emission spectral patterns.

We will use the chemical models of Chapter 8 as a platform to demonstrate the phenomenon of radiant absorption. Figure 9.5 presents the same methane molecule floating aimlessly around in our atmosphere. A photon from the sun interacts with the methane. The photon transferred its energy to the methane molecule. In so doing, a hydrogen was ripped away from the carbon.

In this case, the photon would have to transmit 413 kJ/mole of energy. That was the energy value used in Chapter 8. Photon energies are very accurately known and can be accurately calculated.

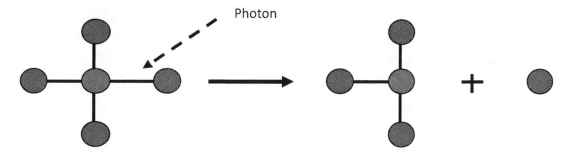

Figure 9.5 Photon Interaction

The photon interacted with one C-H bond in the methane molecule to produce a methane molecule minus a hydrogen atom and a separate hydrogen atom.

1. The 1st Law of Thermodynamics dictates that the incoming photon energy must have at least the C-H bond energy or hydrogen removal from methane will not happen. This is a must-know concept that applies to our utility grade solar energy.

2. If the separated hydrogen and the methane (minus a hydrogen) recombine, the energy released will be the same as the original photon. The recombination may release a lower energy photon, and also may convert to some heat energy, but the total energy released will be exactly the same energy as the original photon from the sun.

Figure 9.5, in a simple model, presents atomic separation of a molecule. However, this simple case is not particularly useful in our radiant energy science. Photon absorption-reemission also has what can be considered as a very complicated science. Figure 9.6 presents a more universal model of an atom (and the same holds true for all molecules) in which chemical electron energies are only allowed at certain levels as dictated by quantum mechanics. These energies between allowed levels will be less than the total removal energy as presented in Figure 9.6. Figure 9.6 is the same as Figure 8.2 of the Hydrogen atom. Higher (exited) levels of hydrogen are allowed even when only one electron is present as in hydrogen. The amount of energy between allowed levels of electron to nucleus attraction are very accurately known. For simplicity, hydrogen is the example.

Not only are the energies only allowed in these energy states, electrons can temporarily exist in any of these energy states. This means that energy transitions for photon absorption can also occur between electron states and then a little while later emit that same energy as the electron returns to its former state. The key concept about photon absorption is that an atom or molecule can absorb a higher energy photon and later re-emit that energy as lower energy photons.

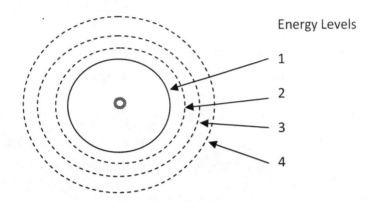

Figure 9.6 Energy States

Figure 9.7 is presented in order to graphically reinforce this key concept

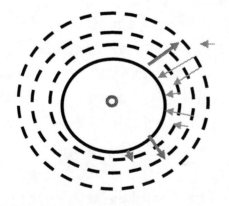

Thick lines are photon absorption

Thin lines are photon re-emission

Figure 9.7 Typical Re-emitting

VIII. Familiar Re-emitted Radiant Energy Observations

We have observed the many phenomena involving re-emitted radiant energy, but few are interpreted fundamentally as explained in **Section VII.** Think a little about these familiar observations.

1. On a sunny day, when we return to our automobile after lunch, we observe that the temperature is unexpectedly high. Rather than think about how this high temperature occurred, we wait for the air conditioner to cool the car. Some people temporarily open a window to help in the cooling process.

   What happened was that the higher energy photons (rays) arrived from the sun. The photons passed through the automobile's windows (which are obviously light spectrum transparent) and converted their energy to heat as they interacted with the automobile's interior.

   The photons are either converted to heat energy immediately or re-emitted as lower energy photons (See Figure 9.7). Here is the reason for the unexpected heating. The windows, transparent to high energy photons from sunlight, blocked the re-emitted low energy photons emitted from the automobile interior. The heat energy is trapped in the automobile, raising the temperature more than expected.

   Some people buy a light reflector to place in the windows of the car. The reflectors reflect the high energy solar photons back out the window before they interact with the automobile interior. They do reduce the automobile's temperature rise during lunch time.

2. We utilize trapped heat in a plant greenhouse by the same radiant photon conversions in the automobile described above. In this case we utilize the **"greenhouse"** effect.

3. The popular subject of global warming and the contribution of carbon dioxide (a greenhouse gas) to the global warming is a "heated" debate. The greenhouse effect is the same as the mechanisms described above.

Carbon dioxide exists in our atmosphere. The higher energy radiation from the sun does not interact with carbon dioxide. Carbon dioxide is transparent to our visible solar spectrum. The major components of our atmosphere can be considered transparent to incoming solar radiation. But the earth itself emits radiant energy of a lower energy based upon the temperature of the earth. Carbon dioxide does interact with these lower energy photons. This is exactly the "greenhouse" effect we explained as an example of photon re-emission within an automobile. Only now the earth, rather than the car, is warmer than expected.

Re-emitted photons from the earth do not interact with the major constituents of air (nitrogen, oxygen, and argon) because they do not have enough energy. Water and carbon dioxide do substantially interact with the re-emitted photons from the earth and block low energy photons from leaving the earth. This warms (increases the temperature) of the earth to the comfortable temperatures that we enjoy today.

The current debates are centered about the recent increasing level of carbon dioxide measured in our atmosphere. This text will not speculate upon this issue.

IX. Conclusions

Radiant energy is energy independent of matter. Radiant energy heats the earth and provides the biological environment necessary for life. Radiant energy is a major contender for our future utility grade energy systems (see Chapter 17 – Solar Power)

The must-know elements of radiant energy are:

1. **Radiant energy is electromagnetic energy.**

2. **Radiant energy exists as packets (quanta - photons) travelling at the speed of light.**

3. **Photons interact with matter in a manner not known by our senses, but quite well scientifically understood.**

4. **Photon energy depends only upon frequency of the electromagnetic wave.**

5. **Quantum energy intensity spans heat radiation to beyond X-rays.**

6. **Re-emission of photons from matter produces many of our observed phenomena.**

Chapter 9 Insight

Plank's Constant and The Ozone Layer

Two terms were alluded to within Chapter 9: Plank's constant and the ozone layer. Neither topic is directly associated to energy science, but both provide a unifying view of view of radiant energy.

Plank's constant

The joule is the standard of energy using the Metric measurement system. A simple relationship was discovered by Max Plank to determine the energy value of a photon in joules. If we can determine the frequency of a photon (electromagnetic packet) in waves per second (and we can accurately do that), then we can precisely determine the energy of the packet with this simple equation:

Energy (joules) = (Plank's constant) x (quantum frequency)

$$E = h\nu$$

ν is the frequency of the electromagnetic wave in the quantum. ν is pronounced "new". It is not the English letter "vee".

The h is *Plank's constant*. Max Plank, through clever methods, determined that h is 6.6×10^{-34} joule – seconds.

If we look at Section VI, the energy of radiant energy was repeatedly calculated using the simple E=hν formula. This is the link between radiant energy and other kinds of energy.

The Ozone Layer

In Section VI, we calculated the quantum properties of radiant energy capable of separating an oxygen molecule (O_2) into two oxygen atoms.

But we left out the story of ozone production. Refer back to Section VI. When a radiant quantum from the sun is equal or greater than 8.22×10^{-19} J of energy, an oxygen molecule can separate into two oxygen atoms.

The oxygen atoms react with other oxygen molecules (O_2) to produce ozone molecules (O_3). Now this occurs over a large span of altitudes in our atmosphere. Ozone is not a dense layer, but spread out.

We now have a ozone "layer" in our atmosphere. Ozone absorbs almost all of the solar photons in the range of 200×10^{-9} m to 320×10^{-9} m. Those photons never reach the earth.

These photons are called ultraviolet radiation (UV) with more energy than our life forms can handle. Biologically, we have evolved within the "ozone UV shield" and if the ozone layer was removed from our atmosphere, we would struggle to survive.

Chapter 10:

Electrical Energy

Sections:

I. Introduction to Electrical Energy

The challenge in writing a chapter about electrical energy is being able to communicate a library of electrical energy information within a single chapter without trivializing this vital topic. That challenge is met by 1) concentrating only upon basic electrical energy science and 2) limiting the electrical fundamentals to observed phenomenon. The effectiveness of this approach contains substantial compromise.

II. Some Overlooked Background

Before we proceed into the description of electrical energy, the physical background of the electron must be clearly understood as a prerequisite to a meaningful description of this topic

1. The electron is the lightest of the natural three basic particles (electron, proton, and neutron) that compose all of our atomic elements. See Figure 8.1 for the absolute masses.

2. The electron also has a property called "charge." Charge means that electrons and protons forcefully repel each other as like charge and forcefully attract opposite charge. The electron to proton attraction creates all of our known atoms in our universe.

3. All electrons have precisely the same amount of charge (-1) and all protons have precisely the same amount charge (+1). One electron cannot be distinguished from another electron. This greatly simplifies our understanding of electron behavior.

4. In Chapter 8, we described chemical energy in terms of electrons attaching to positive nuclei (plural for nucleus) in atomic-molecular reactions. In chemical energy descriptions, the electrons were "bound" to the nuclei to form stable molecules. But electrons do not have to be bound to positive charges as they are in a neutral atom. Within metals, electrons move freely. Electrons are independent particles with mass. In this chapter (Chapter 10), the electrons are "free" to neutralize their negative charge by moving to a positive charge. The electron charge neutralization process produces electrical energy.

These four facts are often overlooked as the framework of electrical energy investigation.

III. One Electron in a Charge Separation

Figure 10.1 presents a graphic model that is central to all electric energy phenomena. This is a simple graphic and concept, however it is crucial that this visual description be clearly understood ! ! !

Figure 10.1 presents two parallel metal plates with different electrical charges. The upper plate has more electrons than the bottom plate and is therefore negative in relationship to the bottom plate.

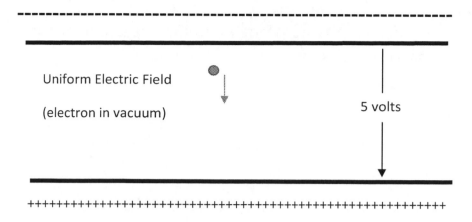

Figure 10.1 Electrical Charge Separation

The "free" electrons in Figure 10.1 cannot flow from negative to positive because the region between the plates is a vacuum and does not *conduct* electrons. Until something else happens, the electrical charge is stored on the plates.

We are going to place 5 volts of attractive electron force (called voltage) between the plates. This is an arbitrary value, it could be any voltage. The voltage can be thought of as extending across the gap between the plates. Scientists call that voltage in the gap the *uniform electric field.*

Without intervention, the electrons remain on one plate, as well as the charge neutralization energy stored between the plates. Figure 10.1 also presents a mental proposition where we pull one (1) loose electron from the negative plate to start movement towards the positive plate across the gap between the plates. This electron will be allowed (mentally) to move freely towards and into the positively charged plate. The attractive force between the electron and the positive plate will accelerate the electron into the positive charge. The energy of charge attraction (force x distance) is being converted to the kinetic energy of the electron.

Figure 10.2 presents a visual graphic which establishes the energy created by an electron when it falls with decreasing voltage across the electric field. Figure 10.2 presents the very predictable energy behavior for electrons passing through an established voltage of an electric field. The kinetic energy of a single electron traveling freely to a lower voltage of one volt in an electric field is 1.6×10^{-19} joule.

When the electron "crashes" into the positive plate, the charge is neutralized and the electron's kinetic energy is transferred into the positive plate (usually as heat energy). Energy is always conserved.

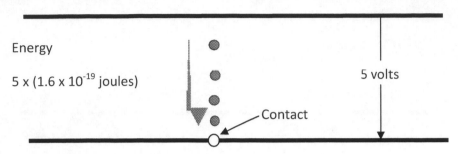

Figure 10.2 Electron Volts (eV)

Electrons can never travel from a negative charge to be neutralized by a positive charge without transferring their energy.

The attractive force between electrical charges is measured as volts. The standardization of voltage will not be described in this text. Measuring voltage, to a high degree of precision and accuracy, is commonplace.

From Figure 10.2, the total electrical energy can be measured as change in voltage of force x the number of electrons undergoing that change. We will utilize the voltage x (# of electrons) to calculate energy repeatedly in the chapter.

Figure 10.3 displays a graphic of our frequent observation of lightning. Figure 10.3 is fundamentally Figure 10.1 under extreme conditions. The vacuum between the plates is replaced by air.

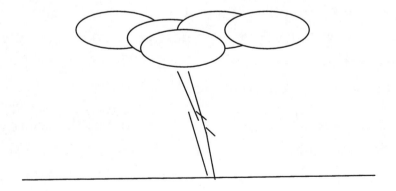

Figure 10.3 Lightning

In the case of lightning, the clouds have accumulated charges by physically rubbing together, collecting many electrons in certain clouds. When the charge voltage exceeds the "break-down voltage" of the air, the electrons neutralize the charges with a "bang".

The "break-down" voltage occurs when the electrical field strength (in volts) forcefully pulls the bound electrons from the air molecules. This forms a conductive path of "free" negative electrons and positive air atoms. That formation of charged particles is called *ionization*. The charged particles (ions) immediately form a path (like a metal wire) for the electric charges to neutralize themselves. The energy and behavior of lightning is scary. The electrical energy transfer into sound, heat, and air expansion make lighting a dangerous phenomenon.

Metals conduct "free" electrons to flow from a negative charge to a positive charge. Observed examples are so obvious that we don't even notice. All electrical power cords and power lines are conductors that allow the electrons' negative charge to flow to a positive charge. Materials (primarily metals) that permit electron flow are called *conductors* and materials that relatively prevent flow are called *insulators*. Every electron must convert charge separation energy to another kind of energy before it neutralizes a positive charge. Charge separation energy is *electrical energy*.

IV. Scaling Up to Usable Electrical Energy Measurements

In Chapters 8 and 9, we viewed chemical energy and radiant energy as products of the positive charge and negative charge behavior of particles in nature (electrons and protons). In the chemical and radiant energy explanations, the charge behavior was described using a single chemical atomic unit or a single electromagnetic photon unit. Individually, these were extremely small physical examples. In this chapter (Chapter 10) we will describe charge behavior and electron movement from the viewpoint of our sensible observations. Our sensible observations require us to use a larger, convenient scale of measurement. We are more familiar with our larger electrical scale than the atomic level scale used the scientists.

Section III described the energy of a single electron moving through an electric field. While a single electron's energy may be a working quantity for small particle physicists and can be used as a fundamental example as in Section III, the small amount of electrical energy generated by one electron is not applicable to our utility grade energy systems. Just as we don't measure distances between towns in inches, but miles; we have to change our measurements of the number of electrons to a more convenient scale.

One electron falling through one volt of an electric field produced 1 eV (electron volt) of energy. 1 eV of energy is 1.60×10^{-19} joule. If we have 0.624×10^{19} electrons falling through one volt of an electric field, then we would have an electrical energy of 1 joule $((1.60 \times 10^{-19}$ joule$) \times (0.624 \times 10^{19}$ electrons$)) = 1.00$ joule.

Now 0.624×10^{19} is a huge number. But we don't even have to use this number again or even memorize it. What we are going to do is change measurement scales and call 0.624×10^{19} electrons "1 Coulomb."

A "**Coulomb**" has many convenient uses in electrical energy and power: but is not a measurement familiar to the public. In this section some electrical energy definitions are presented and in the next section electrical energy applications, using the definitions, will be presented using the common electrical energy observations.

An "**Ampere**" is a coulomb of electrons flowing current of electrons in a conductor every second. A familiar automobile gauge is an ammeter. It measures the amount of electricity (electrons) flowing into and out of the battery. My latest vehicle has a peak electrical generating capacity of 75 amperes. That means that the peak electrical flow from the generator is 75 coulombs per second.

A "**Volt**" is a measure of the electrical force (historically called the electromotive force or EMF). 1 ampere of electric current flowing through 1 volt of EMF will generate 1 joule of energy per second. This logical sequence of power generation by electrons must be clearly understood. My automobile vehicle generates 12 volts (EMF).

A "**Watt**" is a unit of power (energy over time) universally used in measuring electricity power. It is simply "Volts x Amperes" as stated in the last paragraph. It is possible for my automobile to generate 12 volts x 75 amps = 900 watts.

Electrical power bills are measured in (kilo)watt hours (energy over time). A little imagination is required to define electrical energy as a force through a distance. But we will do exactly that conversion in the next section.

I realize that this section presents a very difficult logical sequence of electrical energy (and power) derivation. It is not critical that you learn electrical fundamentals. What is most important is that you understand that electric power is based upon solid scientific elements. **Our utility grade power amounts are expressed in the convenient scale of *megawatts*.** Megawatts are a convenient quantity that relates to the fundamental measurement of one electron used to explain electrical behavior in Section III.

V. Electrical Energy Conversion to Mechanical Energy

Electrical energy is our prime example of available energy that can be converted into usable energy. The basic process of converting available electrical energy into usable mechanical energy is given in this section.

Soon after the discovery that electrons would flow in a conducting wire from negative to positive regions, it was discovered that electrons flowing in conducting wires also produced a magnet like the magnets found in nature. Figure 10.4 presents examples of electrons flowing in wires in two different directions.

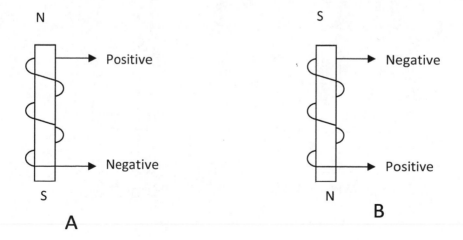

Figure 10.4 Electromagnets

The metal within the coil of wire is magnetized when current flows in the wire. Figure 10-4(A) presents current flowing in one direction that creates a magnetic n (north) upward and a magnetic s (south) downward in the electromagnet. Figure 10-4(B) presents current flowing in the other direction that creates a magnetic s (south) upward and a magnetic n (north) downward.

In Figure 10.5, bar magnets, with a permanent magnetic orientation, are placed above and below the electromagnet. The electromagnet is fixed in position.

1. In Figure 10.5 (Attraction), the electromagnet will mechanically attract (force) the bar magnets and rotate the shaft.

2. In Figure 10.5 (Repulsion), the electromagnet will mechanically repulse (force) the bar magnets and rotate the shaft.

These mechanical forces of attraction and repulsion created by the electromagnet are the basis for electrical to mechanical energy conversion.

A mechanical rotational shaft power conversion from electricity is made by a motor. Figure 10.5 presents a model of an electric motor. All electric motors are based upon this simple energy utilization.

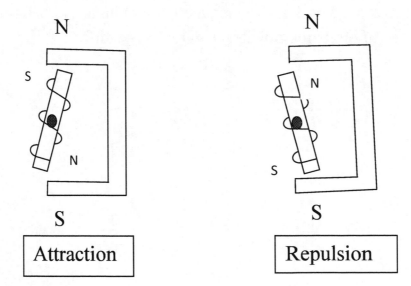

Figure 10.5 Electric Motor

An electromagnet (Figure 10.4) rotates around a mechanical shaft. The electromagnet changes magnetic polarity when we change the direction of the electrical current (Figure 10.4). The change in magnetic polarity generates a rotational force by magnetic attraction or repulsion to the permanent motor magnet (Figure 10.5). A few moments of introspection of the electrical motor concept will solidify this basic energy conversion concept.

VI. Electrical Energy Conversion to Heat Energy

A fundamental property of electrons flowing within a conductor is the electrical (electron) energy conversion to heat energy. "Free" electrons are not exactly free in terms of their flow within a conductor. The resistances to flow of electrons within a conductor are precisely known for pure conductors and many conductors composed of a well defined mixture of elements. The conversion of energy from flowing electrons to the material in which they are flowing is complex. A helpful, but oversimplified, model is to consider that the electrons "bump" into the fixed atoms of the conductors as they flow within the material. This "bumping" converts electron kinetic energy to heat energy at the atomic level.

The relationships between voltage (V), Current (I), and Resistance (R) are well established:

1. Voltage x current = (VxI = Power [in watts])

2. Voltage = current x resistance = (I x R)

3. Power = (current)(current)(resistance) = I^2R

It is very easy to continue into electrical engineering at this point rather than continue with our focus upon energy.

At the energy consumer level, the electrical to heat energy is easy to measure. Commercial applications have a watt capacity. For example:

1. A hair-drier has a 1500 watt power rating. That means conversion of 1500 watts of electrical energy to heat energy will be produced for the time (power) as the hair-drier operates.

2. A portable electric heater has a power rating of 1000 watts. For the time in use, the heater will consume 1000 watts of electricity and produce 1000 watts of heat.

3. A 100 watt incandescent light bulb emits usable photons (light) when the filament is heated to approximately 4500 degrees centigrade. It converts 100 watts of electricity to heat and light during time of use. This common application is not often considered as a heat conversion from electricity. The incandescent bulb conversion of electrical energy to light energy is very inefficient.

4. Our electric clothes-driers use a variety of electric heaters depending upon the complexity of a certain model. The power for a batch of clothes may be about 1 hour at 3000 watts or 3 kilowatt-hours of electrical power.

Rather than continue with specific observations, it is instructive to assume that all electrical energy coming into the house will eventually be converted to heat energy.

A utility grade power distribution system (our grid) has a fundamental condition with electricity distribution between the electricity power generator and the electricity power consumer. The resistance to current flow in the electricity distribution lines is translated into energy heat loss. This power loss is substantial. Electrical resistance within power lines of the grid cause about a 6.5% loss of our electricity generation due to heat conversion during transmission.

VII. Conclusions

The Chapter 10 focus is upon elementary electron behavior and electrical energy utilization in terms of universal dimensions.

The must-know elements of electrical energy are:

1. Mobile electron charge neutralization is the basis of electrical energy.

2. Electrical charge separation is measured in volts of electromotive force.

3. "Free" electrons produce energy when they neutralize charge.

4. Conductors pass electrons and insulators do not pass electrons.

5. A single electron moving 1 volt lower towards neutralization gains 1.6 x 10^{-19} joule. (1.6 x 10^{-19} joule is 1 electron-volt.)

6. The electrical energy conversion to mechanical energy uses electromagnetism.

Chapter 10 Insight

Capacitors

Figure 10.1 within Chapter 10 presents the basic source of electrical energy. Figure 10.1 presents two conductors of "free" electrons separated by an insulator. The two conductors have an electronic charge (EMF or Volts) difference.

Figure 10.1 also presents a ***Capacitor*** where electrical energy is stored. The practical amount of energy that can be stored in capacitors is insufficient for utility grade power applications. However, capacitors are a key fundamental component of electronics and electrical energy utilization. Capacitors are too important to ignore in this text.

Capacitors can be precisely quantified for electrical and electronic designs. This insight only qualitatively describes to people unfamiliar to capacitors, several basic elements:

Capacitors are measured according to 1) the amount of energy storage capacity (joules or farads) and 2) the safe operating EMF (Volts).

1. Capacitors are classified by energy storage capacity in joules for power applications and farads for electronic applications.

   Reduction in physical size and higher breakdown voltages of capacitors can be substantially improved by using a special material between the capacitor plates. That special material is called a ***Dielectric***.

2. Breakdown voltage

   Similar to the lightning being caused by voltage exceeding the insulation of air, the capacitor will arc when the voltage between the plates exceeds the insulation of the dielectric. A common reliability failure of capacitors is "popping" caused by an overvoltage or structural flaw within the capacitor.

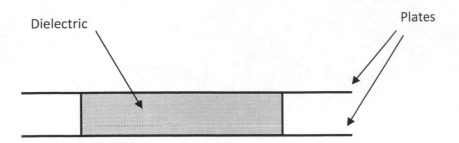

Figure 10.6 Capacitor

A specific application in capacitor development for renewable energy is the use of an automotive super-capacitor. A 100% electrical battery powered automobile has design limitations to the surge of electrical power needed upon occasion. An example is the extra power required when passing a semi truck. Hybrid (internal combustion engine/battery) vehicles use the internal combustion engine and batteries to supply occasional surges of power. A 100% electrical battery powered automobile can use a super-capacitor to provide that surge of power. The super-capacitor would then be recharged during average battery power conditions.

Chapter 11:

Gas Pressure-Volume Energy

Sections:

I. Introduction to Gas Pressure-Volume Energy

Gas Pressure-Volume is an intuitively recognized energy that produces a force through a distance. The energy produced is easily measured in mechanical energy terms. The significant importance of gas pressure-volume energy to utility grade energy production is that gas pressure-volume energy is the major energy path conversion element between heat energy and mechanical energy.

Our first task is to clarify the word "Gas" used in this chapter title, <u>Gas Pressure-Volume Energy.</u> The meaning of "gas" in this chapter is the gas phase of matter, such as air, methane, nitrogen, etc. The word gas does not have the meaning of the common short version of gasoline used in our automobiles.

Our second task is to reduce the proper name Gas Pressure-Volume Energy to the simpler proper name Gas Energy. Since Pressure-Volume is energy by definition of force through a distance, the proper name Gas Pressure-Volume is redundant with Gas Energy.

The investigation of gases has produced fascinating insights into gas physical behavior. Unfortunately, we have to bypass that interesting subject.

II. The Kinetic Theory of Gases

The central concept of the **Kinetic Theory of Gases** is that the total kinetic energy of a gas is equal to the sum of the kinetic energies of all individual molecules within the gas. The kinetic theory of gases has been successfully validated to be a true model.

Models of neon gas and nitrogen gas were presented in Figures 7.3 and 7.4. The figures did not have any solid boundaries and only represented the isolated gas phase molecular movement.

At any gas temperature, we can accurately calculate the distribution of the gas velocities and energies. This means that we also can calculate the kinetic energy for each molecule of the gas from the average velocity and its molecular weight. Figure 11.1 presents the velocity distribution of nitrogen at 0 $^\circ$ C. and 1200 $^\circ$ C. The energy scale, given in the extremely small value of ergs/molecule, is presented on the upper axis of the graph. That is the energy of each nitrogen gas molecule. That energy scale is not a joke. We can calculate the gross nitrogen energy per unit volume directly from those values. It would be a good homework assignment in physical chemistry. We will remain with the subject of energy.

Figure 11.1 displays the measurements of gas velocity distributions at two temperatures. The total kinetic energy of the gas can be calculated directly from the distribution measurements. The velocity distribution of air molecules is a fundamental part of aerodynamic engineering.

Ergs / Molecule(x 10^{-13})

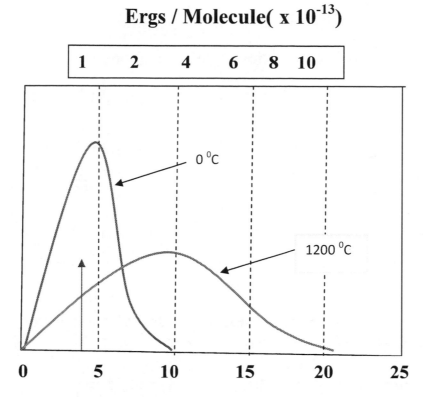

Meters x 10^2 / Second

Figure 11.1 Nitrogen Gas Molecule Speed Distributions

Figure 11.1 leads to many interesting insights into the behavior of gases. Just from the velocity distribution, we will present one insight.

The upward arrow is the speed of sound in air in our atmosphere at sea level. Our air consists mainly of nitrogen. And sound is a compression-rarefaction wave in this case traveling in air. But the compression-rarefication wave can't travel any faster than the air molecules can travel. The speed of sound is measured to be 343 meters / second at sea level, just about what we would expect from the nitrogen gas molecular distribution presented in Figure 11.1.

III. Gas Pressure and PV Energy

Figure 11.2 presents a visual of the following air conditions:

1. Within the body of a gas, molecules travel in a straight line until they collide with another gas molecule. The total energy after the collision doesn't change, but the velocities of each of the colliding molecules does change. This process goes on continuously and the average kinetic energy remains constant.

2. At the boundary where the gas molecules encounter the fixed solid wall, the molecular kinetic energy is reflected back into the gas volume.

3. The average change in velocity of the molecules reflecting from the solid wall material creates a force. If the wall doesn't move a distance, no energy conversion involved.

This force is measured in English PSI (pounds per square inch) or SI Kilopascals (Newtons per square meter). The huge number of reflecting molecules involved result in a pressure (force) average at a stable value

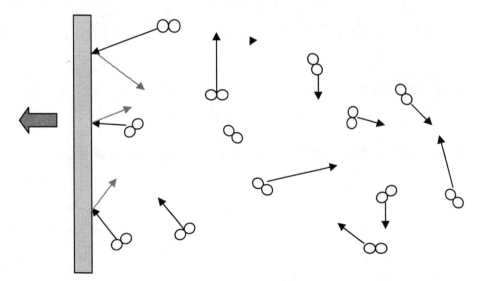

Figure 11.2 Gas Pressure

Figure 11.2 presents the link between molecular kinetic energy and the observed phenomenon of pressure.

The next step is to consider what happens if we let the force of the reflecting gas molecules move the wall. Figure 11.3 presents a gas pressure (now arbitrarily set at 10 PSI) moving a wall (think of the wall as a piston in a cylinder) 3 inches.

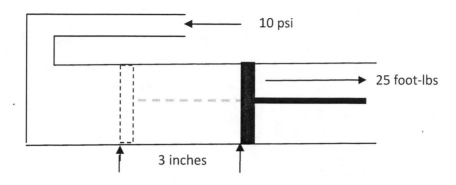

Figure 11.3 Gas Energy

The gas pressure (10 PSI) has moved the piston 3 inches. If the piston's surface area facing the gas were 10 square inches, we would have:

Total pressure = 10 pounds/inch^2 x 10 inch^2 = 100 pounds

and if the piston moved 3 inches or ¼ foot, so we would have an energy of (force x distance) of 100 lbs x ¼ ft = 25 foot-lbs.

This is a description of Watt's steam engine in terms of molecular kinetic energy (heat). The source of the 10 psi gas is not identified. This example is considered ideal. The 25 ft-lbs of energy was converted from gas energy to mechanical energy in this machine.

All applications of heat energy conversion to mechanical energy follow the path of heating a gas to create pressure, then utilizing the pressure x gas volume to convert to mechanical energy. The gas energy to mechanical energy machine was presented in the last section. The application of heat energy conversion to mechanical energy has two established and noteworthy developments:

1. The internal combustion engine

2. The electrical utility grade turbine

Both applications follow the 1st and 2nd Laws of Thermodynamics. Both applications need scientific understanding of gas pressure generation.

IV. The *Stirling* Engine

The Stirling engine is an excellent example of heat energy conversion to mechanical energy.

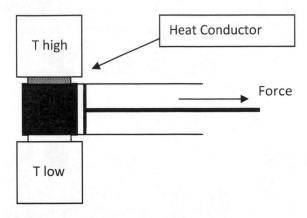

Figure 11.4 Stirling Engine (heating)

The Stirling engine has a fixed volume of gas within a cylinder that is heated from a higher temperature source as presented in Figure 11.4.

The only difference between Figure 11.4 and Figure 11.3 is that the gas pressure is created within the machine's cylinder.

If we cool the fixed volume of gas after it has reached the high temperature, by shutting off the high temperature heat conduction and turning on the low temperature conduction, the gas will cool resulting in a lower pressure. Figure 11.5 presents this action.

The cooling gas will lower the internal pressure, creating a volume retraction within the cylinder. The mechanical energy is realized at the piston.

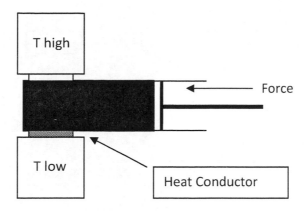

Figure 11.5 Stirling Engine (cooling)

The practical physical limits in engineering design of heat transfer and low power-to-weight ratio have limited practical applications of the Stirling engine.

V. The Internal Combustion Engine

The greatest success in converting heat energy to mechanical energy is the internal combustion engine. The basic engineering process has been to convert the heat energy to gas energy within (internal) the engine cylinder. The science of energy conversion flow is nicely demonstrated in the internal combustion engine.

Chemical energy within hydrocarbons is converted to heat energy internally within the machine cylinder through reaction of the hydrocarbons with oxygen from air. The heat energy raises the temperature of the air within the cylinder with a corresponding increase in air gas energy. The gas energy is converted to mechanical energy during the expansion of the gas.

The engineering (realization) of internal combustion power is based upon oxygen and fuel delivery into the combustion chamber, the timing of the spark to initiate combustion, and the efficient flow of gases in order to improve energy conversion efficiency. The present (2010) internal combustion engines are products of excellent engineering designs.

The internal combustion engine cycles are presented in Figure 11.6.

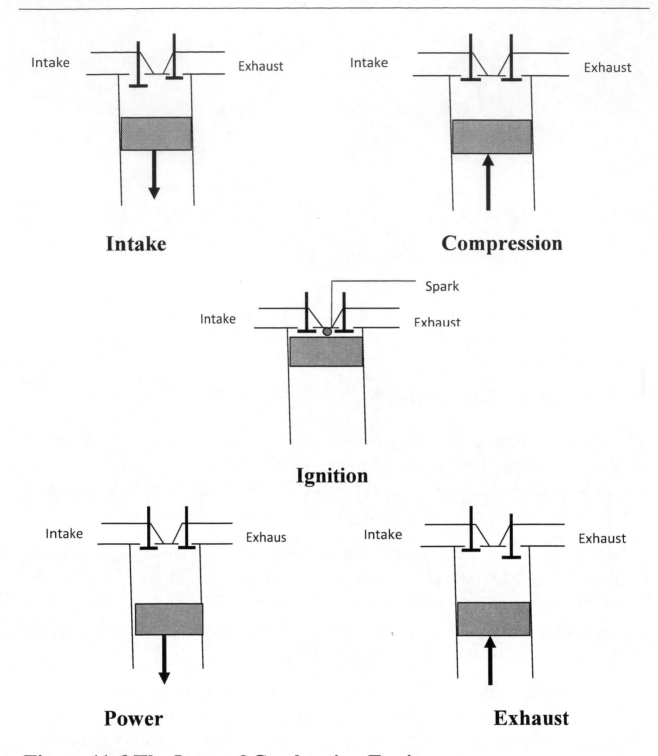

Figure 11.6 The Internal Combustion Engine

The internal combustion engine (heat engine) also has the limitations of the 2nd Law of Thermodynamics and the Carnot Cycle. An observed example is that a

Diesel cycle engine has a greater intrinsic efficiency of chemical energy to mechanical energy conversion.

Heat engine design is a fascinating subject. A chapter directed at heat engine design was written for this text and then discarded because of the extensive non-utility energy (power) related content. However, heat engines remain as our prominent observed energy conversion application.

VI. Gas Kinetic Energy Applications (Turbines and Jets)

Sections III to V present gas energy conversions to mechanical energy within a machine that utilizes energy as presented in Figure 11.2. The mechanical energy (force x distance) was converted from gas expansion.

Another method of gas pressure to mechanical (shaft) energy is presented in Figure 11.7.

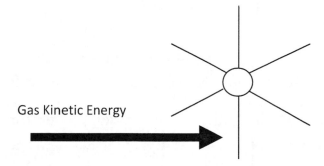

Figure 11.7 The Turbine

The gas energy at the combustion chamber is converted entirely to kinetic energy. We have all observed balloons propelled by escaping gas under pressure. In Figure 11.7, the kinetic energy is transferred, with an adequate conversion efficiency, to mechanical shaft energy when the gas contacts the lever arm of the shaft. A continuous transfer of kinetic energy to mechanical energy occurs when turbine blades enter the kinetic stream of gas. Figure 11.7 only presents the basic concept.

Figure 11.8 presents a model of the sophisticated level of turbine development.

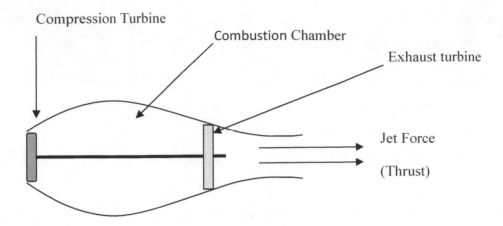

Figure 11.8 Turbine Design

Figure 11.8 presents a *jet* engine used in aircraft. The air is compressed into a combustion chamber and the resulting PV energy upon combustion is divided between an outlet turbine that drives the compression "fan" and the kinetic energy that exits (as a jet) the engine. Although simple in concept, jet engines are very complex engineering designs.

When the design optimizes the mechanical energy of a mechanical shaft, then the shaft can be used to rotate a propeller. That application is called a *"turbo prop."*

Turbines are used directly in utility grade power production of electrical energy from natural gas hydrocarbons. The utility electrical generator shafts are turbine driven by steam in the case of coal fired and nuclear steam generation. Hydroelectric power is turbine driven by a water gravitational energy source. The natural gas power drives the electrical generation shaft similar to the "turbo prop."

Note that the turbine power conversion is fundamentally simple, but optimum designs for specific applications are quite complex.

VII. Conclusions

Gas Pressure Energy is the major conversion path between heat energy and mechanical energy. It must be considered as an important conversion efficiency factor in utility grade applications.

The three laws of thermodynamics are the limiting energy science demonstrated in gas pressure energy. This was explicitly presented in Chapter 7 – Heat Energy, where the heat to mechanical energy is presented.

The must-know elements of gas pressure energy are:

1. Gas energy is the sum of all the kinetic energies of the gas particles.

2. Gas temperature is a measure of the average kinetic energy of the gas particles.

3. When gases expand (and do external work), heat may flow into the gas and maintain the gas temperature, or the gas may expand using its own heat energy and lower the gas temperature.

4. The most efficient conversion of heat energy to mechanical energy (using gas pressure) is described by the Carnot cycle.

5. Jets and turbines are advanced applications of gas pressure energy.

Chapter 11 Insight

Ideal Gas Relationships

All gases can be understood in observable terms (pressure, volume, and temperature) that are easily measured and universally understood. The amazing feature about gases is that they all behave the same to a high degree in terms of their physical properties.

A fixed relationship among all gases is:

P(pressure) x V(volume) = n (amount of gas particles) x T(temperature)

PV = nT

In order to account for the various universal dimensions (measurement systems), an equation proportionality constant R is furnished to allow numerical calculations.

PV = nRT

Values for R are:

      1. = 0.082 Liters x Atmospheres / mole x degrees Kelvin

      2. = 8.3 joules / mole x degrees Kelvin (energy)

      3. = 8.3 kilopascals x liters / mole x Kelvin

For any gas, if we know four values of P, V, n, or T, we can calculate the fifth value with confidence. The insight into gas energy is substantial:

A mole is the molecular weight of the gas in grams. For example, nitrogen has a weight of 28 grams per mole. So 7 grams of nitrogen gas would be 0.25 mole. This is an inconvenient physical chemistry term for amount.

Many aspects of the ideal gas law directly apply to our scientific understanding of PV energy.

An entire science of gas behavior can be developed from the ideal gas equation. Ideal gas behavior has been helpful in understanding the heat energy to mechanical energy conversion of the Carnot Cycle and to provide physical estimates of solar fission limits during hydrogen gas compression during gravitational contraction.

During all Chapter 11 presentations of Gas Pressure applications, the fundamentals of the ideal gas laws provide the scientific limits for energy engineering.

The physical chemistry of gases is a fascinating subject.

Chapter12:

Utility Power

Sections

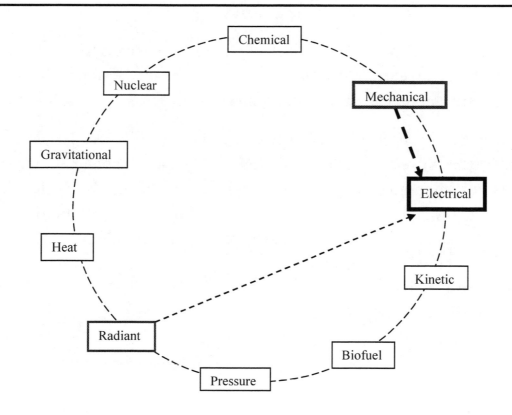

I. Introduction to Utility Power

Chapter 12 is focused upon electrical power utilized by consumers. The 1st Law of Thermodynamics states the fact that energy only flows from one kind to another. There is no absolute source of energy, only energy flow. The energy flow diagrams presented at the beginning of each power topic visually project the topic limits of energy flow within that specific chapter. In Chapter 12 the energy source is mechanical (generator shaft) and radiant solar. The usable form of energy is utility grade electricity.

In Chapter 10, we investigated the fundamentals of electricity. The chapter was divided into four pertinent topics:

1. An electron in an electric charge field

2. Scaling up to useable electricity measurements

3. Electric energy conversion to mechanical energy (motor)

4. Electric energy conversion to heat energy

The Chapter 10 focus was electron behavior, measurement, and electrical usage. The observations of electrical energy usage are well understood by the public. Electricity is substantially a utility grade power.

Figure 12.1 is a recollection graphic from Chapter 10. Chapter 10 presented the major electrical power utilizations of heat, light, and mechanical power. Now lighting is a little more complicated. Light is produced from electricity by incandescence (hot radiant energy-Chapter 9) in classical light bulbs, chemical electron transitions (re-emitted quanta-Chapter 9) in phosphorescent tubes, and light emitting diodes (photovoltaic cells running backwards-Chapter 17). Significant light efficiency has been realized by avoiding the "heat" path of incandescent lights.

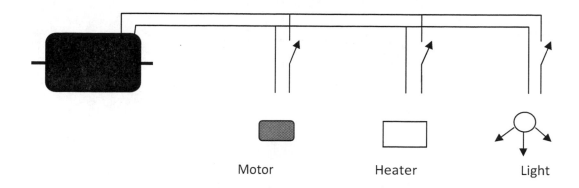

Motor   Heater   Light

Figure12. 1 Electrical Power Usage

All electrical power originates from the amount of electrons (amperes) traveling through an electromotive force field (EMF or volts). That is volts x amps = watts (power). But not a single word was spoken in Chapter 10 about how we get that voltage and amperage to our consumers. This chapter is directed at that electrical power generation and distribution.

In Chapter 12, we will investigate the production of utility grade electric power.

II. The Electricity Generator

In Chapter 10, the electric motor was explained at a basic level as the interaction between magnetic attractions and repulsions created by electron movement within the magnet wires. The observed energy conversion is from electrical power (watts) to mechanical power (horsepower). The electromagnetic behavior was not explained.

Unfortunately, one cannot escape basic magnetic energy phenomenon when explaining basic electricity generation. Figure 12.2 presents a model of the phenomenon of a dynamic magnetic force field. The magnetic phenomenon is not sensed and requires imagination. This is the fifth attempt to visually present this obscure concept, and it still needs improvement.

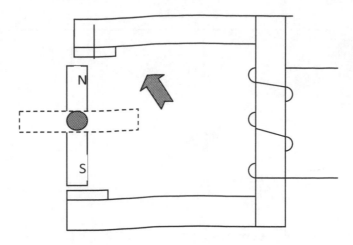

Figure 12.2 A Basic Electrical Generator

Figure 12.2 presents a rotating permanent magnet within a horseshoe external metal loop. As the permanent magnet rotates, the external metal loop will have changing magnetic energy pass through it. The permanent magnet's energy transfers magnetic energy to the horseshoe external metal loop. This energy is felt as a mechanical energy (force x distance) as the rotating permanent magnet physically approaches the external metal loop. When the rotating permanent magnet is forcefully rotated (by mechanical energy) away from the external metal loop, energy is increased in the rotating permanent magnet. Mechanical energy is converted to magnetic energy.

When we rotate the permanent magnet, the external metal loop will change polarity (magnetic north and south) as the rotating permanent magnet changes orientation relative to the external metal loop. The mechanical energy (at the rotating shaft) caused by the attraction of the permanent magnet to the external metal loop during parts of the rotation is exactly the same as the mechanical energy (at the rotating shaft) required to separate the permanent magnet from the external metal loop during parts of the rotation. It may help to understand this phenomenon by recalling that the energy felt (force x distance) when we stick a magnet to the refrigerator is the same as the energy required to remove the magnet. At this point, the magnetic system does not convert any mechanical energy to electrical energy. The net conversion between magnetic energy and mechanical energy is zero upon each rotation of the permanent magnet.

The Figure 12.2 mechanism can become a potential electrical generator when we wrap the external metal loop with wire (as shown in Figure 12.2). Two non-sensed physical principles apply to electricity generation:

1. Electrons are physically forced by a **changing** magnetic field.

2. The electron's force opposes the **changing** magnetic field.

With a little thought, the statements above are the same thing with slightly different points of view.

The wire wrapped around the external metal loop has free electrons (an electron conductor). When we switch the permanent magnets polarity as it rotates, we also switch the magnetic field within the external metal loop. This changing magnetic field within the external metal loop forces the electrons one direction in the wire and then in the other direction as the shaft rotates and the magnetic field reverses. The electrons are physically forced the same as we would mechanically force a mass. This will result in more electrons (negative charge) on one end of the wire and fewer electrons (positive charge) on the other end of the wire as the external metal loop changes magnetic polarity. And that difference in charge strength is measured as electromotive force (EMF) or voltage.

Now that we have electrons flowing, let's investigate some key aspects of electrical generators (Figure 12.3):

1. If the generator wires A and B are not connected to anything (open), there will be no electron movement. The electrons have no place to go. The generator shaft requires no net mechanical power upon each rotation as stated above.

2. When an electrical path is placed between A and B, electrical power will flow according to volts x amperes. Figure 12.3 connects our generator mechanism (Figure 12.2) to our energy utilizations (Figure 12.1).

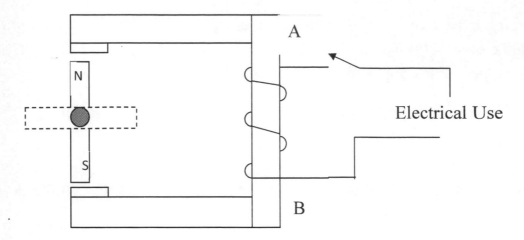

Figure 12.3 An Electrical System

3. When an electrical switch is placed to "on", a path for electricity to flow is created. As the permanent magnet rotates, the electrical voltage (EMF) is created by the magnetic field change in the external metal loop wires. The magnetic field provides force to push the electrons down the wire. The magnetic force needed to push the electrons is converted from the mechanical force of the generator shaft.

This phenomenon is not sensed when we turn on the lights or start an electric motor. But actually, somewhere out there, an electrical generator (or generators) has to add more mechanical power to a shaft in order to power the lights and motor. This electrical generation response is noticeable when I turn on the air conditioning unit on my RV. The gasoline generator motor "grunts". The electrical generator motor has to produce more electrical power. Electrical power is not stored within the utility grid electrical systems. This is obvious during a "blackout", as electrical power is required 24/7.

III. Electricity at the Domestic Wall Plug

Having described the basic electrical generator mechanism, it is convenient to relate our experienced domestic electrical power to the existing utility grade electrical generation system.

At our electrical receptacle we have 120 volt, 60 cycles per second power. This is the form of electrical power that used in our energy utilizations.

First, let us investigate the 60 cycles per second. If we look at the voltage from the electric generator (Figure 12.2) when the generator shaft is turning 3600 revolutions per minute (the same as 60 revolutions per second), we would see a voltage output with time as presented in Figure 12.4. Figure 12.4 looks as though three 60 cps voltages are applied to the electrical power distribution at once. That is true. See Chapter 12 Insight for an explanation.

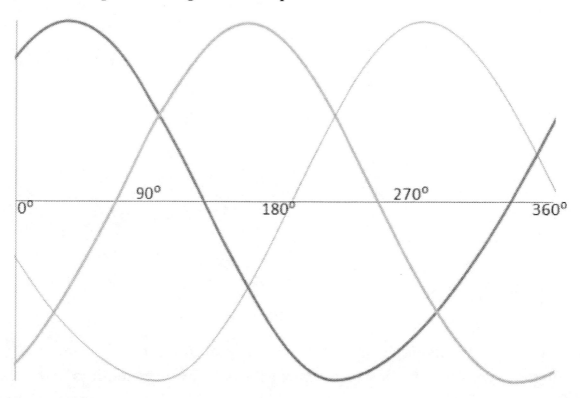

Figure 12.4 60 Cycles per Second Electricity

The voltage would change from positive to negative as the polarity of the permanent rotating magnet changes the magnetic field within the external metal loop. This voltage causes an alternating current to be available at your wall plug. This is called *alternating current or AC.* Contrast that electricity with our electric energy examples in Chapter 10 where electrons only traveled one direction from a negative charge to a positive charge. One direction current flow is called *direct current or DC.* Our domestic voltage alternates at 60 cycles per second, so we have 120 volt, 60 cps electricity in our homes.

IV. Electric Power on the "Grid"

Utility grade electric power has evolved into a single distributed power network called the *grid.* All utility electrical power generators are connected together. The complexity of the grid requires an extensive and detailed understanding beyond the scope of this text. A model of the grid is presented in Figure 12.5.

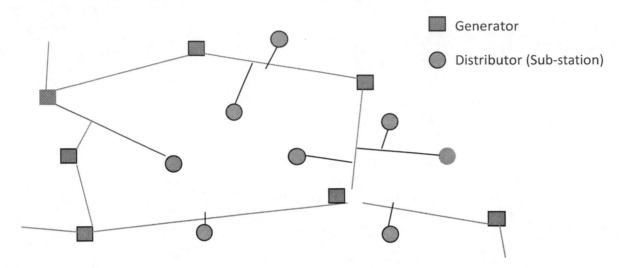

■ Generator

● Distributor (Sub-station)

Figure 12.5 The Grid

The grid allows all electrical power generators to connect to a central power distribution system. An obvious requirement for AC power generators is that they all apply voltage (EMF) in synchronization or else the electrical power generators would randomly be forcing electrons into each other without a net power output.

A memorable fact is that all AC electrical generation are synchronized to be exactly in phase by a master clock signal. Every generator is exactly in sync (phase) with all other generators in the United States. An AC voltage peak measured in New York is exactly, in time, as an AC voltage peak in New Mexico. One observable result is we have to reset our electric clocks only when the electrical power is interrupted. The grid alternating voltage keeps perfect time. All electric clocks are in phase with the master clock. All utility grade AC electricity alternates voltage at exactly 60 cycles per second. As a trivial point, the electrical force field (not the electrons), travels at the speed of light down the electrical power conductors. This allows the timing of all electrical generators in the United States to be synchronized.

It is a fascinating fact that, when we turn a light "on", we are proportionately using power from about 2000 electrical generators

The United States 120 volts AC is derived from historical precedent. Europe has 240 volts AC. From a power utilization and cost perspective, both systems are equivalent.

V. The Power Transformer

One more aspect is included in our fundamental knowledge of utility grade alternating current power. A logical sequence of explaining this aspect is now presented without basic mathematics:

1. The rotating magnet (Figure 12.2) produced an alternating electrical current when it was spun between the external metal loop terminals.

2. The rotating magnet can be replaced by an electromagnet with AC current in the wires. The external metal loop would not sense any difference from the rotating magnet. The electron generating wire coil responds to magnetic changes in the "external metal loop" the same with a magnetic change generated from either a permanent magnet or an electromagnet. Figure 12.7 presents such an electrical device. Figure 12.6 is a *transformer*. We observe many utility grade transformers.

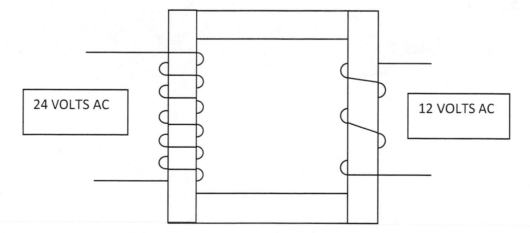

Figure 12.6 Transformer

The first key transformer behavior is that, for any magnetic change in the transformer magnetic core, the electrical voltage (EMF) at the wire wrapped around the core depends only upon the number of turns in the wrapped wire.

The second key transformer behavior is that power from the changing (AC) voltage in the wrapped wire produces the same changing magnetic field power in the core. The transformer only converts electrical power to magnetic power and magnetic power back to electrical power. No energy or power is lost in agreement with the 1st Law of Thermodynamics. In actuality, transformers do lose a little power in the form of heat.

A transformer only converts the electrical power to magnetic power (input wire winding) and at the same time converts the magnetic power to electrical power (output wire winding). The transformer only changes the output AC voltage relative to the input AC voltage.

Figure 12.6 presents electrical values only for comparative reference.

We do not have to clearly understand this bit of electrical engineering. The value of the electrical transformer is that it can change AC voltages in an efficient manner. This transformer aspect is the basis for efficient electrical power distribution.

Figure 12.7 presents a model of our electrical power distribution: (The numbers are for reference only)

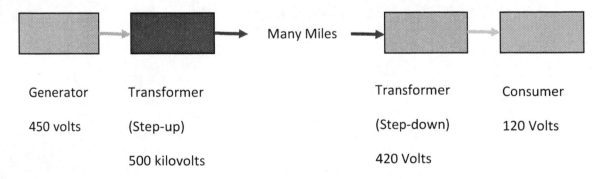

Figure 12.7 Electrical Power Distribution Voltages

The electrical generator is designed to produce 60 cycles per second AC power at 450 volts. There is no need to specify the current or power in this exercise.

A transformer at the generating station converts the 450 volts of 60 cycles per second AC to 500,000 volts or 500 kilovolts (kV) of 60 cycles per second AC. This is a step-up transformer.

500 kV is the grid voltage for power distribution.

At the local electrical power consumer substation, the 500 kV AC grid voltage is converted to 420 volts AC by means of a transformer. This is a step-down transformer.

The substation 420 voltage AC is converted to 120 volts AC for safe end user consumption. One can't imagine a consumer with a 500 kV toaster.

Our explanation of utility power distribution ignores many details involved in actual practice, but does point to the following operational conclusions.

1. By increasing the grid voltage between the generating (step-up) and the using (step-down) locations, we can operate electrical devices at reasonable design voltages.

2. By increasing the grid voltage between the generating (step-up) and using (step-down) locations, we can reduce electrical heat loss for the same amount of electrical power delivered.

Using the AC high voltage electrical power transmission lines, we can reduce the amount of electric power converted to heat power during the electrical power distribution. In the United States, that power loss is now (2010) about 6.5% of the total power. High voltage electrical AC is an efficient method of transmitting power.

VI. Conclusions

Electricity is the established method to distribute utility grade power. The distribution system is the electrical grid. Energy is not stored on the grid. The electrical power is measured as Volts x Amps = Watts.

The must-know elements of electrical power are:

1. Electric power is converted from magnetic power and magnetic power is converted from mechanical power.

2. Electrons are forced by magnetic change.

3. AC is alternating current and DC is direct current.

4. Utility grade generators are connected together by the grid.

5. Utility grade generators are synchronized.

6. The transformer is used for power transmission efficiency.

Chapter 12 Insight

3-Phase Electrical Power Transmission

The distribution of electricity has been simplified in Chapter 12 to improve focus upon electrical power fundamentals. The actual electrical power distribution is reconciled with this simplified version in Chapter 12 Insight.

If you observe closely the usual AC electrical power lines, you will find four wires between the suspension poles:

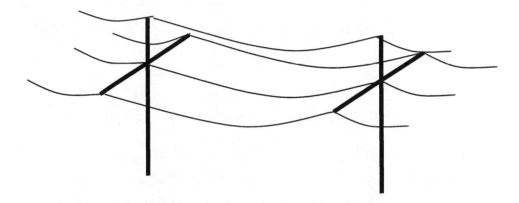

Typical AC Electrical Transmission

The voltage on three of the conducting lines is supplied by the generators as separate voltages, with the voltages of all three conducting lines alternating at 60 cycles per second. However, the voltage cycles of the three conducting lines is shifted (in time) so that THE VOLTAGE BETWEEN EACH OF THE THREE WIRES IS ALWAYS CONSTANT. The proper name, *3-phase*, is derived from the fact that the voltages in the three conducting lines are permanently out of phase with each other. The forth wire is a common ground for other three electrical wires.

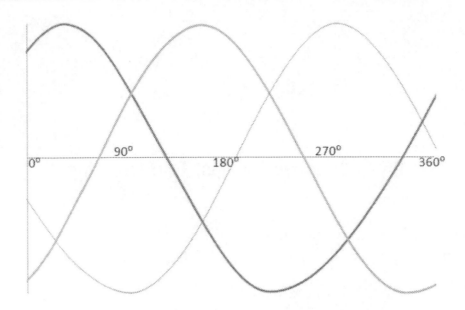

3-Phase AC Electrical Distribution

While this energy engineering insight has nothing to do with utility grade power, it does explain consumer electrical energy applications:

1. The consumer wall plug voltage is 120 volts AC. This voltage is obtained by connecting any two of the AC electrical conducting power lines.

2. When a greater amount of power is required on appliances such as an electric stove or electric dryer, then 2 times the voltage can be obtained by connecting first between two of the AC electrical conducting power lines and then secondly adding the obtained voltage to the third AC electrical conducting line. The voltage is doubled and the current halved by the 240 volt wiring connection. That significantly reduces heat energy "loss" in the power cord and increases the electrical power transmission capability.

All we observe is that we have a different wall plug and power cord for our stove and dryer. We also observe that large air conditioners require a higher voltage connection. The electrical connection (plug) is always grounded for safety reasons.

Chapter 13:

Petroleum

Sections

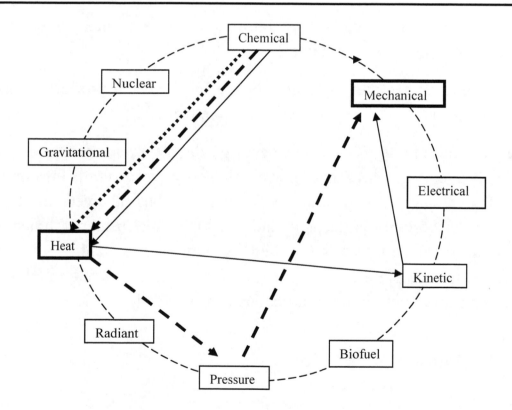

I. Introduction to Petroleum

Chapter 13's energy flow diagram presents the major energy flows from petroleum, indicated as the source of chemical energy. Petroleum is used directly as a heat source (home natural gas), the predominant transportation mechanical power (gasoline and diesel) and as a major mechanical source of electrical generation using the natural gas turbine.

To repeat, as indicated on the energy flow diagram above, three major usable applications are realized from conversion of the petroleum chemical energy source:

1. Heat is an energy realized from burning methane (natural gas) and fuel oil, both petroleum sources. (dotted line)

2. Mechanical power for transportation is realized by burning petroleum in our internal combustion engines. (dashed line)

3. Electrical power is realized by burning methane in many methane (gas) electrical generators. (solid line)

(Casually mentioned, is the fact that propane, a petroleum product, is used for home heating, grills heating and as an automotive fuel.)

Petroleum is a liquid and gas source of energy. Petroleum is a source of portable, affordable, usable, and concentrated chemical energy. Petroleum is the commercial kingpin of our energy dependent economies. It has allowed us to afford commercial transportation (shipping and trucking) and personal transportation (trains and automobiles). It has supplied us with an affordable source of heat energy. The existence of natural petroleum, a fossil fuel, has transformed us from a localized, agrarian society into a mobile, business interactive society.

II. The Origination of Petroleum

The past formation of petroleum is based upon reasonable speculation. I think that speculation is adequate, since precise knowledge how petroleum originated is very difficult considering the amount of variation in this petroleum creation. Our organized approach in explaining the history of petroleum formation is to provide a firm association between the origination of petroleum and energy science.

1. Early Petroleum Origination

The physical process for generating petroleum for our four kinds of petroleum sources is described as follows:

Millions of years ago, carbon was expelled from the center of the earth in the form of volcanic eruptions. The carbon reacted with atmospheric oxygen to form carbon dioxide. The total atmospheric weight, at the time of the eruptions, was about the same as now. The atmospheric composition before the carbon eruptions was about 20% oxygen and 80% nitrogen. The expelled carbon reacted with the atmospheric oxygen to produce carbon dioxide. The carbon dioxide concentration increased to about 1 percent of the atmosphere by weight. This is speculation without quality supporting data.

Starting with an atmospheric carbon dioxide concentration of 1 percent, we enter an energy conversion process that is understood in terms of modern science. It is the conversion of solar radiant energy to chemical energy. Living biological species called plants utilize radiant energy from the sun (sunshine) to convert carbon dioxide into organic molecules that propagate their species. Only plants can use carbon dioxide to produce these organic molecules. Natural selection permits the most adaptable plants to survive.

The key idea is that plants do naturally convert carbon dioxide into organic molecules.

These prehistoric plants lived in the water on earth. The plants thrived in waters that were warm, had sunshine, and abundant carbon dioxide to meet their organic synthesis needs. Now these plants are not the decorative house plants we observe, but are microscopic in size. Today these microscopic plants are commonly called algae. We observe one kind of algae as the green slime in our swimming pools when we forget to add algaecide.

Some algae, by natural selection, survived probably due to their evolved biological process that produced hydrocarbon molecules. Some of these algae exist today. The hydrocarbon molecular structure will be explained shortly. In plants and animals, hydrocarbon type molecules are labeled fats.

It is only a slight overstatement that these plants produced fat. I find it very difficult to imagine a fat microscopic plant. However, the algae with hydrocarbon production may have survived due to the inherent fat (hydrocarbon) energy storage. This will become clear by the end of this chapter.

The prehistoric plants converted carbon dioxide into the beginnings of crude oil. Over millions of years, these plants lived in the water. When they died, they settled to the bottom of the water, taking the stable hydrocarbon precursor molecules with them. Over millions of years, the accumulation of these plant remains formed a thick coating on the bottom. These oily coatings can be observed today. The key idea is that the plants, using radiant energy, created the petroleum starting material.

Again, the key concept regarding petroleum origination is that all petroleum molecules came from the hydrocarbon molecules created by algae. Petroleum is hydrocarbon molecules created by hydrocarbon precursor producing plants.

These algae exist today. We can construct an algae "farm" that uses carbon dioxide and water to immediately produce diesel fuel. Natural petroleum (fossil fuels) was created over millions of years.

Figure 13-1 presents a visual display of the first step in the creation of petroleum.

2. Later Petroleum Origination

All petroleum molecules first originated according to the process shown in Figure 13.1. However, we have four distinct commercial sources of petroleum that supply the petroleum resource material for consumer products. The four distinct sources of petroleum are a result of geological action upon the hydrocarbon accumulations shown in Figure 13.1.

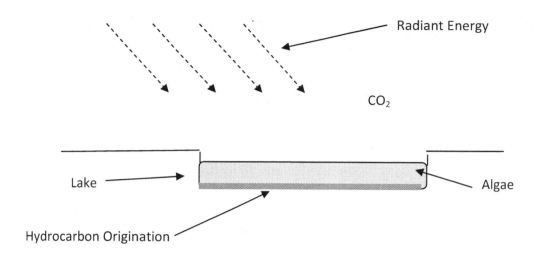

Figure 13.1 Hydrocarbon Origination

Crude Oil – Petroleum Source "One"

Crude oil is a sticky, smelly sludge useless for any application in its natural state. Crude oil is an important source of energy used for applications to our quality of life. Crude oil is a familiar public topic regarding economics, politics, and national security.

Crude oil originated as presented in Figure 13.2. A geologic surface movement (shift) encapsulated the hydrocarbon accumulations. The encapsulated hydrocarbon accumulations had the oxygen and water molecules squeezed out of them. Also, the composition has changed over time because of the interactions among the various hydrocarbon molecules. These interactions are not precisely understood due to the inherent process variations of composition, temperature, and pressure. But we have now created crude oil. Crude oil differs in composition depending upon the original hydrocarbon accumulations and the geological history. In general, crude oil deposits are in areas where ancient bodies of water existed proximate to geological activity.

Natural Gas – Petroleum Source "Two"

Natural gas also originates from the hydrocarbon accumulations shown in Figure 13.1. Natural gases are the small, gaseous hydrocarbon molecules trapped underground in impermeable chambers. We can conveniently assume that natural gas evolved from the hydrocarbon accumulations <u>after</u> being trapped by the geological shift (the same as crude oil above). Logically, if the natural gas wasn't trapped, it would have travelled into the air and, over time, chemically reacted with air and disappeared. Also, the natural gas is a product of the hydrocarbon accumulations after being trapped because it is commonly found in oil wells. Any natural gas prior to hydrocarbon entrapment would have immediately vaporized.

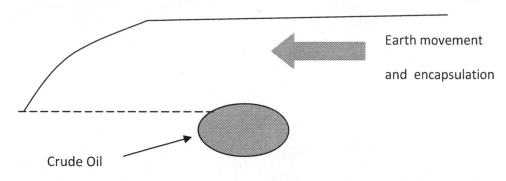

Figure 13.2 Crude Oil Origination

Figure 13.3 shows the two types of natural gas chambers. When the natural gas occurs above the crude oil pools in a chamber, the natural gas is called *"associated."* When the natural gas chamber occurs independent of crude oil it is called *"non-associated."* The compositions of associated and non-associated natural gas are approximately the same.

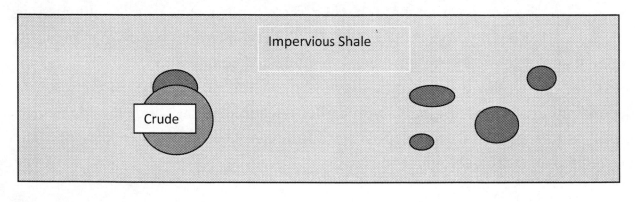

Associated   Non-associated

Figure 13.3 Natural Gas

Shale Oil – Petroleum Source "Three"

Another variation of geological hydrocarbon entrapment occurs when the waters where hydrocarbon accumulations are muddy. Over time, the hydrocarbon accumulations became mixed with the mud (for lack of a better common word). The mixture, with the increasing weight of accumulations, becomes shale with distributed entrapped hydrocarbons. The various areas where ocean bottoms have uplifted into shale mountains indicate that large amounts of petroleum can exist in the shale. The actual amounts of crude oil within the feasible oil shale are about 4 to 40 gallons per ton of shale.

Figure 13.4 presents the visual shale oil source:

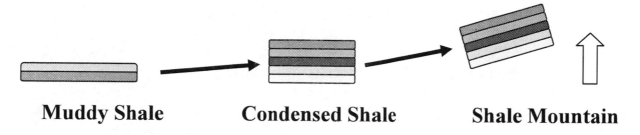

Muddy Shale   **Condensed Shale**   **Shale Mountain**

Figure 13.4 Shale Oil Formation

Tar Sands – Petroleum Source "Four"

Tar sands are already a commercially developed source of petroleum. The process of origination is different. Using the basic concept of hydrocarbon accumulation presented by Figure 13.1, the tar sand origination occurred when the hydrocarbon accumulation deposited simultaneously with sand particles. The hydrocarbon accumulations adhered to the sand particles. However, the resulting mixture did not transform into shale, but remained as a physical mixture of hydrocarbon accumulation surrounding the sand particles. With geological action, the physical mixture was lifted from the water.

When the hydrocarbon mixture was removed from the water, over time the light hydrocarbons evaporated, leaving heavy hydrocarbons surrounding sand particles. The heavy hydrocarbons are known as tar.

This source of petroleum is presented in Figure 13.5.

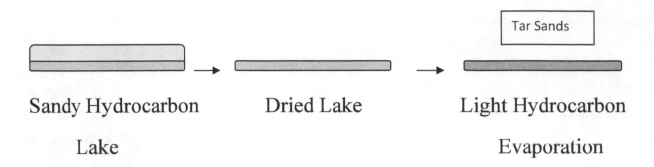

Sandy Hydrocarbon Lake → Dried Lake → Light Hydrocarbon Evaporation

Tar Sands

Figure 13.5 Tar Sand

The commercial significance in terms of economics and political policy vary substantially according to these four sources of petroleum.

It is prudent to understand the categorical origin of your specific petroleum.

III. Creating Petroleum Usable by the Consumer

Section II presented the four major kinds of natural existing petroleum resources available for processing into desirable consumer products. The following processes create the usable chemical energy products.

Crude Oil:

The main activity of petroleum production is crude oil refining.

We begin with the sticky, smelly sludge called crude oil. We convert the crude oil into useful petroleum products by means of a fractionating tower. A fractionating tower is presented in Figure 13.6. I will openly apologize to the knowledgeable petroleum engineers for using such an oversimplified model. The purpose of Figure 13.6 is to convey only the basic principle of petroleum fractionation. This process is exercised within a crude oil refinery.

We will restate the observation that crude oil is a thick liquid that can be transported by ordinary means. So the crude oil refinery can exist remotely from the crude oil extraction wells. This physical process is usually the case.

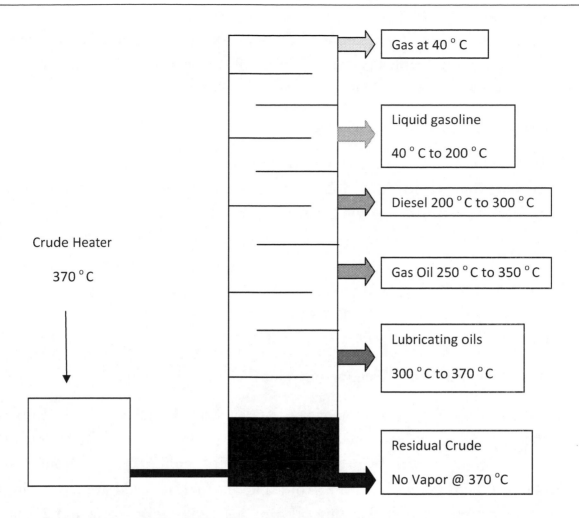

Figure 13.6 Petroleum Refinery Vapors

First, we pump the crude oil into the bottom of the fractionating tower at a temperature of about 370 degrees Centigrade. So everything in the crude oil that vaporizes above 370 degrees Centigrade fills the tower with vapor and the faction of crude oil that doesn't vaporize above 370 degrees Centigrade remains on the bottom. The top of the tower (in this example) is at about 40 degrees centigrade.

Fraction #1: Petroleum Gas

When the crude oil is heated to 370 degrees Centigrade, all of the very light hydrocarbons (1-4 carbons) are boiled from the crude oil as a vapor. They will rise to the top of the fractionating column at 40 degrees Centigrade and be extracted as a gas. The rest of the hydrocarbons (>4 carbons) in the crude oil will not be a vapor at the very top of the tower. They would condense into a liquid and remain lower in the fractionating column. The heavier the hydrocarbon molecules (greater number of carbons) the lower they will exist in the column because they have a higher boiling point.

Fraction #2: Conventional Gasoline

This fraction of crude oil vapor contains hydrocarbon sizes (5-12 carbons). This vapor is removed and condensed into a liquid. This fraction is very familiar to all of us. It is the gasoline used by our automobiles. Yes, you can use this gasoline directly and it will perform without any additional processing. Note that commercial gasoline is a mixture of various hydrocarbons, not a single hydrocarbon compound. Now, any hydrocarbons with greater than 12 carbons will not be vapor for fraction #2. They would be a liquid and exist lower in the fractionating column.

Fraction #3: Diesel fuel –Heating oil – Jet fuel

This fraction of crude oil vapor contains hydrocarbon sizes (12-16 carbons). This vapor is removed and condensed into a liquid. At room temperature, this is a thicker petroleum fraction. Our observation is that Diesel fuel is almost commercial lubricating oil. Diesel fuel is used in trucks in the transportation industry. Heating oil provides heat energy for about 2/3 of the USA homes. Jet fuel usage is obvious. All of these energy needs are met by this crude oil fraction.

Fraction #4: Gas Oil

What a strange name! This fraction of crude oil vapor contains hydrocarbon sizes (15-18 carbons). This crude oil fraction will undergo another step before it becomes a valuable energy product. This crude oil fraction is processed to split into hydrocarbon sizes (7-9 carbons). The name of this process is "cracking" based upon the chemical operation that breaks the molecules sort of in half. We crack gas oil to produce gasoline so that we can get a larger fraction of usable gasoline from each barrel of crude oil. The processes of joining hydrocarbons and breaking hydrocarbons are casually referred to as "reformulation." Reformulated gasoline constitutes about 1/3 of the gasoline that we consume.

Fraction #5: Lubricating Oil and Grease

This fraction of crude oil vapor contains hydrocarbon sizes (16-20 carbons). It is familiar to everyone lubricating mechanical machines. It is a crude oil fraction that is used for its lubricating properties rather than the heat energy produced upon combustion.

Fraction #6: Residual crude oil materials:

As presented on the refinery graphic, there is a portion of crude oil that does not vaporize at the 370 degrees Centigrade. Although this fraction varies with the source of the crude oil, it typically is about 3%. Many valuable products are derived from this crude oil residue. One product observed by everyone is the residual used in our asphalt roads. We even use a petroleum mixture to fix the potholes!

Crude oil is the source of petroleum products burned for energy and used as materials such as asphalt pavement and plastics. In this text we are only concerned with petroleum products burned for energy.

There are about 150 crude oil refineries in the United States. Refineries are not static operations, but can be adjusted to changing petroleum fractions that meet market demands. Refineries have little waste product. Refineries are a crucial business in our economy and way of life. Refineries deserve a greater acknowledgement than the oversimplified model presented in this text.

Crude oil finishing

We have not completed all of the processing required to convert natural hydrocarbon deposits into valuable consumer products. First, let us look at the fractions of crude oil leaving the refinery as presented by Figure 3.6.

Fraction #1 has two significant additional processes before becoming a consumer product:

1. The light gas hydrocarbon molecules in crude oil fraction #1 can be reacted with one another to produce heavier (liquid) molecules. Then these heavier molecules

can be mixed in with the gasoline fraction. This is a method of getting more gallons of a desirable petroleum product from each barrel of crude oil.

2. Fraction #1 can be processed to produce propane. Propane is the convenient gas we use to operate our cooking grills. Propane is a liquid under pressure (110 pounds per square inch at 70 °F). Propane has many applications due to the fact that it liquefies under pressure, allowing a very convenient storage. The natural pressure of liquid propane is ideal for minimum pressure regulation during use. Propane is used in our industries, gas grills, for home heat, tractors and automobiles. Everyone has seen the familiar initials LPG (Liquid Petroleum Gas) signs at petroleum service stations. The separation and distribution of propane is a major industry.

Fraction #2 contains the hydrocarbon distribution of ordinary gasoline. However, additional blending of gasoline with, for example ethanol, reduces the unwanted emission molecules expelled from automobile engines. Gasoline is blended to improve engine performance and emissions before being sent to gas stations. Gasoline is also processed to optimize performances in engines. We all are familiar with regular and high test gasoline. Of course, we have to pay extra for the optimized high test gasoline.

Fraction #3 contains hydrocarbon molecules heavier than gasoline and can be used as diesel fuel and home heating oil. Continuing our theme of crude oil finishing, diesel fuel does undergo a process that removes sulfur from the refinery fraction before it is delivered for end customer use. I know this isn't an energy subject, however we should be aware of the complexity of petroleum product preparation.

Fraction #4 is gas oil. As the name infers, it is oil that is converted to gas. Heavy hydrocarbon molecules are broken into lighter molecules by a process called "cracking." Cracking oil gas significantly increases the amount of gasoline from each barrel of crude oil.

Now we have crude oil petroleum products prepared for use. The value of the crude oil fractions #1 to #4 is realized when we convert the chemical energy in the petroleum to heat energy (and beyond). This concludes our description of the crude oil source of energy.

Natural Gas. Preparation for Use

Another source of energy is natural gas.

Natural gas consists predominately of the smallest hydrocarbon called methane. Each methane molecule is composed of one carbon and four hydrogen. Natural gas historically was discovered along with oil wells (associated) or by itself as pockets of compressed gas (non-associated).

Natural gas prehistorically originated as part of the same process that was described for crude oil. However, some distinctions are needed. We can think of associated natural gas formation as the compressed natural gas separating from the crude oil mixture to create a pocket above the liquefied hydrocarbon sludge. The encapsulation of the hydrocarbon mixture would require, by physical reasoning, a tight methane gas seal to retain the crude gaseous fraction. Therefore, it is reasonable for us to find varying amounts of natural gas associated with crude oil depending upon the original crude oil composition and the possible natural gas leakage. This is observed.

We have also discovered non-associated natural gas isolated from crude oil wells. The non-associated natural gas is formed from the same plant to hydrocarbon formations, but with different temperature-pressure conditions during the natural gas consolidation process. The non-associated gas was trapped in geological chambers. In the past, any escaping methane reacted with oxygen in the atmosphere and disappeared. We can only speculate how much of the methane hydrocarbons have escaped into the air, reacted with the air, and disappeared.

Natural gas has several notable attributes:

1. Natural gas requires processing before it becomes suitable for customer use. The natural gas we use is anything but "natural". The big problem is that gas direct from the natural storage chamber contains a small fraction of hydrocarbon molecules with carbon molecules 3 and larger. If these are not removed, they could and do condense into liquids at cold temperatures. These liquids then block the natural gas distribution pipelines, shutting off the natural gas supply when the temperatures are the coldest. This is not good! Natural gas is processed so that the heavier than methane hydrocarbon

molecules are liquefied and removed, primarily to prevent distribution pipe blockage.

2. Natural gas cannot be conveniently transported like the liquid propane petroleum product. It does not form a convenient liquid under pressure option. Predominantly, natural gas (as a gas) is piped to the point of use. The natural gas distribution pipelines used for heating to residential customers are established in a large scale, economic manner. Natural gas supplies 40% of the energy (2007) for USA industry requirements.

3. Natural gas is sometimes compressed into tanks for transportation. The natural gas in compression is called CNG (Compressed Natural Gas). It is also liquefied at very cold temperatures (by liquid nitrogen) for transportation in ships. That is called Liquefied Natural Gas (LNG).

4. Natural gas is a significant source for electric power generation. Natural gas provides the most completely burned hydrocarbon fuel with the benefit of fast availability as a power source for emergency power generation.

5. Natural gas, before it is sent to consumers, has added to it a small amount of a smelly sulfur based gas. This provides a level of safety as the natural gas mixture will be detected by smell before an explosive gas concentration occurs.

Shale Oil and Tar Sands

Our basic process of developing our topics of energy resources is to first note observations then explain the observations in terms of energy science. Shale oil and tar sands are an exception to that process. Few people are informed about shale oil and tar sands. The public information channels such as newspapers and TV rarely mention these two sources of energy. I really don't know why! Based upon USA imports from Canada, do you realize that, when you filled your gasoline tank, that on the average more than one gallon of the gasoline came from Canadian tar sands (2009). Shale oil and tar sands are a dominant source of our future petroleum energy. So we will spend some time investigating this third and forth source(s) of hydrocarbon energy.

Shale Oil

Petroleum from shale oil formations has significant energy potential

Shale oil originates by the process of plants using solar radiation to create the hydrocarbons. However, the geological process was different. Rather than encapsulation of the hydrocarbon material in the mass geological over-shift over water sludge as presented in Figure 13.2, the hydrocarbon material was trapped within the shale formation. The shale composition and formation can be considered as mud collecting at the bottom of a body of water. The plant petroleum residue was forming at the same time. The shale was formed by the pressure from increasing layers of mud. The prehistoric slate formations are most noticeable where geological uplifts changed the lake bottoms into mountains. This is graphically presented in 13.4.

We have mountains of shale mixed with hydrocarbon oil. Shale is a porous, soft material which allows the shale oil to seep out under heat or be extracted out of the shale by solvents. Some raw shale oil rocks even support combustion.

The initial investigations of shale oil areas indicate that 4 to 40 gallons of hydrocarbon can be extracted from a ton of shale. The process to extract hydrocarbons (kerogen) from shale has yet to be commercially developed (2009). The hydrocarbon is called *kerogen* rather than crude oil. The kerogen is processed the same as crude oil. It provides the same hydrocarbon products as crude oil.

Tar Sands

Tar sands are a significant source of Canadian petroleum

Again, the hydrocarbons in tar sands originate from plants in water using solar radiation. However, this creation of tar sands is slightly different. Instead of having mud surround droplets of hydrocarbon sludge like shale oil, tar sands has a process where the plant hydrocarbons are attached to the exterior of sand particles. There is little mud here, only sand. Over time, all of the low carbon material evaporates from the sand hydrocarbon sludge surface. This leaves a thick hydrocarbon residue as a sand particle coating. It is tar, hence the name "tar sand."

Processing the tar sand into a commercial petroleum product has already been developed. The primary task is to remove the hydrocarbon tar from the sand particle. Using steam at high temperature, we can separate the hydrocarbon coating from the sand particles. The hydrocarbon coating is crude oil of a high molecular weight composition. The crude oil is fractionated, Figure 13.6, into the commercially available petroleum products.

IV. Conclusions

There are many facets to being informed and educated about petroleum. Several salient points regarding petroleum were included, then removed, from this text. The reason for the indecision stems from the reality that petroleum science to very difficult to separate from petroleum engineering. However, two points of information, not emphasized in the text, are now presented for your awareness:

1. As stated in Chapter 8, the energy of carbon to carbon and hydrogen to carbon chemical bonds is very close to the same for all hydrocarbon molecules. And the amount of chemical stored energy per unit of weight or mass (pounds or grams) is about the same for all hydrocarbons.

   a. A pound of gasoline, diesel fuel and propane all have about the same chemical energy content.

   b. A pound of fat on my body has about the same energy content as a pound of gasoline.

   These examples are scientifically based. But most petroleum information is based upon efficiency during a specific application, and that is engineering. A diesel automobile gets better mileage than a gasoline automobile. That is a result of energy conversion efficiency due to engineering rather than a significant measureable difference in the intrinsic energy of gasoline versus diesel fuel sources.

2. The availability of existing natural sources of petroleum is misinterpreted in terms of quality of the hydrocarbon source. Repeatedly, the concept that the "good" petroleum sources are depleted before the "inferior" petroleum sources are explored is presented. The availability of any petroleum source

bears no relationship to the composition or quality of any of the four types of petroleum. That is enough said about this reoccurring theme.

The must-know elements of petroleum are:

1. **Petroleum supplies portable and high energy fuels.**

2. **Petroleum products are hydrocarbons (Chemical energy).**

3. **Petroleum originated from algae.**

4. **There are four categories of petroleum sources**

5. **Refining is a required step in making crude oil, shale oil, and tar sands usable.**

6. **Natural gas requires processing before commercial use.**

Chapter 13 Insight

Hydrocarbon Reserves

A re-occurring topic, that doesn't relate to Energy and Power – Fundamental Knowledge, is hydrocarbon reserves. Energy science is based upon enduring principles and certainly doesn't include hydrocarbon reserves. This is not to diminish the importance of hydrocarbon reserves to our social and economic structure.

The chemically stored energy of available hydrocarbons and coal are both included to provide a comparative viewpoint.

The correct public viewpoint is that crude oil and coal (fossil fuels) are limited in amount and therefore alternate utility grade energy sources will be required in the future. A required input to future energy (power) planning is the accurate determination of fossil fuel reserves.

Fossil fuel reserves are difficult to determine for several reasons:

1. Fossil fuel discoveries are still in progress.

2. The economics of fossil fuel recovery is very complex.

3. Fossil fuel reserve data has business confidentiality.

4. Governments control fossil fuel surveys.

A "best estimate" of fossil fuel reserves is included in this insight. This "best estimate" can be reduced to conclusions that seem very reasonable. Those conclusions contain the intrinsic variables and are easy to manipulate. Be very, very careful!

From experience, two hints are now included:

1. Fossil fuel recovery is different than an absolute like running out of gasoline in your automobile. Realize that economic factors (such as 2x in extraction cost) can substantially impact fossil fuel utilization.

2. Coal and crude oil are variables (composition and availability) in themselves. Only compare existing (benchmark) operations with proposed applications. (ONE TO ONE)

Hydrocarbon Reserves 2010

World:

	Present	Proven	Estimated
Crude (Billion Barrels)	810	1200	(2300)
Gas (Trillion Cubic Meters)	160	280	650
Coal (Billion Short Tons)	1600	5600	(?)

United States:

	Present	Proven	Estimated
Crude (Billion Barrels)	21	64	(860)
Gas (Trillion Cubic Meters)	5.5	18	80
Coal (Billion Short Tons)	470	1700	4000

Chapter 14:

Coal

Sections

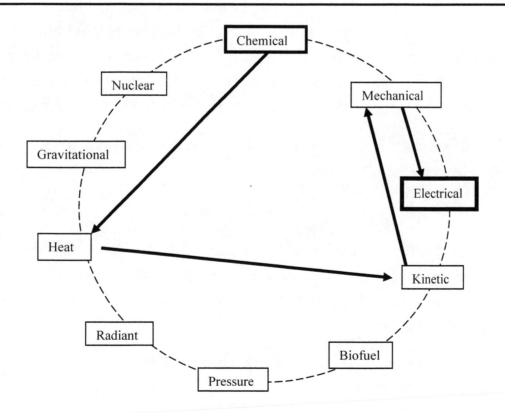

Coal is a source of stored chemical energy that is utilized according to the energy flow diagram presented above. Coal power plants burn coal carbons, produce heat, create steam under pressure, convert the kinetic energy of the steam to shaft mechanical power, and use the shaft mechanical power to produce electricity

I. Introduction to Coal

Coal is a fossil fuel. Coal is the largest source of hydrocarbon chemical energy available. Coal energy is predominantly converted to electrical energy for consumer use.

Coal energy process utilizations represent the earliest applications of available energy converted to create a better quality of life for humans. The ability of humans to use available energy is the significant difference in behavior from animals. That statement is an obvious observation.

The conversion of chemical energy into heat by fire was a key step in human evolution. The heat energy was initially the chemical energy within wood, then evolved into the chemical energy within coal. Coal as an energy process utilization is associated with the industrial revolution. Recall that James Watt's steam engine operated from coal energy and was used to extract coal from under the ground.

An oversimplified chemical reaction of the coal carbon producing heat energy upon combustion is:

$$C + O_2 = CO_2$$

This equation should be used only as a mental construct since the chemical bonding of the carbon in typical coal is extremely variable and complex. For our purposes, it is better to just quantitatively use the measured value of specific coal for energy policy and coal utilization design.

A large natural variation exists in the composition and energy content of coal. This natural variation requires one to have an in depth evaluation of each coal used in each specific application

The focus of this chapter is to explain the scope of the natural energy variations within coal in an organized manner. From this focused explanation, the important information regarding coal utilization will be presented.

II. The Origination of Coal

Coal originates from organic material. The original organic materials are large plants, not the microscopic water based plants associated with the origination of petroleum. Similar to the description of the origination of petroleum, coal can be speculated to have been formed from natural processes.

Figure 14.1 (A-B-C-D) presents the evolution of coal formation.

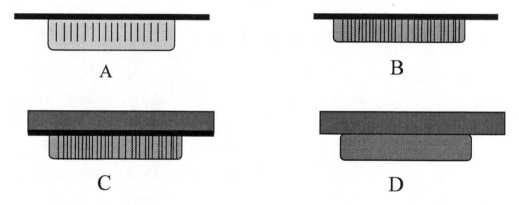

Figure 14.1 Coal Formation

Figure 14.1A presents the accumulation of plant residue (trees and grass) in the bottom of a shallow lake or swamp. The accumulation eventually fills the shallow lake or swamp with organic plant residue. The accumulation is wood product along with smaller residual vegetation. The key chemistry in coal formation from organic residue is that organic residue is isolated from air. Without the oxygen from air, the residue mixture is not initially decomposed to lose its energy content. It retains organic molecules that contain usable chemical energy. Think of this as organic residue within a swamp.

With time and plant concentration, the organic plant residue evolves into Figure 14.1B, peat, presently used as a heat source. The organic structure of the vegetation retains a substantial portion of the chemical energy originating from photosynthesis during plant growth.

Figure 14.1C indicates a geological shift (earth) that encapsulates the organic plant residue. The encapsulated residue is chemically converted by heat and pressure from dead plant material (lignin, cellulose, fiber, etc.) into a material with a greater proportion of carbon (carbonization). The carbonaceous material is called coal. The material evolves from lignite to bituminous coal.

Figure 14.1D indicates a high carbon content material called anthracite or hard coal. Ultimately, with time and pressure, even the hydrogen is removed from the original plant material.

Remember, that coal evolution is a continuum from plants under water to hard coal. There are no distinctive divisions of coal.

Coal is the most abundant source of fossil energy. However, the extent of carbonization of organic plant residue varies greatly. Recent plant residue (wood) has no carbonization and anthracite coal is highly carbonized. Figure 14.2 presents in chart form the levels of carbonization of organic plant residue along with the common names ascribed to the coal of those categories. Remember the coal is a mixture of varying carbonized compositions, even within a specific coal mining area.

Figure 14.2 present the continuum of chemical stored energy from hydrocarbon (gasoline) to wood. The heat energy content is given for each type of coal. Keep this chart handy. It allows us to compare heating source options.

The 1st passing comment about Figure 14.2 is that the energy content per pound of coal increases with the time that the organic material spent under geological pressure. That is an observed fact. A simple version of the coal evolution is that the pressure over time squeezed the hydrogen and oxygen atoms right out of the original cellulosic material. This simple version is speculated to be correct. This results in more carbon content with time. Figure 14.1 presented an oversimplified visual of this process. However, consistent with the 1st Law of Thermodynamics, the squeezing energy (force X distance) was converted to chemical energy within the organic material during the geological pressure process. For this process, the ultimate product is anthracite coal.

The 2nd passing comment about Figure 14-2 is that the energy source(s) are from natural origins and therefore contain natural variations. In fact, the wood-coal sources are a continuum in nature and are only listed in Figure 14-2 as major overlapping categories. You may encounter slightly different values of measurements depending upon your information source selection.

Energy Source	BTU / Pound	Kilojoule / Gram
Gasoline	19,200	44.4
Anthracite	13,000	30.1
Bitumenous	13,000	30.1
Subbituminous	10,300	23.8
Lignite	7,000	16.2
Peat	5,600	13.0
Wood	5,600	13.0

Figure 14.2 Fuel Heat Values

From Figure 14.2, it is easy to estimate how much coal I would have to buy in order to supply my house heating needs per year. My utility bill (natural gas) indicates that I use 80,000,000 BTU's per year. Figure 14.2 indicates that the heat from bituminous coal (locally available) is 13,000 BTU's per pound.

Pounds coal / yr = (80,000,000 BTU's / yr) / (13,000 BTU's / pound)

= 6,100 pounds / year (or a little over 3 tons)

3 tons of coal is reasonable and can be considered an option. Coal would be the least expensive heating fuel for my house (2009).

Heat diagrams of coal combustion are misleading since coal is not a pure substance and produces a large variation (see Figure 14.2) in heat per unit weight. A heat diagram of coal similar to Figure 8.10 was removed from this text for that reason. However, the concept of chemical energy being released during coal combustion is valid for each chemical bond conversion from carbon to carbon dioxide. Only the quantitative measure is of limited value.

The use of coal energy is fundamental to the industrial revolution. The products of heavy industries such as steel beams for buildings, steel structures for ships, locomotives and rails, and so forth could not be met without the abundant available energy source of coal. Coal energy became the fundamental part of the steel industry. Coal energy use for railroad transportation paralleled the petroleum energy use in the personal automobile. A significant inroad temporarily was made for coal supplying home heating.

The coal chemical energy to heat energy conversion is the major source for electrical energy. The steam turbine converts the steam kinetic energy to the shaft power that drives the electric generator. Figure 14.3 presents our coal as our largest source of utility grade electrical power.

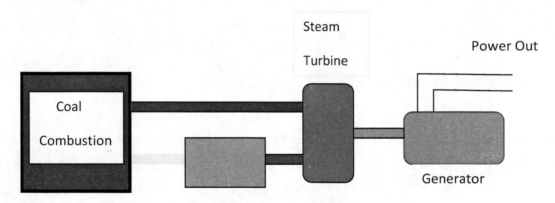

Figure 14.3 Coal Combustion to Electric Power

There isn't any question that coal is an abundant source of energy. However, coal's positive factors are balanced by some negative factors:

1. Coal does not burn completely. The origination of coal itself was a mixture of non-combustible materials along with combustible organic material. We are all familiar with ashes. This intrinsic composition mixture of coal presents problems in coal usage applications and in residual ash disposal.

2. Part of coal composition includes natural sulfur and metallic elements that need containment during the combustion process. This adds expense to coal

burning applications. The development of *"clean coal"* processes is a response to this problem. This engineering aspect of coal combustion is stated for your awareness.

3. Smoke and soot particles are known by everyone to be part of coal burning. The industrial cities of the coal burning era have left an indelible image. The efforts to remove the particulates from coal burning power plant emissions are continuing developments.

4. Coal is a carbonized fuel that produces carbon dioxide upon combustion. In order to utilize the coal energy, this has remained an unavoidable issue. The relationship between carbon oxidation energy and carbon dioxide generation is given in Chapter 8.

III. Synfuel

Coal is an abundant source of energy. It can, with extensive and expensive processing, be converted into viable liquid petroleum products such as gasoline and Diesel fuel. ***Synthetic Fuel (synfuel)*** is the hydrocarbon product produced from coal. Synfuel products cannot be distinguished from natural petroleum products for all use applications.

Synfuel was used extensively by Germany during World War II when coal was available and petroleum was scarce. Synfuel is currently being produced in South Africa where synfuel from coal competes economically with the imported petroleum products.

Synfuel has unfavorable energy efficiency in terms of coal conversion to liquid hydrocarbons. Synfuel is a possible option for producing liquid hydrocarbon products, but it is not considered economically favorable. The analysis of synfuel production costs will not be explored in this text. However, engineering advances such as using nuclear power to facilitate the coal to liquid hydrocarbon conversion may create a viable future energy path for production of liquid hydrocarbon fuels. That energy process is speculation beyond this text. Be aware of this proposal.

The predominant method of gasification of coal is the Fischer – Tropsh process, named after the German discoverers of this process:

The gasification of coal chemical reactions is very simple:

$$C + H_2O = H_2 + CO$$

Both H_2 and CO are gases. The mixture is called Syngas.(sometimes water gas)

This reaction requires a lot of energy!!

To produce hydrocarbon fuel from syngas is theoretically simple:

Syngas is passed over iron oxide where it reacts to produce a variety of hydrocarbons. This reaction produces a lot of heat energy. The hydrocarbons are refined like petroleum to produce commercial products.

Syngas has an old application history. Syngas (then called coal gas) was used for early street lighting in several cities. Cost considerations made electrical street lighting the reasonable replacement choice. The name lamplighter remains.

The possibility of producing liquid hydrocarbon fuel from our abundant coal reserves is tantalizing. But remember that the energy efficiency of the Fischer – Tropsh gasification is about 50% on a heat energy basis. Unless a method is developed to utilize the heat requirement, the coal gasification will not compete economically.

IV. Other Coal Applications

Coal was the fundamental energy source that drove the industrial revolution. This was especially true in the production of steel. The substantial users of coal energy have migrated to the less particulate emissions of natural gas or to electricity, where coal is only part of the electricity power source. This migration of energies by substantial users is a separate topic. Coal has vanished from home heating use and is not universally observed by the public. However, the abundance of affordable coal will be a major factor in consideration of our future energy sources. At home, the chemical energy in coal for home heating has been replaced by the cleaner, more convenient home heating by natural gas, fuel oil, and electricity. The only residential use of coal is the coke (coke product) used in our barbecues.

Coal still remains the major source of energy for generation of electricity.

V. Conclusions

Coal is the historic source of industrial heat energy. The chemical energy stored in coal originates from plants in the solar radiant energy conversion into carbon molecules. Coal is a very abundant source of energy as a fossil fuel.

Wood is the first fuel of significant energy value in Figure 14.2. In Energy and Power – Fundamental Knowledge, wood is considered as a biofuel (Chapter 20). Wood is a sustainable energy source but is currently (2010) non-competitive in providing a significant part of our utility grade energy needs.

Synthetic hydrocarbon fuel can be produced from coal. Although synfuel is interchangeable with petroleum products, it is cost prohibitive.

The must-know elements of coal are:

1. Coal originated from organic plant material.

2. Coal has significant natural variation.

3. Coal is the most abundant fossil fuel.

4. Coal is the least expensive source of heat energy.

5. Liquid petroleum can be processed from coal.

6. Coal has negative factors of incomplete combustion (ashes), air polluting elements, soot particles, and carbon dioxide.

Chapter 14 Insight

Carbon Sinks and Cycles

Most chapter insights are directed at mathematical logic to clearly describe energy relationships. Chapter 14 Insight is different in that the subjects of carbon sinks and cycles are only a qualitative descriptions. The advent of ecological awareness has produced many well intentioned investigations of carbon (and carbon dioxide) without the normal mathematical rigor associated with scientific conclusions. The lack of comprehensive data and natural complexity have resulted in a large variety of conclusions presented to the public, by well intentioned people, in bewildering contradictions.

You do not need in Energy and Power – Fundamental Knowledge another opinion about carbon dioxide. Instead, a framework is presented to only understand the proper nouns of carbon dioxide discussions. Here is the carbon story.

The element carbon was initially uniformly distributed among all other elements in a molten earth. As the earth cooled, the surface became a solid crust. Upon further cooling, the elemental carbon condensed (mineralized) from the molten interior. The coalesced carbon, due to its lower density, burst through the solid crust mantle as volcanic activity. This happened at several time periods. Please don't quote this paragraph. It is only a mental construct with very little supporting evidence.

The volcanic carbon was oxidized by the earth's atmosphere to carbon dioxide. The pure elemental carbon mineral doesn't exist.

All elemental carbon compounds exist today in sinks and cycles:

1. *Inorganic carbon* exists today as 1) carbonates, such a calcium carbonate or 2) carbides, such as carbon tetrachloride. This is a sink for that carbon coming from the earth.

2. *Biosphere carbon* exists today as the element that supports living organisms. Biosphere carbon has the fundamental property of dynamically cycling between living animals and providing carbon dioxide for plants to produce, from solar energy, the higher energy carbon compounds that provide fuel (food) for the same living animals. The carbon that we exhale is used to produce carrots that we eat to stay alive.

The dynamic biosphere carbon cycle is extremely complex. But it is a popular ecological topic. The overall biosphere carbon is called *carbon neutral* because it does not appreciably increase or decrease the amount of carbon dioxide in our atmosphere. Biosphere carbon dioxide is in equilibrium with atmospheric carbon dioxide.

3.***Atmospheric Carbon*** exists in our atmosphere as carbon dioxide. Atmospheric carbon dioxide is accurately measured. The atmosphere is a sink for carbon as carbon dioxide. The public interest with atmospheric carbon dioxide is that increased atmospheric concentrations of carbon dioxide may contribute to *global warming*. The relationship between carbon dioxide concentrations and global warming is hotly debated.

4. *Ocean Carbon* exists when atmospheric carbon dioxide dissolves in the ocean as a sink. A small percentage (about 0.5 %) of the dissolved carbon dioxide chemically reacts with the water. The chemical equation is:

$CO_2(gas) + H_2O$ (liquid) $= H_2CO_3$ (in water)

H_2CO_3 is a weak acid (carbonic acid).

So with more carbon dioxide in the ocean sink, the ocean becomes more acidic.

The ocean is a complex body not easily analyzed by isolated chemistry.

5. *Carbon fossil fuels* were investigated in Chapter 13 and Chapter 14. Fossil fuels are carbon sinks where the organic chemical energy is stored. Whether or not fossil fuels can be considered as a carbon dioxide bio-cycle is truly a matter of definition. However, the use of fossil fuels as an energy source makes carbon dioxide production unavoidable.

Chapter 15:

Hydroelectric Power

Sections

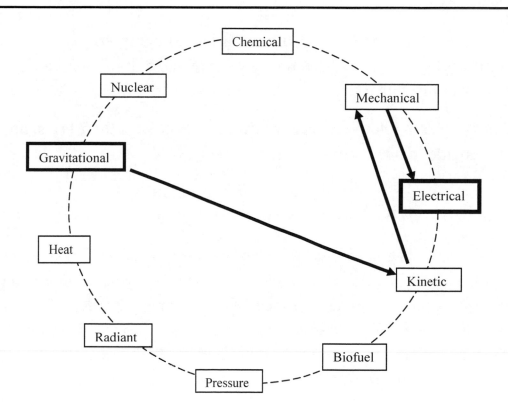

I. Introduction to Hydroelectric Power

Hydroelectric power is known by everyone. Hydroelectric power is produced by exploiting the gravitational energy (power) existing in rivers, and then converts that energy to kinetic power that drives the mechanical energy shaft of a water turbine. The mechanical shaft is connected to an electrical generator.

Hydroelectric power is the conversion of gravitational energy (power) to kinetic energy (power) to mechanical (shaft) power to electric power using water. Within the limits of this text, hydroelectric power will only be understood in terms of utility grade electric power. This is a short chapter.

It is somehow nostalgic to recall our past where water wheels ground flour for domestic consumption. The family name Miller is a derivative of that older very important occupation. Today we build water wheels for decorative purposes. The fundamentals of energy and power apply equally well to that past power application. It was a great improvement over hand grinding of grains to use the power of a water wheel.

Hydroelectricity is the most observed and easiest to comprehend form of utility grade power generation. Hydroelectricity is integrated into our comprehensive energy and power investigations.

Hydroelectric power is relatively inexpensive, available on a 24/7 basis, and can be designed to provide minimal environmental impact.

II. The Hydroelectric Power Generation Cycle

Figure 15.1 presents a graphic of the basic natural rain cycle fundamental to the generation of electric power. The input energy for the cycle is the water, being transported as a vapor, from the surface of the earth to be deposited at higher altitudes as rain water. The water evaporation to rain process is qualitative, but impossible to understand in quantitative terms due to the atmospheric complexity. However, we do quite well with just using the accurately measured rainfall amounts.

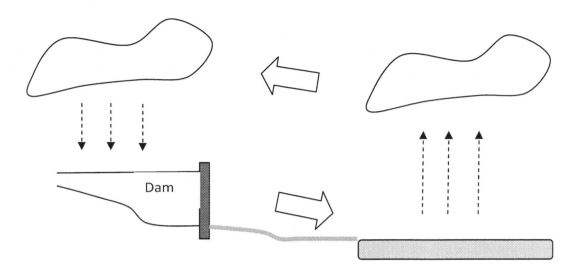

Figure 15.1 The Rain Cycle

Nature has provided us with rivers that conveniently collect the rainfall into potential exploitable power reservoirs. Several comments about the rain cycle are appropriate:

1. The potential for hydroelectric power is determined by regional geology. There are no hydroelectric power plants in Saudi Arabia and many in Norway due to this limitation.

2. The water collected in the river basins is also a variable. The United States Boulder Dam and the Grand Coolee Dam are affected by periodic reduced rainfall (droughts) in their river basins.

3. The global source of hydroelectric power is limited by the amount of economically available rainfall water. And the total amount of worldwide water is fairly constant. The most economical sources have been exploited. In this respect, hydroelectricity is limited.

4. The hydroelectric power cycle is obviously a renewable energy cycle.

These comments are more aspects of the business application of hydroelectricity than explanation of the fundamental science.

III. The Hydroelectric Power Plant

Figure 15.2 presents a generalized hydroelectric dam and power plant. Actually, all hydroelectric power systems have 1) a dam to collect river water, 2) conversion of water gravitational energy to kinetic energy, and 3) A turbine that converts kinetic energy to mechanical shaft energy to the electrical generator.

The kinetic energy to shaft mechanical energy utilizing a turbine is the same as described in Chapter 3.

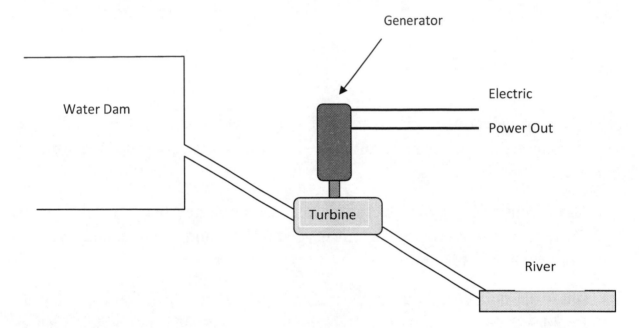

Figure 15.2 Hydroelectric Power Plant

The power efficiency and long term reliability of power dams are outstanding. The careful and successful engineering of Boulder Dam and the Grand Coolee Dam have been historically documented.

IV. Hydroelectric Power Science

Figure 15.3 presents a graphical view of a hydroelectric power in universe constant terms

An arbitrary height of the dam's water level to the turbine inlet is given as 100 feet (It can be any value). The height of a dam to turbine inlet is called a "head". When

1 gallon of water passes into the turbine (Figure 15.3) from a 100 foot "head", it contains the same gravitational energy as a gallon of water being dropped from 100 feet (Figure 15.3). In this example we assign a water flow volume of 500 cubic feet per second. This is an example of the 1st Law of Thermodynamic. The gallon of water converted gravitational energy (height x distance) to an equivalent kinetic energy of the water..

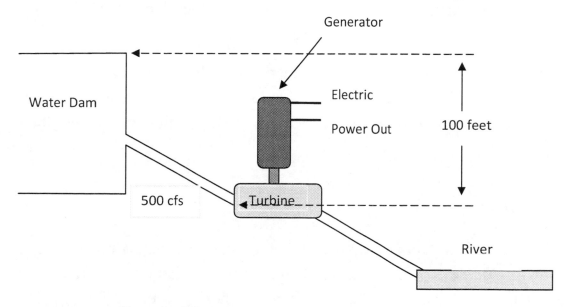

Figure 15.3 Hydroelectric Power

The potential hydroelectric power is now easy to calculate. It is the water's gravitational energy of "head" x the total weight through the turbine inlet.

Example:

Given:

water head = <u>100 feet</u>

Water volume per second = <u>500 cubic feet per second</u>

Water weights 62.4 pounds per cubic feet

(500 cubic feet per second) x (62.4 lbs per cubic foot)

Total weight = <u>31,200 lbs per second</u>

Power: (foot-pounds/sec)

    = 100 ft x 31,200 lbs / sec

    = 3,120, 000 ft-lbs / sec

    = 5670 horsepower or 4,230 kilowatts (4.2 Megawatts)

The numbers in this example have only reference value. However, they do represent a typical hydroelectricity generation plant.

The key idea is that knowing the water "head" and the flow rate, the ideal hydroelectric power is easy to calculate. It should be mentioned that the water gravitational energy conversion to electricity is relatively efficient, greater than 85%.

V. Pumped Storage

Referring to Figure 15.3, it is possible to reverse the hydroelectric power plant and pump water with electrical power from the river into the dam. That process is called "*pumped storage.*" This is a practical way of storing energy. The present pumped storage facilities are both do-able and economically feasible. The present pumped storage facilities are quite efficient (about 90%). Pumped storage provides energy storage for intermittent power production and for meeting peak electrical power demands.

Pumped storage is an obvious option for utilization of the intermittent energy production by wind and solar systems. The existence of the grid makes pumped storage a viable solution to alternate energy intermittent energies.

VI. Conclusions

Hydroelectricity is based upon the conversion of gravitational energy into moving kinetic energy into mechanical shaft energy into electric energy (power). The elements of water power have prehistoric applications.

The must-know elements of hydroelectricity are:

1. **Hydroelectricity is relatively inexpensive, provides constant 24/7 power, and is environmentally friendly.**

2. **Hydroelectricity potential is limited by natural conditions.**

3. **The electric power generated by hydroelectricity is calculated as equivalent gravitational energy (power).**

Chapter 15 Insight

Hydroelectric Storage

The renewable energy systems of wind power and solar power are bound to intermittent power. Economics dictates that we should adapt these renewable energy systems power output to customer demands. This insight is presented to reinforce the concept of hydroelectric storage as a reasonable solution to the electrical power reconciliation of peak demands and intermittent generation.

The proper name for hydroelectric energy storage is *"pumped storage"*. Pumped power storage is widely used by electrical power companies to contain peak power demands such as afternoon air conditioning during the summer.

The pumped power storage is accomplished with an efficiency of around 85% and is a reasonable candidate for intermittent electrical power generation without further development. This insight does not belabor the future pumped storage proposals; but an obvious factor is the required dam altitudes within the distributed systems of water dams.

A sample calculation is given using our Lake Tahoe as a national pumped storage facility. Lake Tahoe is near the home of the author, and I can expect some emotional input after providing this example!

Gravitational Energy in Lake Tahoe (hmg)

Gravitational Energy = (mass)(acceleration of gravity)(height)

1. Mass =(From the Visitor's Authority) 39×10^{12} gallons

   $(39 \times 10^{12}$ gallons$) \times (8.34$ lbs/gallon$)= 325 \times 10^{12}$ lbs

   $(325 \times 10^{12}$ lbs$) \times (1$ kg/2.2 lbs$) = \underline{\mathbf{148 \times 10^{12} \ kg}}$

2. Acceleration = **9.8 meters/sec^2**

3. Height = (1 mile) x (1600 meters/mile) = **1600 meters**

Gravitational Energy = $(148 \times 10^{12}$ kg$)(9.8 m/s^2)(1600$ m$)$

   = **23 x 10^{17} Joules**

Energy in BTU's:

   = $(23 \cdot x\ 10^{17}$ Joules$)$ x $(1 Btu/1055$ Joules$)$

   = **22 x 10^{14} Btu**

A. USA electrical energy per day (From EIA)

   $(40.6 \times 10^{15}$ Btu/yr$)$ x $(1$ yr/365 days$)$ = **1.1 x 10^{14} Btu/day**

B. Tahoe's potential energy/USA electrical energy per day

   22 x 10^{14} Btu/$(1.1 \times 10^{14}$ Btu/day$)$ = **20 days**

The stored gravitational energy due to the height of Lake Tahoe's water is equivalent to the total USA electrical energy used in 20 days.

Chapter 16:

Nuclear Power

Sections:

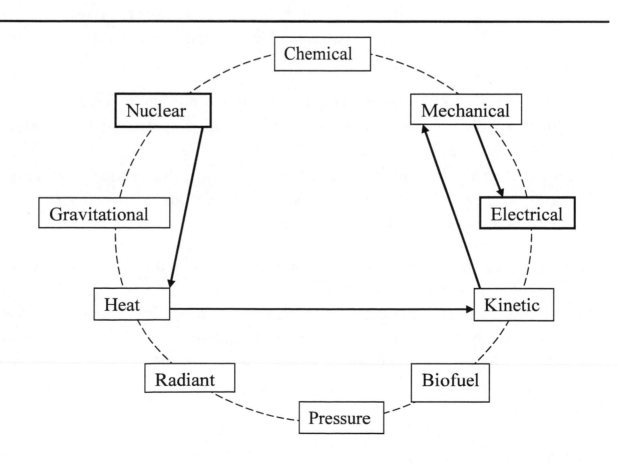

The energy flow diagram represents a nuclear power plant. The nuclear reaction is the source of heat power that flows into the usable electrical power.

I. Introduction to Nuclear Power

Nuclear Energy and Power are available by matter (mass) conversion to energy at the centers (nuclei) of atoms. *Energy and Power – Fundamental Knowledge*, combines the nuclear energy source explanation with the utility power application (as heat for utility power). The reason for this approach is that nuclear energy does not have any familiar sensed components and therefore is impossible to describe in terms of the non-existent observations.

II. Atomic Nuclei

In *Chapter 8: Chemical Energy*, it was explained that all atoms in the universe have a central nucleus where all of each individual atom's protons exist. This is a modern discovery. The condition where all of the positive charges (protons) exist in a small central cluster within each atom could not occur without neutrons gluing the protons together, in spite of the tremendous electrical repulsive force among the protons.

The number of neutrons required to provide enough attractive force to create a stable, in time, atom for each exact number of protons in the nucleus has been determined for all chemical elements. If there are too few or too many neutrons to create a stable nucleus, with time, the nucleus will adjust the neutron / proton ratio to create a stable nucleus. The stabilization process is called *natural radioactivity*. No process on earth can change that rate of natural radioactivity.

Natural radioactivity produces a significant amount of heat when the nuclei of atoms move towards their stable neutron configurations. The heat within the center of the earth is partially produced by this natural radioactivity. The key overview concept is that each occurrence of natural radioactivity is an independent event. The total heat generated within our earth is spread throughout our planet. With time, the heat production from natural radioactivity will slow as all the nuclei evolve into stable atoms.

III. Energy and Matter are Related

Independent of the discovery of natural radioactivity, Albert Einstein mathematically derived (discovered), that by logically considering kinetic energy and the measured behavior of light speed, one could relate energy to mass. This was a milestone in human understanding of the universe. The equation is very simple:

$$E = mc^2$$

The energy to mass equivalence is explained in simple universe constants. An example is given below in Figure 16.1. This formula has been printed on t-shirts for many and understood by few. The derivation of $e=mc^2$ is not that difficult of an extension of our Chapter 4 Insight. This text does not pursue that interesting derivation.

To impress upon the reader the actual values of energy stored as matter, the following example is given:

The mass of a pencil tip eraser is about 1.0 grams.

$$E = mc^2$$
$$= (1.0 \times 10^{-3} \text{ kg}) \times (3.0 \times 10^8 \text{ m / s})^2$$
$$= 9.0 \times 10^{13} \text{ kg} \times \text{m}^2 / \text{s}^2 = 9.0 \times 10^{13} \text{ joules of energy}$$

This is equivalent to 33,000 tons of TNT explosive !!!

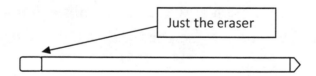

Just the eraser

Figure 16.1 Pencil Eraser

Now that we realize the great amounts of energy produced when mass is converted to energy, we have incentive to investigate the following nuclear energy fundamentals:

1. When a nucleus naturally adjusts to a stable configuration and releases energy (natural radioactivity), the total mass of the electrons, neutrons, and

protons after the adjustment is less than before the adjustment. The created energy came from the loss of mass in this process. This is the prime concept of nuclear energy. The 1st Law of Thermodynamics applies to this process.

2. The earth is losing mass as the natural radioactivity occurs. But don't worry, it is a very small amount of the total mass.

3. The energy from natural nuclear changes is not a viable source of utility grade energy because it is diffuse. It is not physically feasible to concentrate naturally radioactive materials into a utility grade power source.

IV. Nuclear Fission

Natural radioactivity was discovered around 1900, but a key associated nuclear discovery was made about 1938. When the nuclei of heavy atoms are subjected to a kinetically energetic neutrons, the nuclei may not only absorb the neutron to create a heavier nuclei, but the neutron can cause the nucleus to break apart into smaller nuclei (smaller atoms). When that breakage (fission) occurs, a loss of mass and the production of energy results. The loss of mass releases energy according to Einstein's discovery of $E = mc^2$. The discovery of nuclear fission has had a significant impact upon modern society.

The utilization of nuclear fission as an energy source was quickly achieved by the United States (and many counties later) in the war time development of the atomic bomb, appropriately named a nuclear weapon. The observation of the atomic bomb effectiveness validates the nuclear science discoveries, but also places a great obligation upon the social behavior of mankind.

The task of releasing the huge nuclear energy was focused upon:

1. Finding a way to produce the concentrated amount of neutrons necessary to create a significant fission nuclear event.

2. Finding a deliverable nuclear system outside of the laboratory confines.

An ideal natural chemical element was found. That chemical element was uranium. Uranium is our largest (element #92) natural element. The existence of uranium ore for mining is adequate.

Uranium, as mined, comes substantially in two major forms; Uranium 238 and Uranium 235. A chart is provided to clearly present these two forms of uranium:

Uranium	Protons	Neutrons	Weight (AMU)*
"235"	92	143	235
"238"	92	146	238

- *AMU = Atomic Mass Units

The physical process of the nuclear weapon creation was staggering. The developed process is explained below, because it is the basis of our utility grade nuclear energy program:

1. The chemical element used for nuclear weapons and all nuclear power generation is natural Uranium 235 with 92 protons and 143 neutrons in the nucleus. Within this text, U-235 is called only "235" to prevent repetitive confusion.

2. The operational feature of 235 is, when a single 235 nucleus splits into smaller atoms, it produces 2 or 3 more neutrons capable of splitting more 235 nuclei. These excess neutrons produced upon the splitting of 235 are the source of a continuing nuclear reaction as presented in Figure 16.2. The continuing source of neutrons during the 235 fission is called a *chain reaction*. 238 does not produce excess neutrons upon splitting.

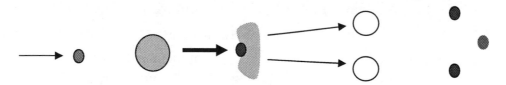

Figure 16.2 U-235 Fission

Neutron + 235 transforms to two smaller atoms plus 3 neutrons

1. The 235 atom, presented as splitting in Figure 16.2, is one example of possible 232 nuclear fission outcomes. In the Figure 16.2 example, 235 may be splitting into one krypton atom and one barium atom. The 235 can also

split into other atoms. But, each of the 235 fissions results in excess neutrons and lots of energy.

2. The excess neutrons create a source for additional atomic fissions. If the 235's are close to each other (concentrated), then enough neutrons can be produced to cause a chain reaction where all of the 235's are soon split (nuclear fission) and all the energy is released at once.

3. The key idea is that each 235 has excess neutrons after fission to cause a chain (continuing) nuclear fission of nearby 235 nuclei.

The requirement for building an uncontrolled mass fission of 235 (atomic bomb) is to concentrate enough pure 235 atoms together (military grade 235) so that when the neutrons created by the initial 235 atom splits (Figure 16-2), the resulting neutrons will hit and split at least another 235 nucleus before they are wasted into non-fissionable contacts or leave the 235 mass. This uncontrolled chain reaction will produce enough neutrons to hit and split most of the concentrated 235. This releases energy beyond all earlier comprehension. And that is an atomic weapon. The key attribute of 235 is that it produces its own source of neutrons to cause a chain reaction and nuclear fission of all the concentrated atoms.

A well defined amount (mass) of 235 is required to cause this chain reaction. Think of that as pure 235 the size of a soft ball. That amount of mass is present in every uranium atomic weapon. That amount of 235 is small enough to be designed into a portable weapon. The amount of mass to sustain an uncontrolled nuclear chain reaction is called the *critical mass*. Figure 16.3 presents the elements of a nuclear weapon. The basic idea is to form a critical mass of 235. An explosive slams the two amounts of 235 into a critical mass.

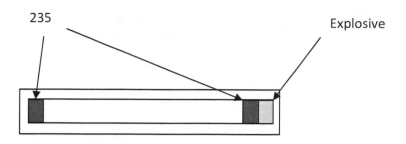

Figure 16.3 Nuclear Weapon

V. Nuclear Power Generation

Within a decade after the creation of the nuclear weapon, a peaceful application of 235 was designed and realized. The fission energy released in a nuclear weapon was engineered to create heat and electrical utility grade power.

A nuclear reactor, presented in 16.4, is designed to control the rate of 235 fission. This allows the 235 nuclear reaction to produce heat energy over an extended period of time that is converted to mechanical shaft energy for use in electrical power generation.

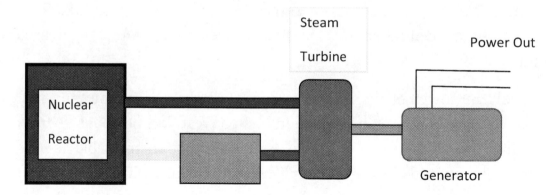

Figure 16.4 Nuclear Power Plant

The engineering design fundamentals of a nuclear power plant are not included in this text. For those interested in nuclear power plant design, even a qualitative investigation is fascinating.

The electrical capacity of a present nuclear power plants is relatively large, on average producing about 1 gigawatts of electrical power. The power output is constant except for periods of nuclear plant maintenance. The physical principles are elementary, we are just converting some matter into energy.

Nuclear power generation has strong political aspects which are not part of energy science, but will be explained as part of the public energy forum:

1. We encounter two forms of uranium atoms when mining. One finds that Uranium-238 (with 92 protons and 146 neutrons) is about 99.4% of the natural uranium ore and Uranium-235 (with 92 protons and 143 neutrons) is about 0.6% in the natural cause a chain fission reaction.

2. A uranium nuclear weapon is created by first increasing the concentration of 235 to over 90% (military grade). This almost pure 235 allows the critical mass required for an uncontrolled nuclear chain reaction. To separate 235 from the 235/238 uranium ore mixture is a monumental task. Chemically 235 and 238 are the same (both uranium); so no chemical method can be used. Centrifuges and diffusions are used to physically separate 235 from 238 based upon the slight weight difference of the atoms.

3. Nuclear reactions in power (heat) plants are designed with fissionable uranium 235 concentrations of about 4% and the rest is 238. This is a convenient concentration of 235 to engineer an operating nuclear power plant.

The 235 "fuel" in power plants is in the form of "rods". With time, the rods will contain less and less 235 as the controlled nuclear reaction proceeds. After about two years, the concentration of 235 will be reduced to an unusable level in the nuclear reactor (spent rods) and needs replacement with a fresh 4% 232 rod.

1. The spent rods consist, in a loose approximation, 2% unused 235, 2% 235 nuclear reaction products, 94% U-238, and 2% of man-made chemical elements.(mainly Plutonium) I am apologizing for this weak model which is stated only for logical purpose.

2. We have some inherent problems with spent nuclear fuel rods. Part of the nuclear reaction products within the spent rod are radioactive chemical elements that naturally adjust (decay) to stable chemical elements. These

chemical elements are radioactive and become stable at determined rates. In this respect, the spent rods are a radioactive health concern.

3. The man-made chemical elements are explained below under the *Plutonium* Section. These elements, called *trans-uranium elements*, are not found on earth, but are created during the 235 nuclear reaction. They too are radioactive.

Considering the national security threat posed by nuclear weapons and the problems associated with spent nuclear rod disposal, the adaptation of nuclear power is highly politicized. The topic of nuclear waste disposal will not be addressed in this text.

VI. Plutonium

When the 235 is in the process of nuclear fission within our nuclear power plant, another nuclear reaction occurs. The excess neutrons, those beyond the amount required to continue the 235 chain reaction, are also contacting the 238 nuclei and some are "sticking' to those 238 nuclei. This is visually presented in Figure 16.5.

Neutron — Uranium 238 — Plutonium 239 — Plus 2 electrons

Figure 16.5 Creating Plutonium 239

The 238 atom plus an extra neutron in the nucleus creates Plutonium. Plutonium does not exist naturally on earth. It is a man-made (in our reactor) chemical element. Understand that plutonium has these properties:

1. Plutonium is also a nuclear fissionable material similar to 235. 239 nuclear weapons have been created and 239 power plants are under development.

2. Concentrating plutonium into a critical mass for use in an uncontrolled reaction is much easier than separating 235 from the 238 in mined material. Uranium and plutonium in nuclear reactor products can be chemically

separated. Terrorists could easily assemble a plutonium nuclear weapon. This is of great concern.

3. Plutonium also presents the possibility of a nuclear reaction path where the 238 atoms can be converted into fissionable plutonium atoms. This means that rather than be limited to the energy of the 4% 235 in a nuclear reactor rod, we could theoretically fission the remaining 96% of 238. This could supply energy beyond our common comprehension.

The design of a nuclear plant that specifically produces 239 from 238 is called a *breeder reactor* and produces fissionable material. The development of breeder reactors has been curtailed for security reasons. However, this remains a huge future source of utility grade energy.

VII. Conclusions

Nuclear energy is created by mass conversion into energy. The only available path for practical mass conversion to energy, to date, is to change (react) nuclei. The earlier explanation of how neutrons "glue" protons to exist together in the nucleus of atoms is a direct relationship to this energy conversion.

The must-know elements of nuclear energy are:

1. Einstein's equation $E = mc^2$

2. U-235 works because of the neutron chain reaction

3. A nuclear weapon is an uncontrolled reaction

4. A nuclear power plant is a controlled reaction

5. Plutonium (239) is produced from 238

6. Plutonium creates a major problem in nuclear arms control

Chapter 16 Insight

Nuclear Fusion

Nuclear fusion is the reaction of two nuclei to form a larger nucleus. Nuclear fusion is the energy source of the sun.

There are several specific nuclear reactions that occur within stars. Our sun has a predominant fusion reaction of two hydrogen nuclei (protons) to produce a hydrogen nucleus with one proton and one neutron.

2 hydrogen nuclei   1 deuteron

A hydrogen nucleus with one neutron is called a deuteron. This reaction is very slow. Even at the sun's interior temperature of 15 million degrees Celsius, it takes an average time of 8 billion years for two hydrogen nuclei to fuse. This is the basis for the predicted longevity of our sun.

Once a deuteron is formed, it immediately fuses with another hydrogen nucleus to form helium:

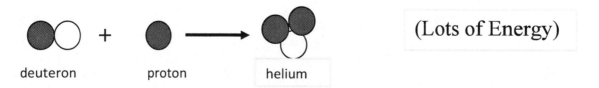

deuteron   proton   helium   (Lots of Energy)

The sun creates energy by conversion of matter during the hydrogen to helium nuclear fusion. The quantities of energy produced by our sun's nuclear fusion can be estimated. A man-made nuclear fusion process is an enticing avenue for future energy production.

Unfortunately, the only man made nuclear fusion has been accomplished by developing the uncontrolled fission reaction to initiate a hydrogen nuclear weapon.

The overwhelming engineering difficulty in developing nuclear fusion power is that a temperature greater than 10 million degrees must be continually maintained to create a continuous fusion reaction. In the hydrogen bomb, the required nuclear fusion temperature is achieved momentarily by a conventional nuclear fission bomb. Of course, this is an uncontrolled reaction. The reality of operational nuclear fusion power generation is far in the future. But the stability of our solar system, as indicated earlier, allows us sufficient time to investigate this potential source of utility grade power.

Chapter 17:

Solar Power

Sections:

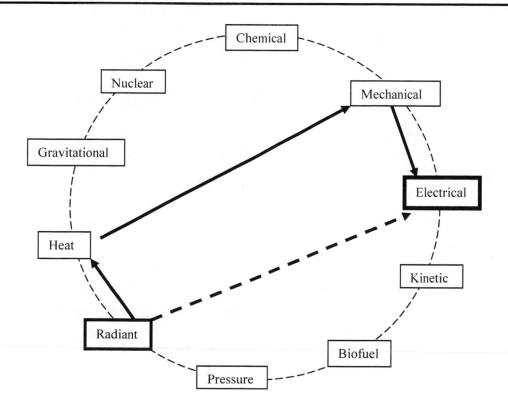

Solar photovoltaic (PV) power is an active candidate in producing renewable electric energy. PV power development is governed by the scientific understanding of radiant energy and photon-material energy interactions.

I. Introduction to Solar Power

Solar energy is the radiant energy transmitted from our sun. Radiant solar energy is observed and felt by everyone. The intensity of radiant energy from the sun to our earth has been relatively stable for millions of years. Our focal question is "Can we convert this abundant and reliable energy source into another kind more suitable to modern societal needs?"

The solar energy from the sun has always been utilized directly to improve our quality of life. Sunshine has been generally associated with pleasant experiences, as long as the ambient temperature is not unpleasantly hot. The beach and afternoon walks in the sun are pleasant experiences.

The solar radiation is explained in depth in Chapter 9. What is investigated in Chapter 17 is the conversion of the available solar energy to useful kinds of energies.

There are presently three main categories of solar energy conversions:

A. Passive solar heating

B. Active solar thermal heating

C. Photovoltaic solar energy conversion

II. Passive Solar Heating

Passive solar heating is solar radiant energy converting directly to heat energy.

An example of passive solar heating is presented in Figure 17.1(A and B)).

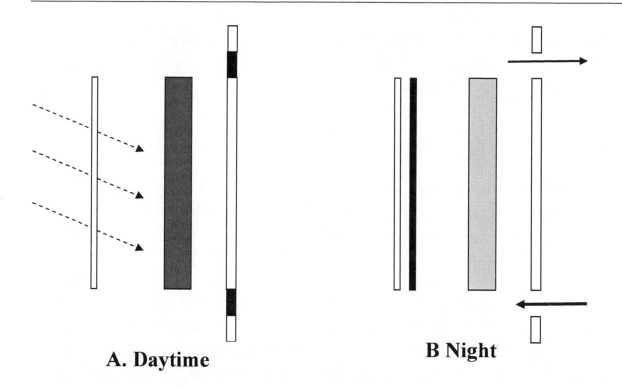

A. Daytime

B Night

Figure 17.1 Passive Solar Heating

The sun's energy can be converted into and stored as heat during the sunshine period of the day. Then the stored heat is released during the colder, dark hours of the day.

During the day, the sun heats the concrete wall inside the house (Figure 17.1A). The temperature of the wall increases according to the heat absorption capacity of the wall and the exposure to the solar energy. The solar energy to heat energy conversion efficiency is maximized by isolating the wall from air heat flow into the house by the dampers.

At night, the curtain next to the windows is drawn to prevent re-radiation of the heat energy within the wall back to the outside of the house (Figure 17.1B). It is common practice to draw curtains to reduce radiant energy transfer. At night, the dampers are opened and that allows the heat within the concrete wall to transfer (pass) into the house.

When designed properly, using proper insulation and solar absorption materials, the passive solar heating can significantly contribute to comfortable house temperatures at lower energy costs.

Another familiar passive solar heating system involves solar energy collected to raise the temperature (heat) of domestic hot water and swimming pools.

The only scientific fact worth repeating regarding solar heating is that the limit of radiant solar energy is about 1000 watts per square meter on a clear sunny day when the square meter faces directly into the sun.

This is a very limiting scientific fact. If I heat my swimming pool with square meters of solar panels, the very maximum heating possible is 5 square meters x 1000 watts/ square meter = 5000 watts. The solar panel's radiant heat to thermal heat (as measured by pool temperature rise) is dependent upon pool temperature, panel design, sun intensity (cloudiness), day length, panel angle to the sun, and piping heat loss. So don't be too surprised if the solar panels won't produce the expected rise in pool temperature. It may be more feasible to use natural gas to heat your pool. Domestic hot water and pool applications of direct solar energy are excellent. The solar energy source cost nothing!

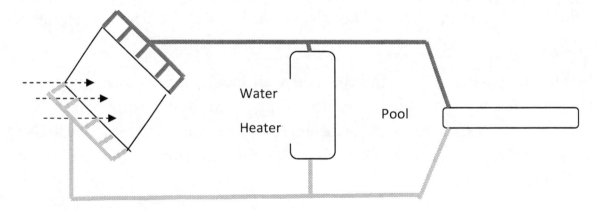

Figure 17.2 Solar Panel Heating

Passive solar heaters are engineered applications where the solar heating effect is optimized to create a more convenient and comfortable living surroundings. This is entirely engineered for a specific application. The science of thermal solar heating is presented in Chapter 7.

III. Solar Thermal Power to Electrical Power

Solar thermal power conversion to electric power involved heat engineering. A substantial effort has been directed at conversion of the solar radiant energy of 1000 watts/ square meter to electrical power. This is a large utility business system operation. Figure 17.3 and Figure 17.4 are graphical representations of this process.

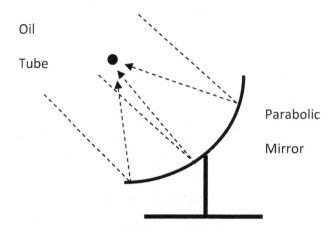

Figure 17.3 Solar Thermal Heat Energy Generation

The electrical generation portion of a thermal heat energy system is explained in Chapter 10: Electrical Energy. Solar thermal electricity generation is a large, utility system.

The solar energy is concentrated by parabolic mirrors which are positioned directly towards the sun. The mirrors concentrate the solar energy into photon absorbing tubes that are positioned at the parabolic mirrors focal points. The tubes are designed to absorb the maximum amount of the concentrated solar radiant energy. The tubes convert the solar energy to heat energy. Inside the tube, oil that can withstand the elevated temperature transfers the heat energy.

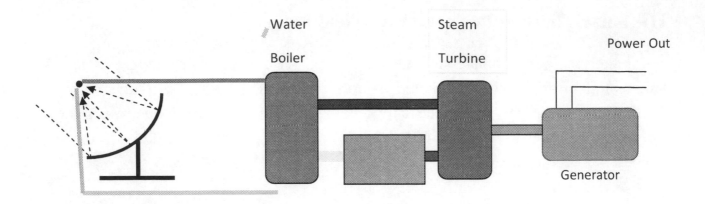

Figure 17.4 Solar Thermal Electricity Generation

The heat energy within the oil is transferred by conduction to a conventional water boiler that produces steam to generate electrical power (See Figure 17.4).

Note that the 2nd Law of Thermodynamics applies and the higher the temperature of the transfer oil travelling to the steam generator, the higher the efficiency of the system.

The solar thermal electrical generation system has been demonstrated; but it is limited by some intrinsic factors:

1. The solar energy input is an absolute variable. Rainy days are a problem. A cloud passing over the solar collection system causes an immediate large change in energy output from the collection system.

2. The sun does not shine at night.

These factors impact the system reliability. This would become a greater limiting factor if solar thermal electric generation became a major source of utility grade power. The inclusion of a short term energy storage system would partially alleviate some of the short term power transients. Major engineering designs could potentially optimize solar thermal electricity generation.

IV. Photovoltaic Power

Photovoltaic power is the conversion of solar radiant power directly to electrical power. As the name photovoltaic suggests, solar radiation (photons) to electrical potential (volts). No other kinds of energy conversions are required. Basically, photovoltaic behavior is not observable, so an extra effort is made to explain the abstract PV phenomenon.

Photovoltaic power is the "Holy Grail" of future utility grade energy systems. And also, like the crusaders and the "Holy Grail," maybe the promise of inexpensive, abundant photovoltaic energy is unattainable. However, the understanding of photovoltaic energy is a science that will be forever a segment of energy education.

Our explanation of photovoltaic (PV) power follows the energy conversion process from radiant energy to utility grade electrical energy.

The semiconductor (PV) material

We have chosen our PV cell material to be silicon. Silicon is the semiconductor material used for the revolution in electronic devices. We do have the options to use other materials for PV cells, but silicon presently provides the most familiar semiconductor material.

Each silicon atom has 14 protons, 14 electrons, and 14 neutrons. But only 4 of the 14 electrons in each silicon atom can bond to adjacent atoms. The remaining 10 electrons (non-bonding) remain fixed to each silicon atom.

A perfect silicon crystal is formed where pure silicon atoms are completely bonded with each other using their 4 bonding electrons. Figure 17.5 presents a silicon crystal showing only the bonding electrons. Figure 17.5 is presented as a bonded sheet in two dimensions. Actually, a perfect silicon crystal has atoms arranged in a perfect three dimensional pyramidal structure. Fortunately, the two dimensional model is adequate for our discussion.

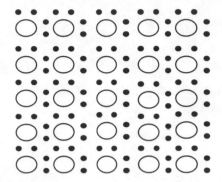

Figure 17.5 Silicon Crystal

Photon interaction with silicon:

The silicon bonds within the silicon crystal have an energy of 1.1 electron volts. That means, if the silicon crystal is exposed to radiant energy, a bonding electron may be "knocked" loose within the crystal by 1.1 electron volt or greater of photon energy.

Figure 17.6 presents a graphic of an electron removed from a bond by a photon.

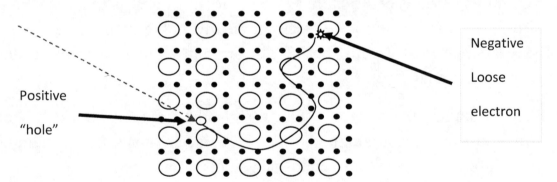

Figure 17.6 Silicon Photon Interaction (in a Slice of Crystalline Silicon)

Figure 17.6 presents interesting behavior within the silicon:

1. The "knocked" loose electron exists away from positive sites. Most of the silicon bonding is complete. The **negative** electron wanders around the silicon crystal. It can only release 1.1 electron-volts of energy if it can combine with a positive center (hole).

2. The departing electron left a **positive** center (hole) within the silicon crystal.

3. In time, some negative electrons will find a positive hole and reestablish a missing bond. That *recombination* of electron and hole will produce a 1.1 electron volt equivalent of heat and photon energy.

4. An exposure to solar radiant energy produces holes and electrons in pure silicon crystals. The total charge of the silicon crystal remains zero. When we stop the solar radiant energy, electron-hole production stops.

Permanent charge barriers

When solar photons interact with crystalline silicon, electron – hole pairs are produced. When one electron recombines with one hole, 1.1 electron volts of energy is released. If we could capture the stored recombination energy by collecting all of the electrons before they recombine, we could have a source of electrical power. And we can!!

Figure 17.7 presents a silicon slice where the upper ½ of the silicone slice has a permanent positive charge and the lower ½ of the silicone slice has a permanent negative charge. The permanent charges within the silicon are the fundamental reason for solar cell behavior. The Figure 17.7 charges are created by a semiconductor process explained in the *Chapter 17 Insight*.

Negatively charged silicone

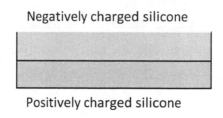

Positively charged silicone

Figure 17.7 Silicon Permanent Charges

V. PV Cell Operation

The permanent charges within the silicone create an electric field. The electric field creates a barrier to electrons and holes as presented below in Figure 17.8.

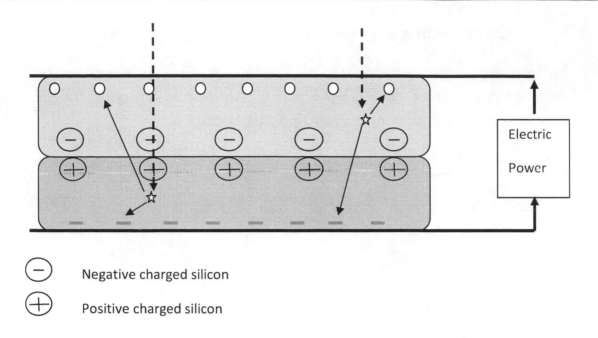

⊖ Negative charged silicon

⊕ Positive charged silicon

Figure 17.8 PV Cell in Operation

Figure 17.8 presents a two incoming photons (dotted lines); one creating an electron-hole pair within the positively charged silicon and the other creating an electron-hole pair within the negatively charged silicon (stars). The electrons and holes will move under the influence of the permanent charges (electric fields) as depicted by the arrows. The holes accumulate on the negative side of the silicon wafer and the electrons accumulate on the positive side of the wafer.

The electrons and holes will accumulate until their total charge (in volts) becomes great enough to overcome the permanent electric charge barrier. That is the PV cell operating voltage. The silicon wafer becomes a capacitor, storing electrical energy as described in the Chapter 10 Insight.

Figure 17.8 presents electric contacts which allow the accumulated electrons in the positive side to bypass the electric field barrier and travel directly to neutralize holes on the negative side of the PV cell. The PV cell electrical flow (current) will transfer electrical energy (power) exactly like the capacitor described in Chapter 10 Insight.

The PV cell can be understood as an electrical capacitor that continually regenerates (at an optimal designed voltage) as long as photons generate electron-hole pairs. The current is a function of the solar radiant power input. Nighttime and cloudy days diminish electron-hole production.

The electrical power produced by PV cells can be electronically converted to 60 cycle 120 volt AC power. This electrical conversion allows universal use of PV power and the opportunity to produce utility grade electricity for our "grid." The "grid" can be the PV power load in Figure 17.10.

Silicon photovoltaic cells are solid state devices without any significant wear-out mechanism. The working lifetime of photovoltaic cells is in excess of 20 years.

The efficiency (Electrical energy out / solar energy in) x 100% is about 17% for a typical silicon PV cell. The radiant to electrical power efficiency of ordinary PV cells (those with reasonable cost) and cost of production are challenges for adaption to utility grade systems.

The complex nature of the solid state physics for the development of PV cells is well understood, assisted by our semiconductor revolution.

VI. Conclusions

Solar energy is the radiant energy transmitted from our sun. A considerable effort is directed at developing solar energy into an important segment of our utility grade energy requirements. The solar thermal heat systems are easy to comprehend from observations, but the photon energy to electrical energy (photovoltaic) conversion is quite obscure. Energy science provides insight and limits to solar energy systems.

The must-know elements of solar energy are:

> **1. Solar energy at the earth's surface is 1000 watts per square meter.**
>
> **2. Solar energy is quite intermittent.**
>
> **3. PV cells are very durable.**
>
> **4. PV generation can be connected to the grid.**
>
> **5. PV applications are cost limited at this time (2010).**

Chapter 17 Insight

Creating Permanent Charges

Figure 17.5 presented a perfect silicon crystal where all bonding electrons are utilized in the crystal. There are no "free" electrons in this material.

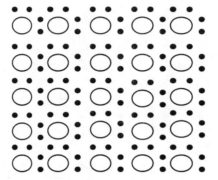

Using semiconductor processes, not described in detail in this text, we can substitute (implant) atoms within the silicon with 5 bonding electrons instead of the silicon 4 bonding electrons, or 3 bonding electrons instead of the silicon 4 bonding electrons.

Since the implanted atoms are neutral in charge, the overall charge of the silicon crystal ("A" and "B" below) is still neutral. At this point, there are locations within the crystal that have an extra electron or are missing an electron within the perfect crystal. Look close to the darkened atoms.

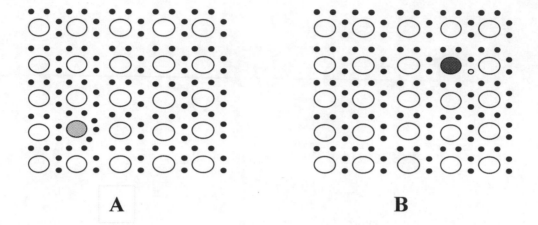

A   **B**

When "A" and "B" are physically joined, an astonishing phenomenon occurs. The extra electron(s) on the atoms on one side migrate and **permanently** attaches to the missing electron site (holes) that exist on the other side. This makes one side **permanently** negative and the other side **permanently** positive.

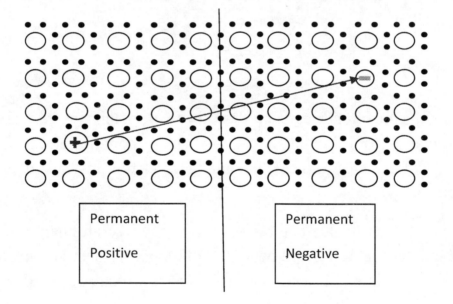

Please note that the electrons have migrated to fill vacant bonds within the silicon crystal.

The silicon crystal is now completely bonded, but the **permanent** charge (positive and negative) remains on the implanted atoms. This is one method of how we create a permanent charge barrier for PV cells.

Chapter 18

Wind Power

Sections:

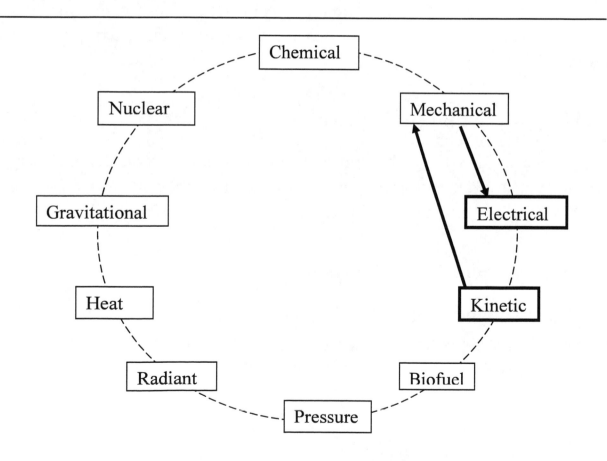

I. Introduction to Wind Power

Wind energy is a leading candidate for renewable energy. The process converting wind energy, an available power source, to usable electric power is intuitively understood. This process application depends more upon engineering, business, and political factors.

Wind power is the conversion of wind kinetic energy (power) into mechanical energy (shaft power) into electrical power. The kinetic energy of wind source can be considered as converted from atmosphere pressure-thermal differences caused by solar radiation. In absolute terms, the winds are very complex in origin and impossible to accurately predict. Wind power electricity generation is intermittent.

Wind power has a long history. We are all familiar with the idyllic farm scene that includes a windmill used to pump water. As children, we have built "pinwheels" that turn as we pass them through the air.

The use of wind power as a source of utility grade power is in its infancy. It is easy to drift into the speculation of the role of wind power in our future utility grade power production. This text only will focus upon the scientific aspects of wind power.

II. Wind Power Universal Dimensions

Utility grade wind power is the conversion of air mass in motion (kinetic energy) into mechanical shaft power that is converted to electrical power by means of a generator. The universe dimensions are explicitly derived in *Chapter 18 Insight*.

III. Wind Turbine Power Basics

There are two type of utility grade energy wind turbines: horizontal (fan) and vertical (egg-beaters).Figure 18.1 is a graphic of the two main types of wind turbines.

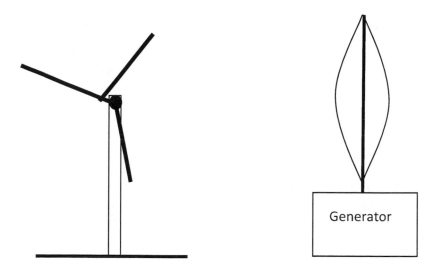

Figure 18.1 Wind Turbines

Utility grade wind turbine designs (100 kW to 5.0 mW) have evolved into 3 blades connected to a hub and shaft. The blade length and tower height of wind turbines has increased with time. The conversion efficiency of wind power to electrical power is increased with increasing wind turbine size. This results in a lower cost (per kW hr) of electrical power production.

The blades of wind turbines are made of fiberglass. The force created by the wind to the turbine blade is the same aerodynamic force created by an airplane wing. Figure 18.2 presents an airplane wing (turbine blade) passing through air with the proper names of the resulting forces.

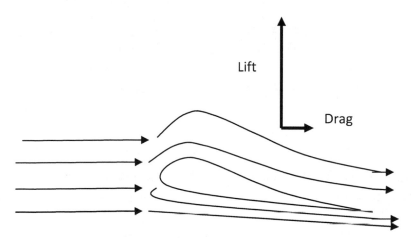

Figure 18.2 Turbine Blade Forces

In a turbine blade, the lift force is the force turning the mechanical generator shaft. In a turbine blade, the drag is the force directed against the turbine generator shaft. The lift force is mostly created by the partial vacuum, during wind passage, formed on the upper (See Figure 18.2) blade surface.

Blade designs are very complex. Blades require maximum efficiency during large variations in wind, gusty winds, and extreme ambient conditions. The maximum theoretic conversion of wind kinetic energy to mechanical energy is 59%.

Figure 18.3 presents the typical electrical power output from a wind turbine. Figure 18.3 is almost intuitive; but is presented to clarify wind turbine performance aspects. Figure 18.3 presents electrical power output versus wind velocity in a graphic example. Different wind turbines have different power versus wind velocity specifications.

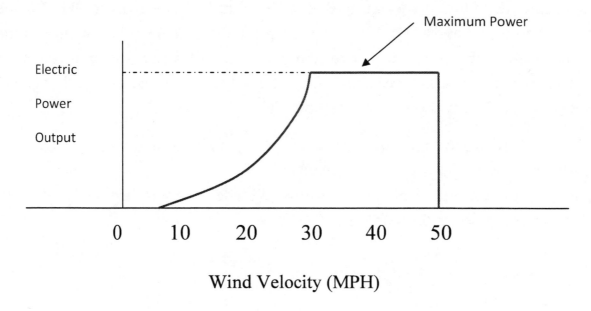

Figure 18.3 Wind Velocity vs. Electrical Power

1. The wind with velocity from 0 to 5 miles per hour does not have sufficient kinetic energy to rotate the electrical generator shaft. Usually, the wind turbine shaft is braked-to-stop for these low wind velocities.

2. The wind velocity of 5 to 30 miles per hour is the designed range where most (in time) wind power to electrical power occurs. As explained below, the

electrical power transfer from a wind turbine to the electrical power grid is a challenge.

3. The wind velocities from 30 miles per hour to 50 miles per hour will produce the maximum electrical output (nameplate) for the wind turbine. The maximum output is realized only a small portion of the time. What fraction of the time does the wind blow over 30 miles per hour? The constant power output between 30 miles per hour and 50 miles per hour is achieved by rotating "feathering" the blades to extract less kinetic energy from the wind.

4. At 50 miles per hour wind speed, the wind turbine will completely "feather" the wind turbine blades to stop rotation. This is for safety considerations, in addition, the turbine shaft will to braked to zero rotation

IV. Intermittent Power

A typical wind velocity with time graph is presented in Figure 18.4. Figure 18.4 is illustrated as an example. The first noticeable presentation of Figure 18.4 is that the wind does not blow at certain times. Wind velocities are unpredictable.

Figure 18.4 presents daily "average" wind velocities. Averages may be misleading. We are all aware of the phenomenon of wind "dying down" in the evening of each day. For instance, it would not be surprising if the wind turbine located at the Figure 18.4 would not produce any electricity on day 7, 8, and 9. But maybe it would produce some electrical power. There is an intrinsic uncertainty. So be very careful when interpreting wind analysis data. It is much better to analyze the actual electrical output rather than wind data !!

The measurement of wind power, in terms of electrical megawatt-hours output, is a source of continual confusion. Please be careful that you understand the following measured values, regardless of the proper nouns that are used by different data sources:

1. The rated maximum capacity of the wind turbine generator as presented in Figure 18.3.This is often called the *"name plate"* electrical capacity. This is the electrical power output if the wind is blowing continuously at optimum velocity.

2. The actual operating and measured output over time (e.g. year 2008). This is often called the *"benchmark electrical capacity."*

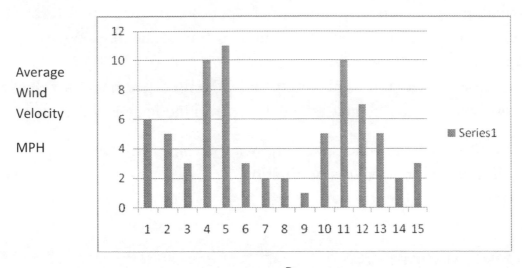

Figure 18.4 Typical Wind Velocity Day

In an acceptable wind area, the actual measured output over time of wind turbine generators is between 20% and 30% of the nameplate maximum rated output at optimum wind velocity.

Wind power storage is an important consideration. Presently (2010), wind power is intermittent and cannot be considered as a reliable peak power usage time electrical utility. The hottest day, requiring the greatest amount of electricity for air conditioning, may occur when the winds are not blowing. Immediate back-up power is presently supplied by natural gas fired electrical generators. It would be great if we could store power for use during peak power requirement times. The pumped storage hydroelectric power storage, described in Chapter 15, is a reasonable method of storing energy. Pumped storage is presently used at several hydroelectric generating plants.

In general, wind turbine based electrical power needs the planning consideration of intermittent power.

V. Wind Velocity Measurement

Wind measurement can be accomplished by an instrument called an *anemometer.* Anemometers are observed as part of home weather stations. Similar to home wind measuring instruments, the rotating cups spin measuring the wind velocity. For potential utility grade wind turbines, the wind velocity is typically measured at a height of 50 meters.

The National Renewable Energy Laboratory (NREL) actively pursues mapping "average" wind velocities throughout the United States. This is part of the renewable energy program. The NREL mapping includes precise data from existing wind farms. The wind "average" measurement involves statistical interpretation. NREL wind maps indicate prime areas for wind power sites. Selecting a wind turbine site with optimum velocity wind is a prime consideration for the generation of competitively priced electrical power.

Since the NREL wind maps are updated often, no sample is given in this text. Current maps are available on the internet. Wind velocities are a crucial part of wind turbine business investments.

VI. Wind Power Grid Connections

When we first see a *"wind farm"*, with many wind turbines, the first correct impression is that the blades eerily turn at the same speed. The synchronization of wind turbine blades is the result of connecting to a synchronized AC grid (Chapter 12).

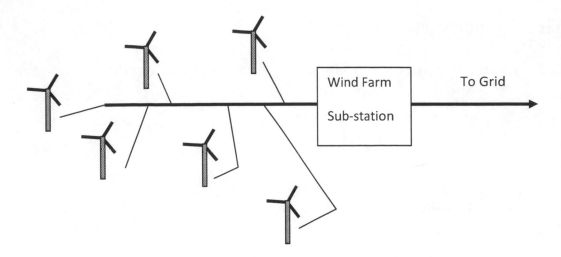

Figure 18.5 Grid Connection

The wind turbine electrical generator forces power unto the grid exactly as presented in Figure 18.5. It is best to consider that the wind turbine generator forces an AC (current x voltage) power unto the grid exactly the same frequency as the mechanical power supplied to the shaft by the wind turbine blades.

The AC of the grid has to be matched to the AC of the generator to have power transmission. That means that the wind power electrical generator must always have an exact 60 cycles AC output. With a fixed turbine shaft to generator shaft ratio, the turbine shaft must also turn at a fixed rotational velocity.

The actual specified blade rotational velocity depends upon the transmission gear ratio (blade rotation to electrical generator shaft rotation) and the generator rotational speed to create the 60 cycles AC of the grid. Figure 18.5 only presents a reasonable example. However, wind turbine AC generators of the same design all spin at the same speed, in time with the master clock.

This is a simplified version of the electrical controls of a wind turbine electrical generator.

VII. Business Topics

The wind energy resource exploitation is limited by cost competitive production of electrical power. The key issues of cost competitiveness are:

1. Most important is selection of a site where the wind velocity is optimum for production of electrical power. Although the Chapter 18 Insight derives the wind to electrical power efficiency in universe dimensions, a common estimate is that the wind generator produces power according to the 3rd power of the wind velocity. For a moment, all non-mathematicians should delete the last sentence. It is sufficient to say that a wind at 30 miles per hour has the potential of producing 8 times the power as a wind at 15 miles per hour.

2. Windy locations are not always accessible for wind turbine construction and maintenance. The cost of accessibility (roads) has to be considered.

3. Delivering power to the grid is a cost factor. Wind "farms" of many wind turbines reduce unit cost by using a single electrical transmission line. This can be a significant reduction in overall cost.

4. The capacity of existing grid lines to handle additional wind power generation is a difficult problem to resolve due to the complexity of the existing grid system.

5. A very important consideration during this early development of wind turbines is reliability. The data regarding reliability is very difficult to obtain because of business sensitivity. However, known examples of maintenance and operation (M and O) costs suggest that wind turbine reliability is a major cost factor of wind turbine operations.

VII. Conclusions

Wind power is the conversion of kinetic energy (wind) into mechanical energy (shaft) into electrical energy. Wind power is a growing utility grade electricity source. The principles of wind power are simple, but the applications are cost competitive and complex.

The must-know elements of wind energy are:

1. Wind energy is the conversion of kinetic energy (power) to electric power.

2. Wind energy is an intermittent source of power.

3. Power storage is an important consideration

4. Utility wind generation connects to the electrical grid.

5. Cost considerations are of basic importance.

Chapter 18 Insight

Wind Kinetic to Electrical Output Efficiency

$$\text{Efficiency} = \frac{\text{Electrical energy out of turbine}}{\text{Wind energy into turbine}} \times 100\%$$

1. Wind kinetic energy = ½ (mass)(velocity)^2 (PER SECOND)
   Mass is the amount of air flowing through the turbine blades every second. To calculate the volume of air each second, we need to know the velocity of the air. We have chosen a velocity of 9 meters/sec. This air velocity is specified for an existing 2.5 Megawatt turbine operating at about ½ power capacity.

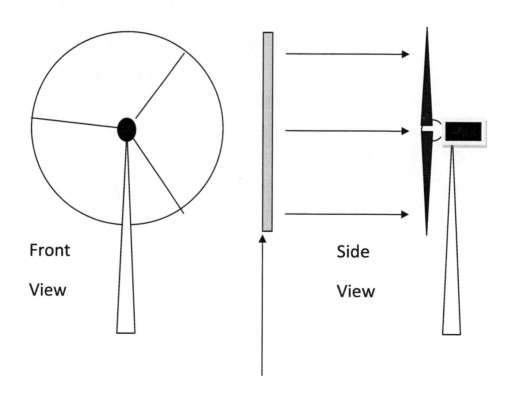

Front

View

Side

View

VOLUME OF AIR THROUGH TURBINE EACH SECOND

The volume of air passing through the turbine blades per second will be 9 meters per second (the velocity per second) times the area covered by the turbine rotors. This volume is presented as the volume above the arrow.

The turbine rotor diameter is 100 meters.
$A = \pi r^2 = 3.14 \ (50 \ \text{meters})^2 = 7850$ square meters
Volume = (9 meters / second)(7850 meters squared)
71 x 10³ cubic meters / second

MASS OF AIR THROUGH TURBINE EACH SECOND

Mass of wind = wind density x wind volume
Wind density given at 1.1 kg / cubic meter
= (1.1 kg/cubic meter) x (71 x 10³ cubic meters)
= 78 x 10³ kg

KINETIC ENERGY OF THE WIND EACH SECOND

KE = ½ mv² = ½ (78 x 10³ kg)(9meters/sec)² = **3500 x 10³ J / sec**

WIND ENERGY INPUT TO ELECTRICAL ENERGY OUTPUT EFFICIENCY

Electrical energy from turbine each second at 9 meters / sec wind velocity from performance specification = 1100 kW = 1100 x 10³ J / sec

Efficiency:

$$\frac{1100 \times 10^3 \text{ J / sec}}{3500 \times 10^3 \text{ J / sec}} \quad x \quad 100 = 31\%$$

31% is a reasonable estimate based upon fundamental dimensions.

Chapter 19:

Geothermal Power

Sections:

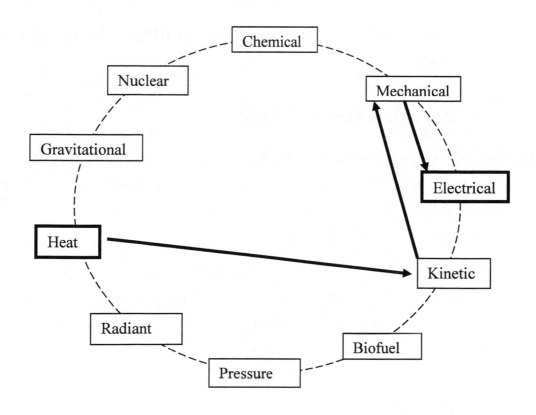

I. Introduction to Geothermal Power

The energy flow for utility grade power is presented. The consumer application of heat pumps is explained in the text.

Geothermal power is converting heat energy existing below the earth's surface into utility grade electric power.

Geothermal heat transfer, used to enhance air conditioning and heating (heat pumps), is also included in this chapter.

Geothermal (hydrothermal) power presently contributes as a utility level generator of electric power. The fundamentals of geothermal electric power generation are explained in this chapter.

Geothermal heat for electrical power production is significant worldwide. Geothermal heat energy usage is neither scientifically complex nor are the engineering applications impossible in most cases. Geothermal systems are explained in this chapter to improve understanding to the public. The maintenance and operation of geothermal power plants is substantial.

Also, the consumer use of ground based heat pumps begged the inclusion of that subject within this chapter.

II. Geothermal (Hydrothermal) Power

Several methods have been presented in the last few chapters where heat energy is the fundamental factor in the energy conversion process. Recently, we have begun to utilize the existing heat below the ground for producing electric power. Geothermal energy is a natural resource.

The generation of electricity has been described in Chapter 10. All we need to understand in this section is that that geothermal energy produces the pressurized vapor that rotates the gas turbine. Producing the vapor to drive the turbine from geothermal energy is not simple; so please have some patience.

The available heat source of geothermal energy is produced by the earth's tectonic plates colliding or by the molten magna from the earth's interior "piping" to the surface. The best example of geothermal energy from tectonic plates is the "pacific ring of fire." The "pacific ring of fire" is also known for its volcanic activity. Countries like the Philippines, situated on the "pacific ring of fire", utilize the geothermal energy. The best example of rising molten magma is the caldera at Yellowstone Park. The Yellowstone Park caldera could be a source of enough geothermal energy to supply the electrical needs of the United States.

Extracting the geothermal heat energy is a difficult problem. Several different geothermal systems are presented for you to have a broad exposure to this engineering problem. To repeat, the geothermal science is simple, but the geothermal engineering is challenging.

There are presently three types of geothermal energy conversions to electrical power utility grade systems:

1. The most desirable geothermal system economically is when the geothermal chamber consists of substantially pressurized steam rather than water. A typical steam pressure may be 80 PSI. The proper noun for this system is "*vapor-dominated.*" In this system the steam in the underground chamber has sufficient pressure to drive the electrical turbine generators directly. These rare conditions are met when the geothermal chamber has a high temperature and the heat transfer to steam capability along with an optimal amount of input water to convert to steam. Since the steam reaching the generator turbine contains only water vapor, this system is commonly referred to as "Dry Steam" or a dry system. The best example of a dry steam system is The Geysers at Santa Rosa, California.

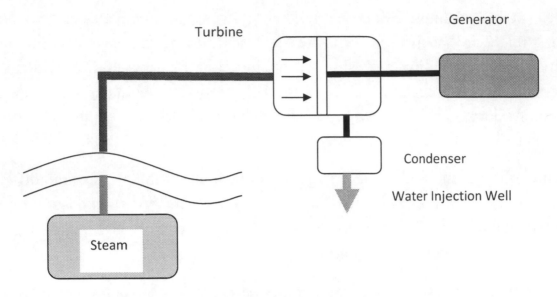

Figure 19.1 Vapor-dominated Geothermal Power Plant

Or Dry Steam Power Plant

Even the dry steam plants need environmental remedial processing to remove sulfur and metals like mercury from the released steam. The remedial actions require a considerable effort.

2. Most geothermal hot water (~200 $^\circ$C) systems produce steam from the geothermal waters (wet) as the water "flashes" into steam near the generator turbine. The excess water is injected back to the underground chamber. The "flash" separators and turbines are exposed to all materials traveling with the water/steam into the turbine. This mainly consists of material from the hot water generation chamber. Materials separation schemes are required. The "flash" evaporator steam generation is the predominant geothermal power system.

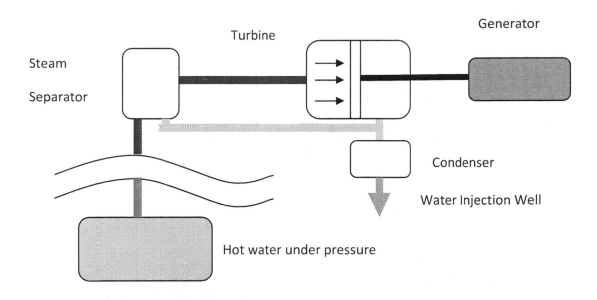

Figure 19.2 "Flash" Steam Geothermal Power Plant

3. Below 200°C the geothermal temperature is inadequate for an efficient production of electric power by means of a (water) steam driven turbine. The geothermal water temperature is too low for efficient steam production. However, the lower temperature is high enough to boil other liquids. By means of a heat exchanger, a liquid such as isobutane can be boiled at a lower temperature than water. The isobutane will produce the required pressure to operate the vapor turbine. The isobutane is in a closed loop heat energy to mechanical energy transfer working fluid. Since this system uses both hot water and a low boiling liquid, it is called a *Binary System*. Binary geothermal systems are an effective method of extracting geothermal energy from chamber temperatures less than 200 °C. Of course, the lower temperature water produces power with a lower efficiency.

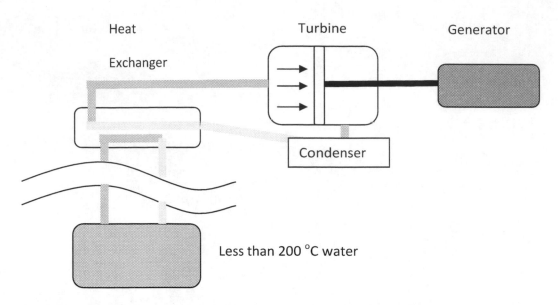

Figure 19.3 Binary Geothermal Power Plant

Figures 17-1, 17-2, and 17-3 are diagrams of the common geothermal systems. Note that water is injected back into the ground in all systems. Water is injected to increase the operating life of each system. Geothermal energy is not a renewable energy source on a predictable basis. The optimum injection design varies with each hydrothermal plant. Each hydrothermal plant behaves differently.

A fundamental and variable limitation of geothermal systems are:

1. The existence of an adequate geothermal heat source. Adequate means with sufficient heat and hot water volume.

2. Heat transfer between the hot earth and the water (steam) heat transfer medium. This is the amount of fractured rock existing in the geothermal source.

3. The opportunity for water injection to sustain the heat energy recovery.

Injecting pressurized water into the geothermal chamber to crack rock formations and blasting the chamber to increase rock surface area have met with some success. However, it is difficult to determine, in these cases, whether the heat transfer limit is a rock surface heat transfer problem or that the total heat capacity of the geothermal chamber is limited. Practically, every geothermal heat extraction well is different.

Geothermal power extraction has been associated with increased seismic activity.

The uncertainties of geothermal systems are substantial. The cost of utility grade development of geothermal energy is predictable in locations such as Iceland, where abundant and lasting geothermal energy is available. In the United States, geothermal explorations have not significantly lowered the inherent risk of investing in a non productive geothermal location. An extensive geological survey of geothermal energy has been documented by the United States Geological Survey (USGS). Any comprehensive investigation of geothermal energy should start with the USGS documentation.

III. "Dry" Geothermal Systems

Another source of geothermal energy is the heat energy that exists without water. Note that the term hydrothermal is missing from this section.

Several attempts have been made to extract heat energy from hot dry rock areas within the earth. Chapter 19 Insight addresses this subject.

IV. Air Conditioners and Heat Pumps

Heating and cooling are substantial usages of consumer electricity. Although air conditioners and heat pumps are not part of utility grade power production, their consumer end use is a significant part of our power usage.

Air conditioners and heat pumps are explained in this section (Section IV) and the related geothermal enhancements, providing electrical energy conservation, are explained in the next section (Section V).

Figure 19.5 presents a graphic of the air conditioner. The two significant components of an air conditioner are 1) the refrigerant liquid-to-gas **evaporator** and 2) the gas- to- liquid **compressor.**

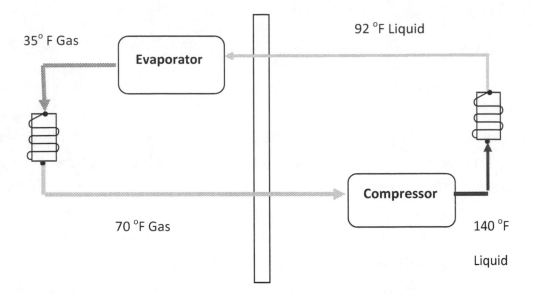

Figure 19.4 The Air Conditioner

Figure 19.4 presents a house being air conditioned (cooled) to an inside temperature of $70°$ F, when the outside temperature is at $92°$ F. The air conditioner presented in Figure 19.4 has a ***"refrigerant"*** that cycles between a hot liquid and a cold gas within a closed system.

Let us trace a refrigerant molecule around the air conditioning cycle:

1. Starting with the evaporator, the liquid becomes a gas. The gas is relatively cold because the refrigerant molecule now can acquire gas kinetic energy that wasn't allowed as a liquid. The difference between the energy of a specific refrigerant liquid and a gas is the ***latent heat of evaporation.***

2. In Figure 19.4, the inside room heat (temperature) has warmed the evaporated refrigerant gas from 35 $°$F to 70 $°$F (room temperature). Remember the 2nd Law of Thermodynamics. Heat flows from the warmer room to the cooler air conditioner coils. A coil of heat conducting material with a fan is provided to assist this process. We observe the air exiting the inside portion of the air conditioner to be cold. That heating the refrigerant gas simultaneously cools the room.

3. At 70°F, the gas is piped to the compressor. The compressor condenses the refrigerant gas into a pressurized liquid. When gases condense, the phase change from gas to liquid produces heat. The refrigerant molecule now is required to transfer its gas kinetic energy to heat. The electrical motor transfers enough pressure-volume energy to overcome the kinetic energy of the 70° F gas. The heat released during this phase change (gas to liquid) is called the latent *heat of condensation.* The gas condenses and transfers to the surroundings the latent heat of condensation upon becoming a liquid. The compressor and coils are hot (e.g. – 140 °F). The air exiting an air conditioner, even on a hot day, it very hot. The power to liquefy to gas is furnished by a "compressor." That is the system input power.

4. The hot refrigerant liquid (e.g. 140 °F) is cooled to 92 °F by outside ambient air. This cooling of the liquid transfers refrigerant heat to the outside surroundings. The next step in the process is returning the 92 °F pressurized refrigerant liquid to the inside evaporator. The closed loop cycle is now complete

What we have just done is cool the room with electrical energy. That process is assisted by a heat conducting coils and fans. The temperatures presented in Figure 19.4 are ideal references. Note that the evaporator coils transferred room heat to the cold refrigerant gas down to the room temperature of 70 °F and that the compressor coils cooled the hot compressed liquid to the outside (ambient) temperature of 92 °F. Actual coils can never exceed the efficiency limits of the ambient conditions.

The total cycle removes heat from the inside and expels heat on the outside. An energy diagram is input compressor electrical power to heat transfer between a lower temperature and a higher temperature.

All refrigerant phase change air conditioners operate fundamentally as presented in Figure 19.4. This includes home and automobile air conditioners and our home refrigerators and freezers.

The key consideration in air conditioner heat flow is that the heat transfer (inside to outside) is directly proportional to the difference in temperature between the inside evaporator and the outside condenser. This is common observed sense. It takes more power to cool our building on a hot day than a cooler day.

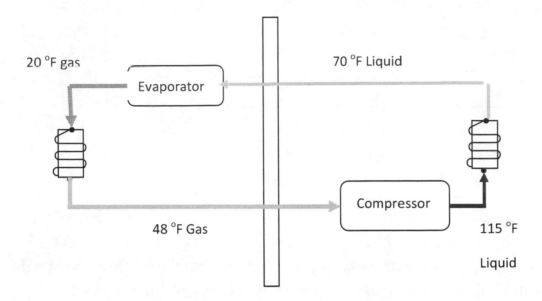

Figure 19.5 Heat Pump

Figure 19.5 uses the same refrigerant cycle to heat the building interior. It is just Figure 19.4with a refrigerant condenser and evaporator reversal. Think of this as putting in our window air conditioner in reverse outside and inside positions. Now hot air is supplied to the interior and cold air is supplied to the exterior. Now the system unit is called a *"heat pump."* And the heat energy is transferred from the electrical energy supplied to the compressor pump. Commercial heat pumps do have a duel role as air conditioner and heater.

Figure 19.5 presents a typical inside temperature as 70 °F and outside temperature as 48 °F. It is the same 22 °F difference in temperature as presented in Figure 19.4, only now we are heating instead of cooling. Without expanding upon heat pump engineering, notice that the outside evaporator now has a refrigerant at 20 °F and we have an icing problem with the outside moisture freezing to the evaporator unit.

For moderate climates, electrical power heat pumps are a cost competitive method of house heating.

V. Geothermal Heat Pumps

A substantial increase in the heat pump system efficiency can be realized by using geothermal heat energy in combination with the air conditioners and heat pumps described in Figure 19.4 and 19.5. The efficiency is calculated as (heat power out / electrical power in) x 100.

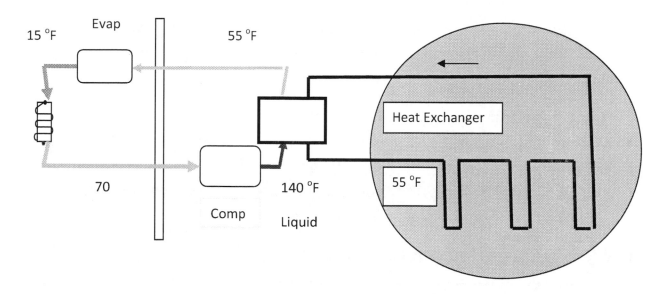

Figure 19.6 Ground Loop Heat Pump (Cooling)

Figure 19.6 is the same as Figure 19.4 except that we have added a heat exchanger. The ground loop will cool the returned hot (140 °F) compressed liquid to the evaporator close to the ground temperature of 55 °F. The evaporator input liquid is kept close to 55°F the by circulating liquid in a ground loop. A ground loop changed the refrigerant temperature returning to the evaporator from 92 °F to 55 °F. With this additional heat exchanger, the liquid refrigerant to the evaporator unit is at 55 °F, rather than the ambient outside temperature (e.g 92 °F). The system operates like the outside temperature is 55 °F rather than the actual 92 °F. A substantial efficiency increase is realized.

This is just a comment to an insightful question. "Why does the system ground loop system perform more efficiently?" The answer is: With the compression pump at the same input electrical power, the evaporator coils have a lower temperature refrigerant gas.

The second insightful question is: "Why is the refrigerant gas colder?" The answer is a little bit longer. When the refrigerant liquid evaporated, the gas was heated from two sources:

1. The room transferred heat to the gas (observed as cooling).

2. The heat from the hot incoming liquid transferred heat to the cool gas.

With the liquid cooling loop, the <u>incoming liquid</u> is cooler (55 °F rather than 92 °F) and less heat energy is now available from the hot liquid for warming the evaporated gas in the evaporation coil.

The refrigerant heat of evaporation is constant and more heat is required from the room to return gas to the compressor at room temperature. With the same compressor energy input, the heat flowing from the room is greater. Our observation is that to keep the room at a constant 70 °C requires that the air conditioner be "on" for less time with a ground loop.

That is more cooling and increased efficiency.

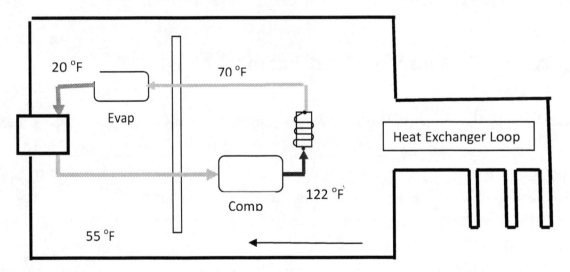

Figure 19.7 Ground Loop Heat Pump (Heating)

A heat pump may be used with a ground loop heat exchanger for an increase in heat efficiency. The evaporator is heated, by means of a ground loop heat exchanger, close to the ground temperature of 55 °F. This increases the heat pump evaporator output temperature from (let us say 48 °F) to the evaporator temperature of about 55 °F. The system operates like the outside temperature is 55 °F rather than the actual 48 °F. An efficiency increase is realized.

Note that when the ambient temperature is close to the ground loop temperature, little heat flow exists. Figure 9.17 presents such an example.

This section presented the geothermal heat pumps in terms of temperatures rather than heat flow diagrams. In all cases, heat flows obey the three laws of thermodynamics:

1. Energy is conserved and never created. Geothermal heat pumps transfer electrical energy from the compressor pump and heat energy from the ground. Again, the system energy flow obeys the 1st Law of Thermodynamics.

2. Heat energy always flows from a higher temperature to a lower temperature.

3. Refrigerants in the gas phase are "ideal" gases, obeying the absolute temperature scale (Kelvin).

VI. Conclusions

Geothermal power from earth heat sources provides a small, yet significant contribution to our utility grade power requirements. Future geothermal developments are also directed at utilization of lower temperature sources in combination with other energy systems (co-generation of power). See Chapter 20 Insight for a proposed usage of geothermal power.

The must-know elements of geothermal energy are:

1. **There are three categories of geothermal power (dry steam, flash, and binary power generation.**

2. **Geothermal resource depends upon water temperature, heat transfer of the rock (fracture) zone, and explicit heat capability.**

3. **Most geothermal wells have extended power producing capability**

4. **Every geothermal well is unique.**

5. **Geothermal ground loops significantly enhance air conditioner and heat pump efficiency.**

Chapter 19 Insight

Geothermal Dry Heat Power

The amount of heat energy stored within the earth provides an attraction for ingenious exploitation. However, like other potentially available energy resources, the difficulties in extracting heat energy from within our earth has been unsuccessful.

In general, temperature (heat) increases with depth from the global surface. This is from about 55° F at the surface to 5500° F at the center of the earth. This global heat is not the best potential for source of heat extraction. It is only mentioned for your awareness. The existence of "hot spots" near the surface of our earth have been mapped by the United States Geological Survey (USGS). As mentioned in Chapter 19, the "ring of fire" tectonic plates and the Yellowstone caldera provide significant heat sources within reasonable exploitation depths.

After identifying the "hot spots', those without the heat transfer capability of water remain as undeveloped heat energy sources. This insight is a brief outline on attempts to exploit this significant resource.

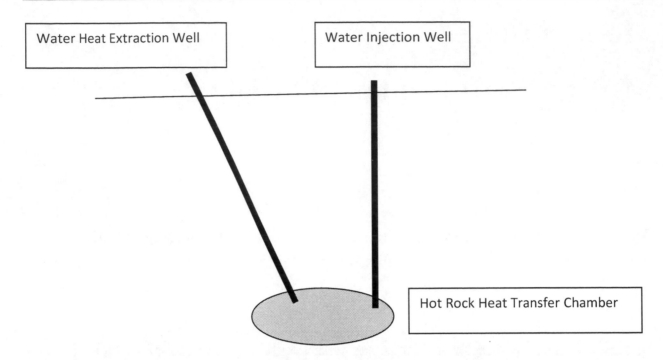

This graphic presents the basic plans and associated problems of dry heat energy extraction.

The distance underground could vary from 1000 ft to 3000 ft. This is similar to crude oil well depths.

1. Note that the hot rock heat transfer chamber must be generated. Detecting a hot rock chamber just waiting for water is not possible at this time. Attempts have been made using high pressure water and explosives to fracture the hot rock into a suitable heat transfer chamber. This requires both adequate heat transfer and non-permeable characteristics.

2. Water has been the only heat transfer liquid to extract earth heat. The reason for using water is because of its high specific heat, making heat transfer economically feasible. Air as a heat transfer material is economically unsuitable. The availability of water immediately becomes an engineering design limitation.

3. The placement of the injection well and the production well at great depths is an overwhelming challenge.

Chapter 20:

Biofuel Power

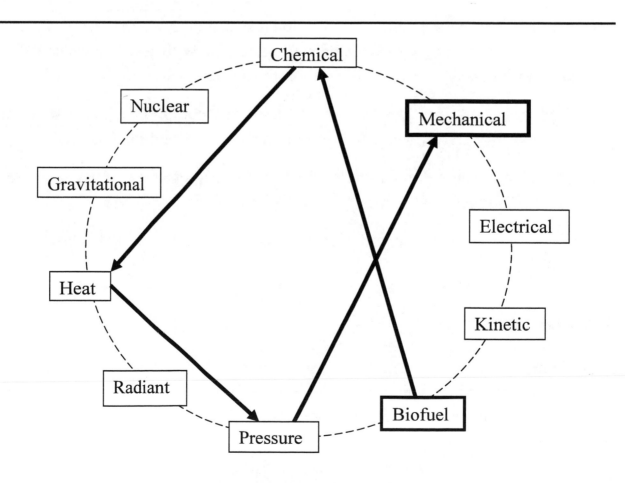

I. Introduction to Biofuel

The Chapter 20 biofuel energy flow only considers using biodeisel as a diesel fuel replacement in transportation. There is not any reason beyond cold temperature behavior and cost that biofuel cannot be a substitute for heating oil. Wood and ethanol, not presented as energy flows, can be considered substitutes for coal and gasoline.

Biofuels are energy sources produced by biological activity during our recent (present) time frame.

This chapter, Biofuel Power, was discarded from this text and then re-instated. Biofuel Power still remains marginally within the central focus of this text. The marginal condition is created by:

1. Biofuel Power processes are not clearly defined in scientific universal terms. Biological measurements are ambiguous and subject to incoherent analysis. This is a valid reason for text exclusion.

2. Biofuel Power is in the stage of intense commercial development. This creates a wide variety of development initiatives with few "benchmarks" of quantitative data. This is a valid reason for text exclusion.

3. Biofuel Power does provide a more complete, comprehensive view of our future utility grade power. This is a valid reason for text inclusion.

The best we can do is to retain the Biofuel Power chapter and emphasize the few basic scientific aspects that occur.

Biofuels will be discussed in order of their societal impact: Wood, Ethanol, and Biodiesel.

II. Wood

The burning of wood for fuel is familiar to everyone. Wood can be considered as a renewable organic fuel. The carbon dioxide contribution of wood is neutral. As much carbon dioxide is consumed upon wood formation as is released during wood burning.

Wood is an interesting source of available energy. It is an existing source of renewable energy that conveniently stores chemical energy for later use when needed. A positive feature of wood is this intrinsic energy storage. Compare this is to the immediate energy conversion requirement of renewable energy sources such as solar and wind (power).

The historic use of wood energy has been recently well investigated by many governmental agencies. A balanced estimation of wood energy conversion from our solar/biological source is now presented using the governmental agencies quantified data. This is a key consideration when evaluating sustainable energy options. This presentation should answer many questions regarding the feasibility of wood as a source of sustainable energy.

Example:

We have a one-acre wood lot of maple trees. Our intention is to use this one-acre wood lot to provide sustainable heating energy for our house.

1. On a continuing basis, the one-acre lot will produce about 25 cubic feet of available maple wood per year. That is the wood growth from all of the maple trees on this one-ace wood lot. This amount of maple growth was found on a credible government web site.

2. One of the features of wood is that it contains about 25% water when first cut (green wood). We will have to split the wood into smaller sizes to promote faster drying. Then we have to wait for the water to evaporate from the wood. As a process, we are only chopping and drying the wood.

3. The weight of maple wood production per year is:

   Maple wood weight = 25 cubic feet x density of maple

   The density of maple wood was found to be 43 lbs / cubic foot.

   Maple wood weight = 25 cubic feet x 43 lbs / cubic foot

   = 1075 lbs (per year)

4. Energy from burning maple wood:

Maple burning produces about 6,800 BTU/lb

6,800 BTU / lb x 1075 lbs = **7,310.000 BTU's**

The 7,310,000 BTU's of heat has significance only when compared to other available heat sources. Looking at my utility bill, I used about 80,000,000 BTU's to heat my house last year. The heat was supplied by natural gas. The conclusion is that one-acre of sustainable maple wood would supply about $1/10^{th}$ of my current annual heating usage.

In order to have a sustainable wood burning option for house heating, I need to have a larger wood lot and/or a more energy efficient house.

Sustainable kinds of energy will be determined by simple energy engineering calculations such as this example of wood energy. These simple conclusive derivations connect the energy science to reasonable options of sustainable energy. Yet it is instructive to estimate the amount of woodland required to replace our current national natural gas consumption. That's a homework problem.

Implicit within our wood energy calculations are many variables. For instance, mature forests do not produce wood at this estimated rate. For instance, many types of wood, with a range of energy contents, are used for heating. This results in inexact calculations from uncontrolled variables. The conclusions are not definitive. The example given above is a subjective best estimate.

III. Ethanol

Ethanol is a very old biological fuel produced by human society. The production of ethanol, as an alcoholic beverage, is as old as recorded history. A central element in the ethanol production is that we currently produce ethanol biologically the same way our ancestors produced their wine. They would take a berry or seed with concentrated chemical energy (mainly sugar) and add yeast to ferment (react) to produce alcohol. Yeast provides the chemical conversion that human chemists have yet to duplicate. The natural variation in this process was stunning. Most alcoholic drinks were barely consumable.

The same process of concentrated chemical energy (corn seeds) converted into alcohol by yeast is now utilized to produce ethanol for use as a liquid fuel. The economic and political aspects of ethanol production are significant.

Ethanol is a chemical presented in Figure 20.1:

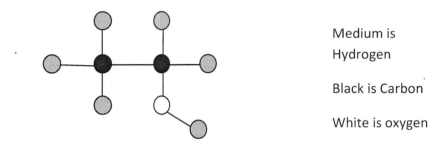

Medium is Hydrogen

Black is Carbon

White is oxygen

Figure 20.1 Ethanol

Ethanol has the following properties:

Energy per gallon	87,000 Btu's
Boiling Point	78.4 °C
Freezing Point	-114.3 °C

Ethanol can be used as a gasoline replacement at a reasonable engineering application cost. It is slightly more volatile than gas and also has lower energy content per gallon. But these factors are not prohibitive to use as an alternate to gasoline. The use of ethanol, as a liquid fuel, is actually constrained by business and social factors; not by scientific and engineering limitations.

The chemical conversion of corn seed to ethanol follows our established yeast fermentations in two steps. It is very similar to the mountaineers production of "corn licker" in one step, only with optimized efficiency. In step one, the corn is ground to a fine powder, mixed with water (making corn starch) and fed to specifically cultured yeast. The yeast produces a sugar. In step two, the sugar solution is fed to a different specifically cultured yeast which converts the sugar to alcohol. Now this sounds simple on paper, but working with organic molecules and yeast strains is very difficult. It can be considered an art form, rather than a science.

The energy flow of ethanol production is very interesting and has been the topic of many debates. Corn seed is a very energy intensive chemical. It contains, on average, 8,000 Btu's per pound. As a heating fuel, it actually competes economically with wood when the corn market price is low. However, it requires about 33,000 Btu's of energy, mainly from natural gas, to convert a gallon of ethanol fuel from seed corn.

One central debate surrounding corn based ethanol production is the energy balance for ethanol production. Considering the amount of energy required to produce the corn (fuel, fertilizer, transportation, etc.) and the energy to process the corn seed, do we use more fossil fuel energy to produce a gallon of ethanol than we derive from the gallon of ethanol fuel energy? The answer is difficult to precisely determine because of the many variables involved. Technically, a good approximation is that the amount of energy we use to produce ethanol is the same as the amount of energy in the produced ethanol. This is based upon existing data. You can, or may, draw your own conclusions.

The second central debate is that the production of corn based ethanol lowers the world food production. As stated earlier, corn is a very high energy source for heat, ethanol, or food. Considering humanity as a fundamental purpose, food production should always take priority over liquid fuel production. Again, the analysis of the food versus fuel production is very complex. The available analysis exists with subjective authority without a major effort to create non-biased data. This cannot be considered as a capitulation in analysis, but I personally find this beyond my comprehension. This situation also points towards a goal of a greater understanding of energy science combined with social policy.

Summarizing this ethanol section:

1. Ethanol production, due to biological variables, is like a brewer's art more than an exact scientific development.

2. The scientific limits still apply. Ethanol will always have a heat of combustion energy of 87,000 Btu's per gallon.

3. The 1st law of Thermodynamics still applies. Energy "in" has to be equal to energy "out".

4. Ethanol is a viable substitute for gasoline.

Ethanol is a viable source of liquid petroleum suitable for power applications. It has a credible history as an alternate to fossil fuel derived from crude oil.

IV. Biodiesel

The common link between many living species and biodiesel is the prevalent chemical in many living species of triglyceride, which is presented in Figure 20-2:

$$R'-CO-O-CH_2$$
$$|$$
$$R'-CO-O-CH$$
$$|$$
$$R'-CO-O-CH_2$$

Figure 20.2 Triglyceride

The "R's" presented in Figure 20.2 are hydrocarbon chains of atoms exactly the same as the hydrocarbon atoms discussed in Chapter 8. The "R" chains have evolved differently, but are not energetically different, in various living organic systems. Of course, these chains contain exactly the same amount of energy as those discussed in Chapter 8. These hydrocarbon chains are how living species store energy. The triglycerides stored, in a concentrated manner, within a single cell, are called fat. Yes, when your doctor said your triglyceride level is too high, this was exactly to what he was referring.

Triglycerides follow the basic rules of organic chemistry. Triglyceride chemistry can be precisely understood in contrast to the yeast mystery involved in ethanol production. The following organic chemistry reactions occur to produce biodiesel:

1. Triglyceride stock

The generic triglyceride molecule presented in Figure 20.2 is found in significant amounts in agricultural crops such as corn, soy beans, canola, sunflower seed, palm oil. Of course, the final biodiesel cost depends upon the cost of the stock. The actual triglyceride can be considered equal among all stock sources and the biodiesel produced is essentially equal among all stock sources. Note that all biodiesel stocks are derived from plant energies concentrated and stored for species reproduction (seeds).

The historic separations of triglycerides are our common kitchen cooking oils such as corn oil, canola oil, palm oil, soy bean oil, etc. That food process will not be discussed. We will just start our process with the kitchen oils. It is mentioned that used deep frying cooking oils from our fast food places are popular stock sources. They are not sufficient in amount to be considered alone as a utility grade energy source.

2. Trans-esters

An established organic chemical reaction can transform triglycerides into usable diesel fuel. The triglycerides are reacted with methanol to produce a chemical called an "R" methyl ester. This is presented in Figure 20.3

R – methyl ester is an equivalent to our established fossil diesel fuel refined from crude oil. The small differences in application engineering are not an impediment for usage. Blending biodiesel with fossil diesel usually requires little, if any, modifications to engine design.

$$R'\text{-CO-O-CH}_2$$
$$|$$
$$R'\text{-CO-O-CH} \quad + \quad 3\ CH_3OH \quad = \quad \mathbf{3\ R'\text{-CO-O-CH}_3} \quad + \quad HOCH$$
$$|$$
$$R'\text{-CO-O-CH}_2$$

with right-hand glycerol:

$$HOCH_2$$
$$|$$
$$HOCH$$
$$|$$
$$HOCH_2$$

Figure 20.3 Methyl Ester

This is an organic chemical reaction of triglyceride and methanol producing methyl ester (diesel fuel) and glycerin. The chemical process to convert organic stock to R - methyl ester is simple on paper, but requires diligence for commercial grade operation. The commercial competitive position of biodiesel depends primarily upon the price of the feedstock. The science and engineering always involve development of improved efficiencies.

Biodiesel has a significant history of use. The "benchmark" applications are generally limited by the competitive price disadvantage of the biodiesel fuel.

V. Vegetable Oils

For the sake of completeness, a mention of vegetable oils as a liquid fuel seems in order. First, note that ethanol (ethyl alcohol) and biodiesel (R - methyl ester) are fuels which are reasonable alternates to the existing fossil fuels. Reasonable means that alcohol and biodiesel can be blended or substituted 100% into the existing fossil fuels without prohibited cost or engine performance. This results in conversion to these sustainable energy liquid fuels only a matter of cost and availability. Second, vegetable oil is in the category where blending with fossil fuels and 100% substitution requires a significant redesign of the heat engines for use. That limitation and primitive engineering of vegetable oil engines have inhibited exploitation. However, the energy source does exist and has considerable public exposure.

VI. Algae

The biological production of hydrocarbon based fuel could also be a modern application and improvement over the prehistoric process that created crude oil (see Chapter 13). This modern application is in the early stages of development and strictly should not be a topic of this text Energy and Power - Fundamental Knowledge. The development of algae as an alternate energy source has little energy science when compared to the art of controlling natural variables.

However, it is a direction in creating alternate hydrocarbon fuels, so the subject of algae is included in this chapter.

Algae are microscopic plants that exist in many species. Algae are everywhere, in the wind and annoyingly in our swimming pools. Some algae produce hydrocarbons, converting radiant energy from the sun into stored chemical energy. As stated in Chapter 13, this conversion process is our speculation of how our crude oil originated.

Basically, all we have to do is grow algae and process them like our soy bean oil process to create a usable fuel. But having algae create hydrocarbon fuel is very challenging for the following reasons:

1. Some strains (species) of algae possess the biological ability to produce energy rich hydrocarbons. That ability can be thought of as the natural selection of algae species that will survive when possessing stored energy. This is the same as bears gaining fat before hibernation. Humans also acquire fat through this same biological process. This adaptive process exists within algae. Algae produce a greater amount of hydrocarbon chemicals when they are stressed (deprived of food and energy).

   It is a challenge to optimize hydrocarbon output from algae.

2. The operative word in "Some strains of algae is **some.** A major difficulty in operating an algae "farm" is that other algae species, that do not efficiently produce hydrocarbons, enter the hydrocarbon producing algae system and compete for food and survival. These interloping algae contaminate and ruin the working process. Remember that these other species are in the air all around us. The green algae observed in our pools is one of those culprits. It is an ongoing challenge to prevent these interloping algae species from entering the productive system.

Algae for the production of liquid fuel is a speculative development. The energy science portion of this chapter is relegated to Chapter 20 Insight. Chapter 20 Insight is recommended reading, since the contained information is pertinent to frequent public discussions.

VII. Conclusions

There is a major development effort towards utilizing biofuels because, when burned to produce heat, they are carbon neutral and do not contribute to increased atmospheric carbon dioxide like fossil fuels. The intense debates surrounding energy balances of biofuel production and biofuel volume capability require a comprehensive understanding of this important energy segment.

The must-know elements of biofuel energy are;

    1. Biofuels are primarily wood, ethanol, and biodiesel.

    2. Biofuels are carbon neutral.

    3. Biofuels impact established plant food cycles.

    4. Algae hydrocarbon synthesis is an energy fuel development path.

    6. Natural solar conversion to biofuels is very inefficient.

Chapter 20 Insight

Power Co-generation

Co-generation of power has significant cost reduction in production of utility grade energy that is realized ultimately as a consumer energy price reduction. After the entire text was devoted to separation of energies and powers, this insight offers examples of engineering solutions that a based upon two existing energy sources:

1. The development of biodiesel from algae plants has a scientific limit of input solar energy as a maximum of 1000 watts / m^2. This limit dictates the algae engineering system and the maintenance and operation (M and O) cost of this energy production. If we could utilize the existing geothermal lower temperature (~39° C) to input energy in to the algae production (growth) cycle, then we could have a greater output of hydrocarbon per unit M and O by combining solar and geothermal energies.

2. The heat removed from our nuclear power plant's steam condensers could be used to provide residential and commercial heat, displacing the present natural gas and fuel oil requirements.

3. Pumping natural gas requires natural gas turbines. The exit heat from some of these natural gas pumps is already being used to produce electricity.

4. Industrial applications of co-generation that retrieves exiting heat are already installed and attracting increased attention.

The reason for the Chapter 20 Insight about co-generation is based upon the increasing press attention to this important activity. Energy conservation exists in both the utility grade production and consumer utilization.

Chapter 21

The Automobile

Sections

I. Introduction to The Automobile

Our goal is to provide the automobile as a familiar model for dynamic energy and power understanding. It is more understandable to use the term power transfer when referring to automobiles. Energy flow (with time) is power transfer.

II. The Automobile Gasoline Engine

The majority of automobiles operate with 4-cycle internal combustion gasoline engines. The energy source is the gasoline that supplies about 118,000 Btu's of heat energy per gallon. Gasoline is a high energy, safe, affordable, and abundant energy source. Exploiting gasoline, a fossil fuel, as the power source, has provided a revolution in the automotive engineering application. The gasoline automobile has the established energy flow of chemical energy to heat energy to pressure energy to mechanical energy. On a continuous time basis, this is power. The 4-cycle internal combustion engine operation is presented in Figure 11.6.

The automobile mechanical drive shaft horsepower is an advertising feature in the sales specification of an automobile. Automobile horsepower is associated with the thrill of acceleration and the ability to sustain desirable vehicle velocity. High engine performance is inferred by relative high horsepower. Performance is not defined in physical terms. The gasoline automobile engine performance is inferred by measured torque and horsepower. Figure 21.1 presents an example of an engine power specification.

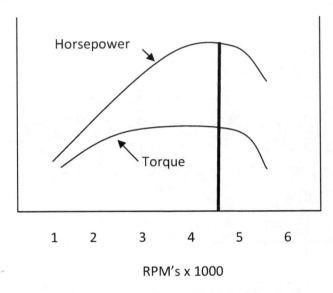

Figure 21.1 Engine Horsepower and Torque

1. The gasoline engine measured in Figure 21.1 has a maximum horsepower at 4600 revolutions per minute (RPM). At 4600 RPM's, the engine produced 180 horsepower. In ordinary driving to our shopping mall, one would use a fraction of the maximum horsepower. However, horsepower is a key automobile sales feature. In automobile racing, we would want to run this engine as close to 4500 RPM's as possible. That would furnish maximum automobile acceleration and speed from the Figure 21.1 engine.

2. Engine torque is a measure of the tangential force at a distance around the drive shaft. The common measurements are called ft-pounds. This common correct interpretation of torque is the amount of tangential mechanical force

at a distance of 1 foot away from the center of the mechanical shaft (see Figure 21.2).

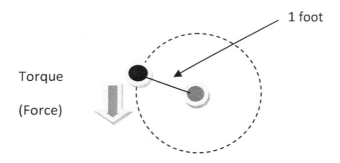

Figure 21.2 Torque (force) of a Shaft

Note that the common measurements of torque are in ft-lbs. But torque is only a tangential "force" as presented in Figure 21.2. It is better described as force at a radius of 1 foot. Unfortunately, torque ft-lbs are **not** the value of "energy" that is also measured in ft-lbs (See Chapter 3). This double meaning of ft-lbs is an institutionalize confusion factor.

3. Foot-pounds / minute (horsepower) can be calculated directly from the torque and RPM values in Figure 21.2. For our automobile:

   a. Our *dynamometer* (defined below) measured 210 ft-lbs of torque (force) and 4500 RPM's.
   b. A formula, not derived in this text, can immediately determine horsepower if we know the torque and RPM's. The formula is just a re-arrangement of James Watt's definition of horsepower.

   Horsepower = (torque x RPM) / 5250 = 180 as we reported

4. Engine design by excellent engineers have optimized the convenience (low noise, economy; and smooth, responsive power) for consumer use. An extreme optimization of horsepower is observed in drag racing. It is hard to imagine why one would take a drag racer (loud and jerky) to the mall. In this section, we will refer only to the specific 180 horsepower engine. The energy input to the gasoline internal combustion engine can be assumed at 118,000 Btu's per gallon, with a slight variation in this value caused by gasoline

source. The engine power output can be accurately measured by a test measurement device called a *dynamometer*.

5. Engine efficiency is [mechanical energy (power) out / chemical energy (power) in] x 100. Unfortunately, the specified engine efficiencies for engines cannot be obtained as a body of data. The reason for not specifying engine efficiency alone is not clear. A reasonable estimate would be 30%. The public awareness rests upon the automobile historic measurement of miles per gallon (MPG). MPG is a good measurement, but it is overwhelmed by variables in the total efficiency analysis of the automobile.

III. A Typical Automobile Trip

The automobile is a machine of modern convenience. For example, we can conveniently shop for goods that improve our living conditions (food, clothes, lights, DVD movies, etc.). A typical trip to the mall is an example. The automobile is always ready for use. All we have to do is drive from our residential area to the freeway and then over to the mall. The conscious thoughts about the trip are air conditioning on hot days and the defensive driving on the crowded freeway. When we arrive back at home we unload the automobile. Unless we were unfortunate and had an automotive failure or accident, we think little of the automobile and its wonderful power systems.

IV. Automobile Power Flow Awareness

The educated person, after reading Energy and Power –Fundamental Knowledge has a different perspective. That ideal perspective is as follows. The mechanical to kinetic energy power conversion of an automobile is furnished by chemical energy from gasoline utilizing an internal combustion engine. But first we will start the engine. The electric starter converts electrical energy from the chemical energy storage battery to crank (revolve) the internal combustion engine. The mechanical power supplied by the electric starter is a significant engineering improvement over hand cranking to start the engine.

Our engine starts and we back out of the garage, Traveling towards the mall, the first common observation is that we start traveling in "low" gear. Note that the engine's horsepower and torque curve (Figure 21.1) starts at the engine 700 RPM's. That is the engine idling speed. Something slips in the mechanical power transfer to get the motive forces (movement) started. This is the slipping clutch in a manual geared transmission and a slipping fluid coupling in an automatic transmission. Slipping infers a mechanical energy to heat energy conversion. The gasoline internal combustion engine requires mechanical force amplification to propel the automobile. A *transmission* converts the available force x distance (in time) of the engine power to a usable force x distance (in time) required at the drive wheels to propel the automobile. After we back out of the garage in "reverse", we shift to "drive" and move forward in "low" gear. We always start moving in "low". This is true for both a manual and automatic transmission. The automobile begins moving with the greatest ratio of engine RPM to drive wheel RPM. This allows the engine to operate in its most powerful RPM region (Section II) and applies the greatest amount of force to the drive wheels. The greatest possible force means the maximum possible acceleration. But an automobile cannot attain an adequate top speed in low gear. The engine can only revolve to a specified top RPM. So it is necessary to shift into higher gears (lower engine to wheel revolution ratios) as less propelling force at the drive wheels is required. We are now operating from the best part of the torque and horsepower curve as presented in Section II. Even after we are moving towards the mall, the transmission has to optimize engine power to wheel power (motive force). Universal observations of shifting gears to meet automobile force requirements are an automatic transmission shifting "down" when we need acceleration to pass or greater wheel force required for traveling up a steep hill.

Until we enter the freeway, we have to stop the automobile for stop signs and stoplights. We are in a 35 MPH residential street and don't normally race from one stoplight to another. We don't utilize all of the engines horsepower.

What we are doing, traveling in the residential area, is converting the chemical energy (gasoline) to kinetic energy (automobile movement) to heat energy in the brakes to stop the automobile. This is stop-and-go driving. The repeated cycle of kinetic energy being converted to brake heat energy lowers the overall efficiency of the automobile. I am not advocating running the red light for the sake of improved fuel efficiency. The observation of this overall lowering of automobile efficiency is legally posted as an EPA mileage on all new automobile "stickers". For instance, an automobile may potentially average 20 MPG in the city (stop-and-go) and 28 MPG in the country (freeway). Of course this is an estimate encompassing many variables.

If we raced to the mall, we would lower our automobile efficiency (burn more gas per mile). We would utilize the maximum horsepower of the engine to attain the highest speed possible (greatest kinetic energy) before braking to a halt. By converting to heat the maximum possible kinetic energy, we have maximized our chemical energy (gasoline) usage per distance traveled. From our understanding of the 1st Law of Thermodynamics, the braking heat energy is the major difference between stop-and-go and freeway MPG. All other automobile energies considered equal, the automobile also keeps idling at the stoplight and consumes gasoline.

Soon we arrive at the freeway on ramp. Entering the freeway traffic is the one time we usually utilize our maximum automobile horsepower to accelerate and match the speeding freeway traffic. The acceleration time to 60 miles per hour is about 10 seconds for our 180horsepower, 3200 pound automobile. The automobile gained 480,000 joules of kinetic energy (if it weighed 3200 pounds or had a mass of 1400 kilograms) in 10 seconds. It may seem fair to you to calculate the specific automobile's efficiency based upon the 480,000 joules and the specific automobile's 180 advertised horsepower (power out / power in). This basic calculation will make you very unpopular with automobile engine devotees. It will be quickly impressed upon you that the advertised maximum horsepower (in our example) was 180 horsepower at 4500 RPM's and this specific automobile engine never gets close to 4500 RPM's in actual use; not even during maximum acceleration. The 180 advertised horsepower measurement was obtained at a test stand. Advertised horsepower is not a precise measure of realized acceleration performance. The goal of internal combustion engine engineering is to maximize the power flow from the highest horsepower RPM region, while preserving overall efficiency from the lower horsepower RPM region. Now we would have both acceleration balanced with economy. The engineers have done a great job.

However, entering the freeway converts gasoline chemical energy to kinetic energy only once during our trip. Driving down the freeway, we don't brake as often to convert the kinetic energy to heat energy as we did in the stop-and-go driving. Our gas mileage increases to the EPA country estimate.

On a level freeway, our 3200 pound automobile requires about 50 horsepower or 37 kilowatts of power at the gasoline engine drive shaft to maintain the 60 MPH speed. This power value is approximated and averaged from existing engineering measurement data. This assumption is validated in that all 3200 pound automobiles will obtain very close to the same mileage (28 MPG). This assumption, without including available measured data, is grossly confirmed by comparing EPA estimated mileages,

Where does our chemical gasoline engine 50 horsepower at constant level freeway speed flow to on a continuing basis?

1. The first portion of the 50 horsepower is converted to heat energy (power) in our differential and bearings in the final mechanical drive conversion of the automobile. We will average, from known and anticipated data, that this amount will be 8% or 4 horsepower.

2. The second significant portion of the 50 horsepower is converted to heat energy (power) within the rotating tires. This is the elastic heat "loss" caused by the flexure and return of the polymeric tire material. The same 3200 pound automobile will have a lower MPG when fully loaded with passengers and luggage (1000 pounds) than just being driven by one individual. An excellent example occurs when we only have the rubber tire as a variable. A semi-truck, with a total weight of 50,000 pounds, will travel at constant 60 MPH on the level on top of a steel railed railroad car using about 25 horsepower. That is about 5 times less horsepower required than traveling on a road with conventional tires.

For better automobile MPG, we are advised to keep maximum pressure in the tires. Of course, the ride will be harsher with the less elasticity in the tires. Tires are being designed to increase gas mileage.

Without dwelling on the process of unraveling the involved variables, a good (but not exact) estimate of power conversion is that 46% of the drive shaft mechanical power at a constant 60 MPH on the level is converted to heat energy from the elastic behavior of the tires. 46% would be 23 horsepower.

3. The third significant portion of the 50 horsepower converts to kinetic energy (power) commonly known as the wind resistance of the automobile. This portion of the energy is easily measured with approximate accuracy. This can be done with a 4-wheel drive automobile. The reason for using a 4-wheel drive vehicle is that we have to measure and calculate the energy (power) flow to all four tires. Place the automobile on a static dynamometer and measure the drive shaft horsepower at the 60MPH speedometer reading. Then take the same automobile on the road and measure the drive shaft horsepower at the 60 MPH speedometer reading. On the road, it should be about 50 horsepower. The difference in total moving (road) drive shaft horsepower and the dynamometer (static) horsepower is close to the wind resistant kinetic energy (power). This is a practical example of the 1st Law of Thermodynamics.

An engineering goal is to make automobiles streamlined to reduce air force (drag) while traveling through the air. The use of aerodynamic designs for the shape of automobiles has caused all 3200 pound, 180 horsepower automobiles, to have the same aerodynamic (teardrop) shape. This is the "claw hammer" effect; where, given enough time, all optimized products will converge to similar designs. Look at all of the major different makes of 3200 lb automobiles. In the parking lot, they all look close to the same. So do all claw hammers.

Rather than become confused with the inherently inaccurate conclusion based upon statistical variations, we will just assume that our automobile traveling 60 MPH on the level highway requires about 46% of out 50 horsepower to sustain its speed against air resistance. This would be 23 horsepower.

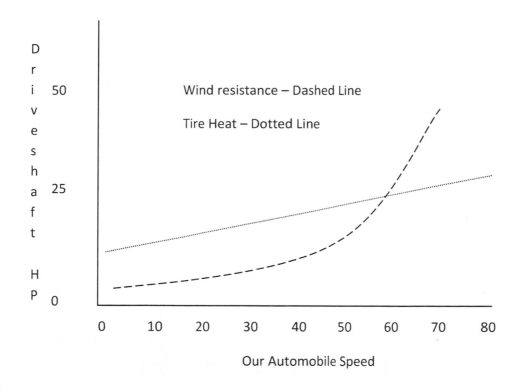

Figure 21.3 Automobile Power Conversions

Please realize that Figure 21.3 is only one example for logical discussion. Wind resistance and tire heat dissipation are quite variable.

In presenting this example of a typical 3200 lb automobile, the tire resistance heat energy loss and the kinetic energy wind generation loss are about the same at 60 MPH on a level highway (Something to remember). A simplified model is that the rate of heat energy (power) loss power tire resistance with constant with speed and the kinetic energy (power) energy loss increases to the square of the speed (speed x speed). This is a fair approximate model for logical understanding; but these values are more accurate when measured for specific automobiles and conditions rather than calculated. This "60 MPH on a level highway" exercise presents a major insight into energy flow within automobiles. Figure 21.3 presents the horsepower requirements of tire heat dissipation and wind resistance of our specific automobile.

4. Another energy flow event occurs on the way to the mall. On the freeway we travel up and down a couple of hills. Our reserve power within the automobile engine could sustain the flow of mechanical power into stored

gravitational energy (power) as we progressed up the hill. Observations are that we pushed down on the accelerator to provide more engine power to ascend the hill or noticed that the engine increased its power (and noise) if we were on cruise control. This energy flow process is so familiar that it is buried in our subconscious.

We store gravitational energy in our automobile while traveling uphill and utilize the stored gravitation energy as we travel (or coast) downhill. On our trip to the mall we only went up and down a couple of 100 foot tall hills. This will not measurably affect overall gasoline MPG. We didn't brake to slow traveling downhill. The gravitational storage cycle is a bit inefficient. However, if we kept a constant automobile speed across flat Kansas, then crossed the Rocky Mountains into Colorado, we would realize a significant change in MPG. Traveling up each Colorado grade, we store gravitational energy into our automobile only to transfer a significant portion of that gravitational energy into heat energy within brakes and / or shifting down to release heat energy by means of our engine. This is particularly concerning to the truck vehicles. A personal integrated value of gravitational energy is an excellent gravitation energy example. I live in Reno (at 4500 ft above sea level) and often travel to San Francisco (at sea level). Gravity provides 10^7 ft-lbs (4500ft x 3200 lbs) of energy to my automobile when I go (down) to San Francisco and I have to provide 10^7 ft-lbs of energy to my automobile as stored gravitational energy when I come back (up) to Reno. I can't escape gravity. The freeway trip from Reno to San Francisco is not a level highway. In fact, recent trips characterize this freeway as a stop-and-go highway (no stop signs, just stopped automobiles).

During our trip to the mall, we travelled in a 3200 pound car, and conveniently ignored the weight of the passengers and purchased goods. However, the following significant power conversions were noted:

1. Mechanical power to the heat power conversion within the automobile machine.

2. Mechanical power to the kinetic energy conversion of movement.

3. Kinetic energy (power) to heat dissipation (power) conversion of braking

4. Mechanical power to heat dissipation (power) conversion within tires.

5. Mechanical power to kinetic energy (power) conversion from wind resistance.

6. Mechanical power conversion to gravitational energy (stored power).

Note that the mechanical drive shaft horsepower is the source of all machine power during the typical automobile operation. That factor is obvious to everyone.

V. Automobile Weight versus Horsepower Requirements

During the analysis of automobile power flow in the Section IV, we kept the weight constant at 3200 pounds. Changing the weight in addition to the rest of the variables makes the analysis too complicated for a presentable logic. Weight is the most important variable of MPG, but there are several other important power variables. A fair average value for vehicle weight effect on MPG was given by a friend. When his truck is empty, on a level freeway at 60 MPH the mileage is about 9 MPG. When fully loaded, on a level freeway at 60 MPH, the mileage is about 5 MPG. There is a strong correlation between weight and MPG. The obvious observation is that lighter automobiles have better MPG's. The prime reason is higher tire heat energy dissipation with higher weight.

The correlation between weight and MPG is often related by using the EPA test mileages as an approximation of the correlation between weight and MPG. This is a poor quantitative measure of the automobile weight variable. Automobiles that are of lower weight generally have a smaller frontal cross sectional area with less wind resistance. Unless you can separate the air resistance variable during comparison of two automobiles, specific relationships due to weight alone cannot be established. The truck example in the last paragraph provides substantially a single weight variable. Measured data calculations separating the wind and tire power data are rare; but not difficult.

Our 3200 pound vehicle was assumed to deliver 28 MPG on the level road at 60 MPH. An estimate is that 3700 pound vehicle will get about 24 MPG on the level road at 60 MPH and that a 2600 pound vehicle will get about 33 MPG on a level road at 60 MPH. These are all gasoline powered automobiles. Of course, the large comparison variables such as loaded weight and tire pressure are not included. The measured data in MPG includes many other intrinsic variables. This very rough estimate is gathered from manufacture's offerings of a series of different weighs in their automobiles.

VI. Automobile Power Engineering

In Section III, we have presented the automobile in terms of fundamental scientific energy and power variables. It is more understandable to summarize the fundamental knowledge in terms of energy and power engineering. We are converting available energy and power science to the automobile application.

1. Mechanical power transfer is required to properly match the gasoline internal combustion engine power output to the most acceptable force needed to accelerate and maintain speed. For a 3200 automobile, this is about 10 seconds to 60 MPH. with adequate passing acceleration. Several engine options may be offered for the same automobile by the same automobile company. The customer can individually select his requirement of the horsepower versus gas mileage trade-off.

   The mechanical transmission is a key design element for increased automobile MPG. The gas engine performance is best at a narrow range of RPM's, but the automobile application of power requires a wide range of RPM's. The general trend is to design a transmission that keeps the engine RPM's close to the designed best efficiency (power out / gasoline in).This is noticeable in the increasing number of gears to improve efficiency by keeping the engine RPM's in the most efficient range.

2. An automobile has to be designed to have adequate (customer choice) reserve power to ascend hills while traveling. This is not a trivial problem. This is a desired customer feature. Remember, the average customer wants both more engine power and better gas mileage. This prevalent attitude also explains the origin of the strange stereotypical inducement pitches by our automobile salesman.

3. Heat transfer from the automobile engine and the brakes is a fundamental design consideration. The braking capacity must be adequate for halting a maximum speed automobile descending a steep (specified) mountain highway.

VII. Engineering Better Automobile MPG's

The global efforts to reduce our energy consumption (gasoline or a substitute) by passenger automobiles rest primarily in three areas:

1. The public acceptance of smaller (less weight and more streamlined) automobiles.

2. The advent of hybrid (explained below) automotive power systems that improve efficiency.

3. Alternate power systems that may enter the automobile market.

All of the efforts are logical extensions of the automobile power flow analyses presented in Sections II, III, and IV.

There has been a perceptible decrease in automobile size in the last two decades. The predominant passenger automobile has migrated from six to five passengers. The availability of two and four passenger automobiles continues the smaller automobile trend. Contributing to the smaller automobile trend:

1. The universal awareness of limited future world wide petroleum stocks

2. The awareness that the petroleum stocks are not domestic.

3. The observation that most automobiles on the road are with only a single driver.

4. The traffic congestion, particularly inter-urban, that is relieved with smaller automobiles

Note that economics is not a universal motivation for smaller automobile size. In fact, the recent popularity of Sports Utility Vehicles (SUV's) reversed the trend toward greater MPG's in favor of convenience, utility, and personal vanity. As the economics driven by decreasing petroleum stocks become significant, the automobile MPG's will adjust to viable levels. We are referring here to the classical gasoline powered automobile.

The hybrid automobile uses an electrical motor in conjunction with an internal combustion engine. The hybrid automobile improves gas mileage significantly through two engineering developments:

1. At low speeds, typical of city driving, the automobile operates as an energy flow from electrical battery power into mechanical power for the drive wheels. When at a stop in the city traffic, the automobile uses no battery power. When the batteries discharge to a low power limit value, the on-board internal combustion engine starts and converts power to a generator that recharges the batteries.

2. The braking system of the hybrid now can also generate electricity while stopping the automobile. Kinetic energy (as power) is converted by a generator into stored electrical battery power.

For small and medium sized automobiles, the hybrid system produces roughly the same MPG's in the city as in the country. Hybrid automobiles have reduced the heat energy lost during braking and use no power during a traffic jam.

Hybrid automobile design is focused upon low weight, streamlined bodies, and optimized electric generation systems.

The low weight desired in a hybrid has to be optimized versus the weight requirement of the additional electrical batteries. This optimization has been engineered to almost perfection. Of course, economically feasible batteries with a higher stored power density would improve this design parameter.

Hybrid automobiles are presently available in the market. For small and medium sized automobiles, the MPG's range from 40 to 50. Presently, the improved MPG's do not universally entice buyers into the hybrid automobile market. For many the increased price of hybrid automobiles, due to the additional electrical system, compares unfavorably to a pure gasoline engine equivalent.

The diesel engine provides an excellent MPG improvement to the gasoline engine. diesel automobile engines are presently market competitors. A diesel automobile engine is quite similar to the gasoline internal combustion engine. The key difference is that the diesel engine compresses the gas to about 23 atmospheres compared to a typical gasoline engine compression of 10 atmospheres. This increased compression raises the internal gas to much higher temperatures (see Chapter 7 Insight). The hydrocarbon fuel cannot enter the cylinder with the incoming air because it would ignite from the increased temperature before the compression cycle was complete. The diesel avoids this pre-ignition by injecting a small amount of diesel fuel at the start of the power stroke. The thermodynamics of the diesel cycle indicates that additional power can be converted to mechanical power at higher efficiency.

Diesel automobile engines have been limited because of smell (of high molecular weight hydrocarbons) and they are expensive. The increased efficiency is about 25% in a narrow power output RPM range. Small diesel automobiles are seriously being introduced into the market.

A highly publicized alternate to the gasoline internal combustion engine is the all electric automobile. This is a hybrid automobile with the on board gas powered electrical generator removed. The scientific challenges of the all electric automobile are:

1. Electrical power storage capacity to provide a convenient automobile operation range. Let us consider for a moment the power requirement for the 3200 pound automobile on the freeway. It was stated as 37 kilowatts at 60 MPH. In simple terms, I need 37 kilowatts of battery power to operate for 1 hour or travel 60 miles.

   If we use a 1200 watt (1.2 kilowatt) lead acid batteries, we would need about 30 to supply stored power for 1 hour of automobile operation. The total battery weight would be about 2000 pounds.

   So we have to invent a battery with more power to weight (power density) and minimize the weight of the rest of the automobile to increase range. That is where development efforts are focused. Notice that all electric vehicles are initially light weight automobiles.

2. Battery recharging The recharging of the batteries is not a trivial problem. With gasoline, we can fill our tank in 10 minutes and then drive 300 miles. Recharging batteries involves limits in the battery charging rate capacity and the electrical power grid connection. Recharging may take hours. Recharging while on the road is a challenge. The infrastructure for recharging does not exist.

The entry of all electric cars provides an option initially for urban drivers that live within the design range and charge limits. Certainly, our observed golf carts have no viable competition for environmentally clean and convenient service.

Departing completely from the guidelines of the text and the focus upon utility grade power, we will mention the futuristic concept of hydrogen powered automobiles.

Hydrogen (H_2) gas has an equivalent energy content by weight to our hydrocarbon methane (CH^4). H_2 is not a power source and does not exist in nature. H_2 does burn efficiently in internal combustion engines and only produces water upon combustion. Nothing could be more environmentally friendly. The use part of hydrogen is very attractive.

The source end of hydrogen is difficult. First, generation of hydrogen requires the energy (plus conversion efficiency) and power equal to that produced by the hydrogen engine (plus conversion efficiency). So to start with, we have to develop power sources equal to or greater than all of the petroleum we use if we intend to replace gasoline and Diesel fuel. The difficulty is one of economics.

Hydrogen distribution would need a pipeline infrastructure. That may be an economic problem for areas of low population density.

Hydrogen storage within automobiles is not fully developed. Storage density and safety issues still exist. The amount of research in this area is fascinating, but voluminous.

An added feature is that hydrogen energy can be converted directly to electrical energy in a *fuel cell*. No Carnot cycle heat to mechanical conversion limit applies. The higher power fuel cells have met with limited success. High powered (bus) applications have not produced clear benchmark data, to my knowledge.

VIII. Conclusions:

The automobile is an excellent familiar machine that can remind everyone about energy and power. The complexity of energy and power applications within the automobile became apparent in this extremely abbreviated text. The social impact of the automobile is a bridge from science to social benefits.

The must-know elements of automobile energy and power are:

    1. The predominant source of energy for automobiles is gasoline.

    2 The heat engine is limited by thermodynamic limitations (see Chapter 7).

    3. During typical driving, drive shaft power within an automobile converts to stored kinetic energy and stored gravitational energy

    4. The automobile drive shaft power is also converted to tire heat energy dissipation and kinetic energy wind resistance

    5. Heat energy is converted from automobile kinetic energy when we brake.

    6. Many development paths for automobile engines are being pursued.

Appendix I – Proper Nouns

Appendix II – Conversion Charts

Metric	Multiply By	English
Weigh (mass)		
Gram (gm) (at earth surface)	0.035	ounces (oz)
Gram (gm) (at earth surface)	0.0022	pounds (lb)
Kilograms (at earth surface)	2.20	pounds (lb)
Newton	0.22	pounds (lb)
Distance		
Meters (m)	39.37	inches (in)
Meters (m)	3.28	feet (ft)
Kilometers (km)	0.62	miles (mi)
Temperature		
Celsius (°C)	9/5 (then add 32)	Fahrenheit (°F)
Heat		
Calorie	0.0039	Btu
Energy / Power		
Joule		Foot - pounds
Watt (J per second)	1.3×10^{-3}	Horsepower
Velocity		
Meters / second	2.3	Miles / hour
Volume		
Liter	0.26	Gallon

Appendix II – Conversion Charts

English	Multiply By	Metric
Weigh (mass)		
Ounces (oz)	28.4	grams (gm)
Pounds (lb)	454.	grams (gm)
Pounds (lb)	0.454	kilograms (kg)
Pounds (lb)	4.45	newton
Distance		
Inches (in)	0.025	meter (m)
Feet (ft)	0.305	meter (m)
Miles (mi)	1.61	kilometers (km)
Temperature		
Fahrenheit (°F)	(subtract 32, then multiply by 5 / 9)	Celsius (°C)
Heat		
Btu	252.	calorie
Energy / Power		
Horsepower	746.	Watt (J / sec)
Velocity		
Miles / hr (MPH)	0.44	Meters / sec (m / s)
Volume		
Gallon	3.79	Liter (l)

Appendix III – Prolog

Energy education is an ascending step – wise process. Energy and Power – Fundamental Knowledge is the step between unawareness and the ability to comprehend the entire scope of utility grade energy. The essential components of energy education of this step are presented in the must-know details summarized at the end of each chapter. The comprehensive understanding of energy is easily summarized below as the Metric utility grade energies.

1. Mechanical energy (Chapter 3)

joule = force x distance = (kilogram mass x g) x (meters)

g = determined 9.8 meters / second^2

kilogram mass x g = newton (weight)

2. Kinetic energy (Chapter 4)

joule = ½ mv^2 = ½ (meters)(meters / second)(meters / second)

3. Gravitational energy (Chapter 5)

joule = mgh = (kilogram mass x g) x (meters height)

g = determined 9.8 meters / second^2

kilogram mass x g = newton (weight)

4. Elastic energy (Chapter 6)

joule = ½ kd^2 = ([kilogram mass x g] / meter)(meters)(meters)

g = determined 9.8 meters / second^2

kilogram mass x g = newton (weight)

5. Heat energy (Chapter 7)

joule = measured specific heat = J / gram x ^{o}C (change)

6. Chemical energy (Chapter 8)

joule = measured heat of chemical reaction = kilojoules / mole

7. Radiant energy (Chapter 9)

joule = hν

$\quad\quad$ h = 6.6 x 10^{-34} joule seconds

$\quad\quad$ ν = wave frequency

8. Electrical energy (Chapter 10)

joule = measured (voltage x coulombs)

9. Pressure-volume energy (Chapter 11)

joule = (kilogram mass x g) / meter^2)(meter^3) = newtons x meters

10. Nuclear energy

joule = (kilograms mass)(c^2)

$\quad\quad$ c = 3.0 x 10^8 meters / second

This text started with the Metric energy listed above. Energy science is required before an intelligent path into energy engineering can be established. This text is written to provide a popular base of energy science information. Note that all energy (joule) calculations are based upon familiar measurements of universal dimensions. This list provides the joule as the unifying factor among all of the utility grade energies. Conversions to the English system are not included, since the conversions add little to the comprehensive view.